London

DIRECTIONS

WRITTEN AND RESEARCHED BY

Rob Humphreys

ROUGH GUIDES

NEW YORK • LONDON • DELHI

www.roughguides.com

Contents

Introduction to

London

London is a very big city. In fact, it's Europe's largest capital by far, stretching for more than thirty miles on either side of the River Thames, and with a population of just under eight million. Ethnically and linguistically, it's also Europe's most diverse metropolis, offering cultural and culinary delights from right across the globe. And after sixteen years of being the only major city in the world not to have its own governing body, London finally has an elected assembly and a mayor who's busy tackling longstanding problems such as public transport.

With no single predominant focus of interest, the city can seem bewilderingly amorphous to newcomers. The key to enjoying London is not to try and do everything in a

When to visit

Despite the temperateness of the English climate, it's impossible to say with any degree of certainty that the weather will be pleasant in any given month. With average daily temperatures of around 22°C, English **summers** rarely get unbearably hot, while the **winters** (average daily temperature 6–10°C) don't get very cold – though they're often wet. However, whenever you come, be prepared for all eventualities; in 2003, summer temperatures hit almost 40°C. As far as crowds go, tourists stream into London pretty much all year round, with peak season from Easter to October, and the biggest crush in July and August, when you'll need to book your accommodation well in advance.

◄ Piccadilly Circus

single visit – concentrate on one or two areas and you'll get a lot more out of the place. London has always been an enthralling city, and the capital's traditional sights – Big Ben, Westminster Abbey, Buckingham Palace, St Paul's Cathedral and the Tower of London – continue to draw in millions of tourists every year. Things change fast, though, and the mushrooming crop of new attractions ensure that there's plenty to do even for those who've visited before. Since the millennium, virtually all of London's world-class museums, galleries and institutions have been reinvented, from the Royal Opera House to the British Museum. With the Tate Modern and the London Eye, the city can now boast the world's largest modern art gallery and Ferris wheel, as well as the Millennium Bridge, the first new Thames crossing for over a hundred years.

Monuments from the capital's glorious past are everywhere, from medieval banqueting halls and the

▶ "Banglatown", Brick Lane

great churches of Christopher Wren to the eclectic Victorian architecture of the triumphalist British Empire. There's also much enjoyment to be had from the city's quiet Georgian squares, the narrow alleyways of the City of London, the riverside walks, and the assorted quirks of what is still identifiably a collection of villages. And London is offset by surprisingly large expanses of greenery, with several large public parks right in the centre as well as wilder spaces on the outskirts.

◀ Berkeley Square

You could spend days just shopping in London, too, mixing with the upper classes in the "tiara triangle" around Harrods, or sampling the offbeat weekend markets of Portobello Road, Camden and Greenwich. The music, clubbing and gay/lesbian scenes are second to none, and mainstream arts are no less exciting, with regular opportunities to catch first-rate theatre companies, dance troupes, exhibitions and opera. The city's pubs have always had heaps of atmosphere, but its restaurants are now an attraction too, with everything from three-star Michelin establishments to low-cost, high-quality Chinese restaurants and Indian curry houses.

◀ Sunset over the the Thames

›› LONDON AT A GLANCE

Soho

The headquarters of hedonistic London, Soho is the heart of the West End entertainment district, with the city's largest concentration of theatres, cinemas, clubs, bars, cafés and restaurants.

◄ Cutty Sark, Greenwich

◄ Soho by night

Greenwich

Well worth the boat or train journey from central London, Greenwich makes the most of its riverside setting, with heaps of maritime sights, a royal park, a bustling weekend market and the famous Greenwich Meridian.

Bankside and Southwark

The traffic-free riverside path takes you past the Tate Modern, Shakespeare's Globe Theatre and several more sights in neighbouring Southwark, while dishing out great views over the water to St Paul's Cathedral.

Covent Garden

With its big covered market hall, cobbled piazza and fantastic range of shops, traffic-becalmed Covent Garden is justifiably many visitors' favourite slice of central London.

◄ Covent Garden Piazza

◄ Natural History Museum

South Kensington

A fashionably smart part of London in its own right, South Kensington is also home to the city's most impressive trio of free museums: the Natural History, Science, and Victoria & Albert.

Hampstead

Although buzzing with cosmopolitan life, Hampstead has managed to retain a more village-like feel than any other London suburb and boasts the wild open space of the Heath as well as a clutch of intriguing small museums.

Westminster

Home to the Houses of Parliament, Big Ben and the striking Abbey and Cathedral, Westminster easily justifies its status as one of London's busiest tourist honeypots.

◄ Hampstead Heath

Ideas

The big six sights

London has lots of hidden corners, obscure attractions and esoteric shops, but amongst the well-known sights, the "**big six**" really do live up to their hype. Westminster Abbey and the Tower of London have justifiably been pulling in the crowds for centuries; the British Museum and the National Gallery have grown in popularity over the last hundred years or so; while the elegance of the London Eye and the stunning collection housed in the Tate Modern have captured the imagination of today's visitors like no other sights.

Tate Modern

Austere former power station that's now an awesome cathedral to modern art.

▶ P.147 ▶ BANKSIDE AND SOUTHWARK ▲

London Eye

The world's largest ferris wheel is a graceful new addition to the London skyline.

▶ P.142 ▶ SOUTH BANK AND AROUND ▲

Westminster Abbey

Venue for every coronation since William the Conqueror and resting place of countless kings and queens, the abbey is an essential stop on any London tour.

▶ P.75 ▶ WESTMINSTER ▲

British Museum

London's most popular museum, worth a visit for its glazed-over Great Court and magnificent Round Reading Room alone.

▶ P.101 ▶ BLOOMSBURY ▲

National Gallery

The vast range of work here, from Giotto to Picasso, ensures that there's something for everyone.

▶ P.67 ▶ TRAFALGAR SQUARE AND WHITEHALL ▼

Tower of London

England's most perfectly preserved medieval fortress, site of some of the goriest events in the nation's history and somewhere everyone should visit at least once.

▶ P.134 ▶ THE TOWER AND DOCKLANDS ▼

What to eat

London is an exciting – though often expensive – place in which to **eat out**. You can sample pretty much every kind of cuisine here, from traditional and modern British food to Georgian and Peruvian. Indeed, London can boast some of the best Cantonese restaurants in the whole of Europe, is a noted centre for Indian and Bangladeshi food, and has some very good French, Greek, Italian, Japanese, Spanish and Thai eateries.

Fish and chips

The national dish – fish in batter with deep-fried potato chips – remains as popular and tasty as ever.

▸ P.167 ▸ HIGH STREET KENSINGTON TO NOTTING HILL ▾

Curry

Attracting top-notch chefs from Bangladesh, Nepal, Sri Lanka and Pakistan as well as all the Indian regions, London is now one of the curry capitals of the world.

▸ P.133 ▸ HOXTON AND SPITALFIELDS ▾

Dim Sum

This bargain spread of dumplings and other little morsels is a Cantonese lunchtime ritual.

▸ P.99 ▸ SOHO   ▲

Haute cuisine

The capital now boasts an impressive array of restaurants serving top-notch, Michelin-starred haute cuisine.

▸ P.163 ▸ SOUTH KENSINGTON, KNIGHTSBRIDGE AND CHELSEA   ▼

Pie and mash

London's most peculiar culinary speciality: minced beef and gravy pie, mashed potatoes and "liquor" (parsley sauce).

▸ P.120 ▸ CLERKENWELL   ▼

Vegetarian

London has a vast range of exclusively veggie eating places, ranging from small, wholesome, informal cafés to smart à la carte restaurants.

▸ P.110 ▸ COVENT GARDEN   ▲

London outdoors

Summer can be unpredictable, and the winter a little damp, but Londoners get out and enjoy the great **outdoors** whatever the weather. Temporary outdoor ice rinks are a regular feature of the winter season, boats ply up and down the Thames throughout the year, and in the summer there are several little-known spots where you can enjoy an alfresco dip.

Hampstead Ponds

Tucked amidst woodland, the Heath's natural ponds are extremely popular for alfresco summer swimming.

▶ P.175 ▶ HAMPSTEAD AND HIGHGATE ▲

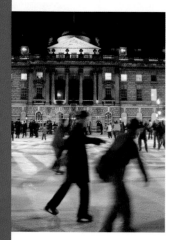

Somerset House ice rink

Set up each winter in the eighteenth-century courtyard of Somerset House, this is London's most picturesque place to skate.

▶ P.217 ▶ ESSENTIALS ▲

Boat trip on the Thames

Zig-zag your way from pier to pier on the central section of the Thames, or take longer trips downriver to Greenwich or upstream to Kew and Richmond.

▸ P.216 ▸ ESSENTIALS ▲

Westminster Abbey College Gardens

Hidden behind the abbey, this secret oasis of green is great for picnics, croquet matches and brass-band concerts.

▸ P.76 ▸ WESTMINSTER ▼

Portobello Road Market

London's best street market (Fri & Sat) offers brilliant retro clothes, bric-a-brac, antiques, and fruit and veg.

▸ P.165 ▸ HIGH STREET KENSINGTON TO NOTTING HILL ▲

Gay and lesbian London

London's **lesbian and gay scene** is so huge, diverse and well established that it's easy to forget just how much it has grown over the last few years. Pink power has given rise to the pink pound, gay liberation to gay lifestyle, and ever-expanding Soho – now firmly established as the homo heart of the city – is vibrant, self-assured and unashamedly commercial. As a result of all this high-profile activity, straight Londoners tend to be a fairly homo-savvy bunch and, on the whole, happy to embrace and sometimes dip into the city's queer offerings.

Old Compton Street

Lined with upfront bars and cafés, and some rather risqué shops, this Soho drag is Gay London's main street.

▸ P.97 ▸ SOHO ▾

First Out

The West End's original gay café-bar still draws in the crowds, and runs a popular weekly pre-club session for women each Friday.

▸ P.112 ▸ COVENT GARDEN ▾

Chariots Roman Baths

London's largest and most fabulous gay sauna features everything you could wish for in the way of hot and sweaty nights indoors.

▶ P.218 ▶ ESSENTIALS ▼

Candy Bar

Central London's hottest girl-bar is a cruisey, upbeat spot that's open until the early hours on the weekend.

▶ P.100 ▶ SOHO ▲

Pride in the Park/Mardi Gras

The up-for-it carnival child of Gay Pride, featuring a whistle-blowing parade through London followed by a huge, ticketed party in a park.

▶ P.215 ▶ ESSENTIALS ◀

London pubs

One of the country's most enduring social institutions, **pubs** remain the focal point of London's communities, offering the prospect of fringe theatre, alternative comedy and live music as well as a pint. The city's great period of pub building took place in the Victorian era, and though many pubs merely pay homage to that period, there are also plenty of genuine, evocative late nineteenth-century interiors, boasting etched glass partitions and lots of authentic polished wood and brass fittings.

Dog and Duck

Victorian Soho pub with real character, real ales and original tiled and mosaiced decor.

▸ P.100 ▸ SOHO ▲

Salisbury

Flamboyant late-Victorian pub a stone's throw from Trafalgar Square, replete with bronze nymphs and etched glasswork.

▸ P.112 ▸ COVENT GARDEN ▲

The Lamb

Classic, beautifully preserved Victorian pub serving London's own Young's beers.

▲

Anchor

Ancient riverside inn near the Tate Modern, where Pepys watched London burn, and Dr Johnson worked on his dictionary.

▼

Ye Olde Cheshire Cheese

A dark, snug seventeenth-century tavern hidden down an alleyway off Fleet Street – look out for the sign.

▲

Art galleries

The astute taste and financial muscle of London's collectors over the centuries has endowed the capital with some wonderful art galleries, many of which offer free entry. The **National** boasts both quality and quantity, stretching from the Italian Renaissance to the Impressionists, while **Tate Modern** is London's magnificent new repository of modern art. In addition, there are several smaller galleries, where the quality is comparable but the collections more manageable.

National Gallery

A comprehensive overview of the history of Western painting, from Renaissance classics in the airy Sainsbury Wing to works from *fin-de-siècle* Paris.

▸ P.67 ▸ TRAFALGAR SQUARE AND WHITEHALL ▾

Courtauld Institute

Quality, not quantity, is the hallmark of this gallery, best known for its superlative collection of Impressionist masterpieces.

▸ P.110 ▸ COVENT GARDEN ▾

Tate Modern

A wonderful hotchpotch of wild and wacky art, from video installations to gargantuan pieces that fill the vastness of the turbine hall.

▸ P.147 ▸ BANKSIDE AND SOUTHWARK ▲

Wallace Collection

Exquisite miniature eighteenth-century chateau close to Oxford Street, housing period furniture and masterpieces by the likes of Rembrandt, Van Dyck, Hals, Fragonard and Watteau.

▸ P.91 ▸ MARYLEBONE ▲

Iveagh Bequest

Small but perfectly formed collection of seventeenth- and eighteenth-century paintings, including works by Gainsborough, Reynolds, Rembrandt and Vermeer.

▸ P.177 ▸ HAMPSTEAD AND HIGHGATE ▼

Tate Britain

The history of British painting from Holbein and Hogarth to Hockney and Hirst, plus copious pre-Raphaelites and lots of Turners.

▸ P.77 ▸ WESTMINSTER ▼

Royal London

Home to the most famous royal family in the world, London doesn't disappoint when it comes to pomp and circumstance. As well as the massing of "busbies" at the daily Changing of the Guard, there are much larger displays of **royal pageantry** to take in throughout the year. The crown jewels are always on public display, guarded by ludicrously overdressed Beefeaters at the Tower of London; and then, of course, there's the city's numerous royal palaces, with Hampton Court by far the most impressive and "Buck House" easily the most famous.

Changing of the Guard

The colourful daily rituals of the Queen's Household Regiments, with the Horse Guards parading behind Whitehall and the Foot Guards looking after Buckingham Palace.

▸ P.71 ▸ TRAFALGAR SQUARE AND WHITEHALL ▲

Trooping the Colour

Suitably spectacular summer show by the Household battalions in the presence of royalty.

▸ P.215 ▸ ESSENTIALS ▲

Tower of London

A place of imprisonment for several monarchs, the Tower remains the safe-deposit box of the crown jewels, which feature some of the biggest diamonds in the world.

▸ P.134 ▸ THE TOWER AND DOCKLANDS ▼

Buckingham Palace

The gaudy London home of Her Majesty is open to the public for just two months in the summer, while the royals holiday in Scotland.

▸ P.80 ▸ ST JAMES'S ▼

Royal Mews

Official garage for the royal family's fancy fleet of Daimlers, gilded coaches and immaculately groomed horses.

▸ P.82 ▸ ST JAMES'S ▲

Hampton Court Palace

Redesigned by Wren, this Tudor pile is without doubt the most magnificent of the country's royal palaces.

▸ P.192 ▸ HAMPTON COURT ▲

Gourmet London

Londoners' sophisticated tastes stretch back a long way. At the height of the British Empire, the capital's dockside warehouses were filled with produce from all over the globe; today, the locals are more cosmopolitan and discerning than ever. From champagne to chocolates, you'll find all the luxury goods you'd expect; seafood – particularly oysters – remains very popular; and there's been a renewed interest in **gourmet British food**: cheese, smoked fish, beer and even wine. As well as being sold in deluxe emporia, top-quality produce is a main feature of London's increasingly popular farmers' markets.

Harrods Food Hall

The Arts and Crafts food hall of the ultimate Knightsbridge department store is a feast for the eyes as well as the stomach.

▶ P.161 ▶ SOUTH KENSINGTON, KNIGHTSBRIDGE AND CHELSEA ▼

Fortnum & Mason

Piccadilly's most famous food emporium, renowned for its picnic hampers, sumptuous food hall and pukka tearoom.

▶ P.88 ▶ PICCADILLY AND MAYFAIR ▼

Neal's Yard Dairy

Experienced, helpful staff encourage customers to sample the outstanding variety of British cheeses piled high on the counters.

▸ P.110 ▸ COVENT GARDEN ▲

Paul

Long-established Parisian café-boulangerie, selling authentic and delicious French breads and pastries.

▸ P.93 ▸ MARYLEBONE ▼

Charbonnel et Walker

If it ain't broke, don't fix it – Her Majesty's chocolatier sticks to its 1875 recipes.

▸ P.88 ▸ PICCADILLY AND MAYFAIR ▼

Borough Market

Stalls at this weekly (Fri & Sat) gourmet food market sell the very best of British produce.

▸ P.149 ▸ BANKSIDE
AND SOUTHWARK ▲

Museums

London has a fantastic number and variety of **museums**, but some stand head and shoulders above the rest. The British Museum and the Victoria and Albert, for example, are both world-class repositories of art treasures. For a balanced view of human conflict, head for the Imperial War Museum, but for exemplary modern, interactive museums that manage to appeal to visitors of all ages, choose the National Maritime Museum or the new Wellcome Wing at the Science Museum. All these are giants compared with Sir John Soane's Museum, a hidden gem with totally unique, treasure-trove atmosphere.

British Museum

Roman and Greek art, Egyptian and Assyrian artefacts, fabulous treasures from Anglo-Saxon, Roman and Medieval Britain, and vast ethnographic collections from all over the world.

▶ P.101 ▶ BLOOMSBURY ▲

Imperial War Museum

The capital's finest military museum puts on fascinating talks and events, houses a huge art collection and gives a sober account of the horrors of war.

▶ P.144 ▶ SOUTH BANK AND AROUND ▲

V&A

The world's greatest applied arts museum, with something for everyone, whether you're into the history of dress, musical instruments, silver, Indian and Islamic art or modern mass-produced design.

▶ P.160 ▶ SOUTH KENSINGTON, KNIGHTSBRIDGE AND CHELSEA ▼

Science Museum

The interactive Wellcome galleries and the daily demonstrations are the most impressive aspects of this enormous complex, covering every conceivable area of science.

▶ P.159 ▶ SOUTH KENSINGTON, KNIGHTSBRIDGE AND CHELSEA ▼

Sir John Soane's Museum

This early nineteenth-century home-cum-studio of the idiosyncratic architect of the Bank of England is crammed with paintings and antique sculpture.

▶ P.116 ▶ HOLBORN ▲

National Maritime Museum

Encompassing the old Royal Observatory as well as the nautical exhibits, this imaginatively designed complex will appeal to all ages.

▶ P.182 ▶ GREENWICH ▲

Churches

As medieval London was almost entirely destroyed by the Great Fire of 1666, the **churches** that survived the flames are all the more precious. The Fire heralded the city's greatest era of church building, much of it under the supervision of Sir Christopher Wren, architect of St Paul's Cathedral. Later, the Victorians added yet more churches to London's burgeoning suburbs, one or two of which are especially worth seeking out.

Westminster Abbey

This former medieval monastic church preserves both its cloisters and chapter house, and boasts some of the city's finest late Gothic architecture and funerary art from every age.

▸ P.75 ▸ WESTMINSTER ▾

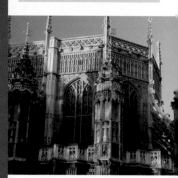

St Paul's Cathedral

The world's first Protestant cathedral is a Baroque masterpiece – test the acoustics in the whispering gallery and climb to the top of the dome.

▸ P.123 ▸ THE CITY ▾

St Bartholomew-the-Great

Much altered, wonderfully ancient church which has the finest Norman chancel in London and some excellent pre-Fire monuments.

▶ P.117 ▶ CLERKENWELL ▲

Temple Church

This early English Gothic church in the heart of the Inns of Court boasts a circular nave featuring battered medieval effigies of the Knights Templar.

▶ P.113 ▶ HOLBORN ▼

Westminster Cathedral

Bizarre, eye-catching neo-Byzantine Catholic cathedral with an ornate but eerily unfinished interior.

▶ P.76 ▶ WESTMINSTER ▲

Diverse London

With around three hundred languages spoken in its confines, all the major religions represented, and with immigrants making up over thirty percent of the population, London is Europe's most ethnically **diverse** city. All the immigrant groups have brought with them traditions and customs that have proved an invaluable and vibrant contribution to London's cultural life. As well as improving the local cuisine immeasurably, they have provided a vast workforce, had a profound impact on the arts and music scene, and are responsible for the Notting Hill Carnival, the country's biggest street party.

Chinatown

London's most distinct and popular ethnic enclave, characterized by its bewildering array of cafés and restaurants.

▶ P.95 ▶ SOHO ▲

Brixton market

Brixton's upfront African-Caribbean consciousness is especially evident around the wonderful market, with its out-door produce stalls and network of indoor arcades.

▶ P.217 ▶ ESSENTIALS ▲

Bevis Marks Synagogue

Built in 1701 in the City, this Sephardi synagogue is the country's oldest, and a favourite venue for candlelit Jewish weddings.

▸ P.126 ▸ THE CITY ▼

Brick Lane

This East End street is the spiritual heart of London's Bangladeshi community, and is best known for its inexpensive curry houses.

▸ P.130 ▸ HOXTON
AND SPITALFIELDS ▲

London Central Mosque

Thousands of worshippers congregate for Friday prayers at this striking modern mosque in Regent's Park.

▸ P.169 ▸ REGENT'S PARK
AND CAMDEN ▼

Kids' London

There's plenty to delight **kids** in London. Top attractions such as London Zoo, the London Aquarium and the Natural History Museum are more or less guaranteed to go down well (and the latter has the added advantage of being free), while further from the centre, Syon Park's child-friendly credentials are ensured by its butterfly house and reptile centre. **Playgrounds** abound in the city's parks, but the mother of them all is the state-of-the-art Diana Memorial Playground in Kensington Gardens. Finally, don't underestimate the value of London's public transport as a source of fun – the no.11 double-decker bus takes you past some of London's chief landmarks.

London Zoo

Opened in 1828 as the world's first scientific zoo, and still a guaranteed hit with children of all ages.

> P.171 ▸ REGENT'S PARK AND CAMDEN ▼

London Aquarium

Large and popular South Bank aquarium, where kids can stroke the rays and gawp at the sharks.

> P.143 ▸ SOUTH BANK AND AROUND ▼

Syon Park

Aristocratic estate that's now home to a butterfly house, a reptile and amphibian attraction, and gardens that feature a miniature steam engine.

▸ P.186 ▸ KEW AND RICHMOND ▲

Natural History Museum

With animatronic dinosaurs and an earthquake simulator, the Natural History is sure to prove a winner.

▸ P.158 ▸ SOUTH KENSINGTON, KNIGHTSBRIDGE AND CHELSEA ▼

Diana Memorial Playground

The city's most sophisticated, imaginative and popular outdoor playground, just a short walk from Diana's former home.

▸ P.157 ▸ HYDE PARK AND KENSINGTON GARDENS ▶

No. 11 bus

Head upstairs for a free double-decker tour of some of London's most famous sights, from Big Ben to St Paul's Cathedral via Trafalgar Square.

▸ P.211 ▸ ESSENTIALS ▼

Indulgent London

If you've got the time and the money, London is a great place in which to **indulge yourself** – whether in the bar of a luxury hotel, the chair of one of the city's leading hair salons or at a table in a Michelin-starred restaurant. Steam baths have been popular here since the Restoration in 1660, and there's an abundance of plush places around, with most offering treatments and massages as an optional extra.

The Sanctuary

Full-on women-only pamper zone, where you can swim naked in the pool, jump in a jacuzzi or loll about in the sauna and steam room.

▸ P.218 ▸ ESSENTIALS ▲

Ironmonger Row Baths

Old-fashioned steam bath, sauna and plunge-pool on the edge of the City, with optional massage and rest beds to collapse on afterwards.

▸ P.218 ▸ ESSENTIALS ▲

Hairdressers

London holds the flagship salons of some of the biggest names in hair, offering spas as well as styling.

▸ P.217 ▸ ESSENTIALS ▾

Cocktails at the Savoy

Britain's first martini was mixed at the Savoy hotel's swish Art Deco American Bar in the 1920s, and it's still *the* place to drink in style.

▸ P.112 ▸ COVENT GARDEN ▴

Dinner at Gordon Ramsay

Experience some of the capital's most sublime cooking at this Michelin-starred restaurant, run by the famously bad-tempered Glaswegian former footballer.

▸ P.163 ▸
SOUTH KENSINGTON,
KNIGHTSBRIDGE AND
CHELSEA ▸

Club-bars

The last decade has seen the inexorable rise of the **club-bar**. Catering for a clubby crowd, with resident DJs, late opening hours and, more often than not, free (or very cheap) entry, club-bars came about as part of the backlash against London's "superclubs", where entrance fees were climbing ever higher and door-policies becoming increasingly draconian. These days, club-bars are ubiquitous, and are ideal if you fancy a laid-back night on the tiles.

AKA

A minimalist adjunct to The End nightclub, this central venue's regular DJ nights pull in a crowd of good-time clubbers.

▶ P.111 ▶ COVENT GARDEN ▼

Cherry Jam

Great west London cocktail bar whose DJ line-ups attract a trendy young crowd.

▶ P.168 ▶ HIGH STREET KENSINGTON TO NOTTING HILL ▼

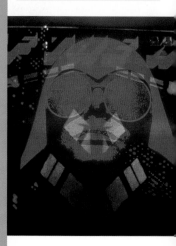

Vibe Bar

Buzzing, busy DJ venue housed in an old East End brewery.

> ▶ P.133 ▶ HOXTON AND SPITALFIELDS ▼

Sosho

Trendy club-bar, doling out lethally good cocktails and best-known for its excellent DJs.

> ▶ P.133 ▶ HOXTON AND SPITALFIELDS ▲

Dragon

Low-key bar popular with a mixed clientele of laid-back locals who like to party on down to the resident DJs.

> ▶ P.133 ▶ HOXTON AND SPITALFIELDS ▼

Victorian London

During the reign of **Queen Victoria** (1837–1901), London trebled in size and became the largest city in the world, at the heart of an empire that stretched across the globe. Not surprisingly, the buildings of the era exude the wealth and confidence of that period. They also reflect the magpie-like tastes of the day, when architects tried to outdo each other in decorative detailing, borrowing from every previous architectural style and from all corners of the empire.

St Pancras Station

Victorian railway station fronted by a gloriously over-the-top red-brick Neo-Gothic hotel.

▶ P.104 ▶ BLOOMSBURY ▼

Brompton Oratory

Experience the smells and sights of an Italianate Roman Catholic church in this wonderfully atmospheric slice of neo-Baroque.

▶ P.161 ▶ SOUTH KENSINGTON, KNIGHTSBRIDGE AND CHELSEA ▼

Leadenhall Market

Cobblestones and graceful Victorian iron-work combine to create the City's most attractive market for luxury comestibles.

▸ P.126 ▸ THE CITY ▲

Albert Memorial

This bombastic monument to Queen Victoria's consort is a riot of semi-precious stones, marbles, bronze and gilding.

▸ P.156 ▸ HYDE PARK AND KENSINGTON GARDENS ▲

Palm House Kew Gardens

Decimus Burton's spectacular curvaceous hothouse is home to most of the world's known palm species.

▸ P.188 ▸ KEW AND RICHMOND ▲

Houses of Parliament

A gargantuan, confident neo-Elizabethan expression of nationhood, best known for its "Big Ben" clocktower.

▸ P.73 ▸ WESTMINSTER ▼

Dead London

In medieval times, only royalty and the nobility were commemorated after their death – and the iconoclasm of the Reformation and the Great Fire of 1666 mean that very little medieval **funerary art** has survived. However, in the nineteenth century, the emergence of an aspirational middle class prompted more and more Londoners to opt for permanent memorials and ever more ostentatious funerals. The legacy of this period can be seen in London's vast suburban **cemeteries**, established during the Victorian period to cope with the new fashion for funereal opulence.

Highgate Cemetery

London's most convincingly Hammer Horror cemetery is most famous as the resting place of Karl Marx.

▸ P.178 ▸ HAMPSTEAD AND HIGHGATE ▼

Kensal Green

This canalside cemetery boasts the capital's most flamboyant funereal sculptures.

▸ P.166 ▸ HIGH STREET KENSINGTON TO NOTTING HILL ▼

Westminster Abbey

When it comes to dead royalty, poets or politicians, the abbey wins hands down.

▸ P.75 ▸ WESTMINSTER ▾

St Paul's Cathedral

The nave features some ludicrously pompous monuments to British imperialists, while the huge crypt specializes in artists.

▸ P.123 ▸ THE CITY ▾

St Mary-at-Lambeth

The tiny graveyard here is home to the beautifully carved John Tradescant memorial and the grave of Captain Bligh of the *Bounty* fame.

▸ P.144 ▸ SOUTH BANK AND AROUND ▴

Cenotaph

Edwin Lutyens' understated Whitehall memorial is a moving commemoration of the "glorious dead" from both world wars.

▸ P.70 ▸ TRAFALGAR SQUARE AND WHITEHALL ▴

Riverside London

Until the 1820s, the Thames was London's main thoroughfare, and some of the city's finest buildings were built along the riverfront; the steady decline in river traffic, though, means that the Thames itself is now quieter than ever before. However the **waterfront** has, if anything, become busier in the last couple of decades. From the revitalized South Bank to the phoenix-like Docklands, the traffic-free portions of riverbank have again become a focal point, with pubs, cafés, restaurants, museums and other attractions jostling for space.

Bankside

Thanks to the Tate Modern, Millennium Bridge and Shakespeare's Globe, the waterside entertainment district of Tudor and Stuart London is pulling in the crowds once again.

▶ P.146 ▶ BANKSIDE AND SOUTHWARK ▼

Old Royal Naval College

This symmetrical Baroque masterpiece enjoys the best riverside setting in the whole of London.

▶ P.182 ▶ GREENWICH ▼

South Bank

The traffic-free riverside path here connects numerous attractions, theatres and galleries, as well as affording by far the best views of the Thames's photogenic north bank.

▸ P.140 ▸ SOUTH BANK AND AROUND ▲

Docklands

The transformation of London's moribund dock system into a world-class business district is a maritime miracle.

▸ P134 ▸ THE TOWER AND DOCKLANDS ▸

Richmond

Elegant Thames-side suburb where you can have a drink overlooking the water, rent rowing boats or stroll along the bucolic towpath.

▸ P.186 ▸ KEW AND RICHMOND ◂

Free London

London can be an expensive place for locals and tourists alike, but there are lots of things to enjoy in the city which are one hundred percent **free**. Aside from the numerous museums and galleries which don't charge entry, there are plenty of slightly more offbeat activities which don't cost a thing, from musical treats and upscale auctions to political sparring matches.

Lunchtime concerts

Free lunchtime classical concerts take place in churches all over the City and parts of the West End.

▸ P.70 ▸ TRAFALGAR SQUARE AND WHITEHALL ▲

Sotheby's auction

Buying might make a dent in your pocket, but viewing and attending an auction costs nothing.

▸ P.87 ▸ PICCADILLY AND MAYFAIR ▲

Evensong at St Paul's Cathedral

The most moving way to experience this great Protestant cathedral is during choral evensong.

▸ P.124 ▸ THE CITY ▼

Foyer gigs in the Royal Festival Hall

One of the joys of a stroll along the South Bank is the chance to catch one of the free lunchtime concerts in the RFH foyer.

▸ P.140 ▸ SOUTH BANK AND AROUND ▲

Kenwood House

An exquisite eighteenth-century interior and top-drawer Old Masters can all be seen for free at English Heritage's flagship property overlooking Hampstead Heath.

▸ P.176 ▸ HAMPSTEAD AND HIGHGATE ▼

London from up high

London is a huge city, but it's only when you take a **bird's-eye view** that you realize just how vast an area it covers. The most far-reaching vistas are from the pods of the London Eye observation wheel, but even here you can barely make out the edge of the city. What you do notice, though, is that London has only a small number of very tall buildings, allowing church spires to rise above the rooftops, and that the city has a wonderfully idiosyncratic patchwork layout, woven over several centuries.

St Paul's Cathedral Dome

A head for heights and the ability to climb 500 steps are needed to enjoy a rooftop view over the City here.

▶ P.122 ▶ THE CITY ▲

London Eye

The city's giant Ferris wheel provides both the most expensive and the most superlative view over the capital.

▶ P.142 ▶ SOUTH BANK AND AROUND ▲

Westminster Cathedral

A lift inside the stripy campanile takes you high above the rooftops of Westminster.

▸ P.76 ▸ WESTMINSTER ▼

Oxo Building

The free public viewing platform on the eighth floor of this former meat-processing factory gives a lovely view over the South Bank.

▸ P.142 ▸ SOUTH BANK AND AROUND ▼

Tower Bridge

The elevated walkways of this landmark bridge provide the ultimate up- and downriver vistas.

▸ P.135 ▸ THE TOWER AND DOCKLANDS ▲

Parliament Hill

North London's favourite kite-flying spot, at the southern tip of Hampstead Heath, offers a fabulous skyline panorama.

▸ P.175 ▸ HAMPSTEAD AND HIGHGATE ▲

London has an endless roster of **festivals and special events**, with something happening somewhere almost every day of the year. The fortnight of grass-court tennis at Wimbledon is one of the great annual social events but, like the Proms festival of classical music, it's open to all-comers provided you're prepared to queue. Carnival, London's mammoth street party, is equally democratic, but it's also worth catching one or two of the more unusual annual events, such as the quaint narrowboat and Morris dancing celebration that is the IWA Cavalcade.

Proms

The world's most egalitarian classical music festival, featuring daily concerts in the Royal Albert Hall (and elsewhere), and culminating in the flag-waving nationalism of the "Last Night".

▸ P.215 ▸ ESSENTIALS ▾

Carnival

Floats, costume bands, sound-systems, legions of food stalls and a fun-loving, heaving crowd make this huge street party unmissable.

▸ P.215 ▸ ESSENTIALS ▾

IWA Canal Cavalcade

Colourful and old-fashioned narrowboat parade at the picturesque Little Venice junction of the Regent's and Grand Union canals.

▸ P.215 ▸ ESSENTIALS ▲

Dance Umbrella

One of the world's leading contemporary dance festivals, with innovative productions staged all over the capital.

▸ P.215 ▸ ESSENTIALS ▼

Open House

Constantly expanding annual event which sees the city's most intriguing historic buildings throw open their doors to the public for free.

▸ P.215 ▸ ESSENTIALS ▲

Wimbledon Lawn Tennis Championship

Summertime grass-court venue of the most singular of tennis's four Grand Slam events – think strawberries and cream, and heroic British failures.

▸ P.215 ▸ ESSENTIALS ▸

Queasy London

London today is a fairly salubrious, modern metropolis, but many of its attractions prefer to glory in the city's murkier past. Medieval London was undoubtedly a muddy, unforgiving place – there were 156 capital offences in the eighteenth-century city – but it was during the Victorian era when it really paid not to be too squeamish. The Gothic horror and hypocrisy of the period is perfectly illustrated by the cult surrounding the Jack the Ripper murders, which still pulls in the punters even today, just as pre-anaesthetic operations did in the past.

Madame Tussaud's

The ghoulish human fascination with murderers and serial killers is indulged in this infamous waxwork museum's Chamber of Horrors.

▸ P.92 ▸ MARYLEBONE

London Dungeon

Ham and Gothic it may be, but the grisly tableaux and ghost-train ride at the London Dungeon are as popular as ever.

▸ P.150 ▸ BANKSIDE AND SOUTHWARK ▲

Old Operating Theatre and Herb Garret

Amputations were performed with great speed and skill at this pre-anaesthetic operating theatre – though often with fatal consequences.

▸ P.149 ▸ BANKSIDE AND SOUTHWARK ▸

Smithfield Market

Each weekday morning around dawn, London's leading market for TK (town-killed) meat is a mass of bloody carcasses.

▸ P.118 ▸ CLERKENWELL ◀

London on stage

London has enjoyed a reputation for quality **theatre** since the time of Shakespeare, and despite the continuing dominance of blockbuster musicals and revenue-spinning star vehicles, the city still provides a platform for innovation. The largely pub-based **fringe** theatre scene is still going strong, and **comedy** is so big that London now boasts more dedicated venues than any other city in the world.

Shakespeare's Globe

This meticulous replica of an Elizabethan playhouse puts on rabble-rousing, open-air performances of plays by Shakespeare and his contemporaries.

▸ P.148 ▸ BANKSIDE AND SOUTHWARK ▾

National Theatre

The South Bank's concrete carbuncle houses three excellent theatre spaces, and stages consistently good productions of everything from classics to new works.

▸ P.142 ▸ SOUTH BANK AND AROUND ▾

Donmar Warehouse

Covent Garden theatre with an outstanding reputation for classy revivals, new writing and star-studded casts.

▸ P.212 ▸ ESSENTIALS ▲

King's Head pub theatre

The most reliable of London's pub theatre venues, the King's Head is always worth a visit.

▸ P.212 ▸ ESSENTIALS ▲

West End musicals

Lavish blockbuster musicals dominate the West End theatre scene.

▸ P.212 ▸ ESSENTIALS ▼

Comedy Café

London's comedy scene is as varied as it is huge, but the acts at this purpose-built Hoxton venue are a cut above the rest.

▸ P.213 ▸ ESSENTIALS ▼

Musical London

For sheer range and variety, there's little to beat London's **live music**. As well as boasting two world-class opera houses and free lunchtime classical concerts held regularly at venues throughout the capital, the live music scene also encompasses all variations of classical, rock, blues, roots and world music. Most major artists include London in any European tour, and there's also a thriving underground scene, with lots of up-and-coming bands working the circuit.

Royal Opera House

Despite the money and effort involved in getting a ticket, it's definitely worth trying to catch a production at one of the world's finest opera houses.

▸ P.213 ▸ ESSENTIALS

Jazz Café

Camden's Jazz Café embraces all kinds of music, attracting top names from world music, roots, folk, R&B and hip-hop, as well as the jazz crowd.

▸ P.214 ▸ ESSENTIALS

Wigmore Hall

Long-established chamber music venue with wonderful acoustics, just off Oxford Street.

▸ P.214 ▸ ESSENTIALS

Astoria

Smack in the centre of London, this cavernous former theatre hosts regular gigs, often with a rock/indie slant.

▸ P.213 ▸ ESSENTIALS

Shepherd's Bush Empire

This old Victorian theatre is probably London's best medium-scale rock venue.

▸ P.214 ▸ ESSENTIALS

Contemporary architecture

The economic boom of the 1980s witnessed London's first wave of **contemporary architecture**. Reflecting the nature of the times, the buildings were generally private office blocks, the most famous of which are the then-groundbreaking Lloyds Building and Canary Wharf. New offices continue to spring up city-wide, and since the turn of the millennium there's been a new wave of lottery-funded structures such as the Millennium Bridge, and public buildings like the new City Hall.

Lloyds Building

Lloyds' high-tech City offices, designed by Richard Rogers in the mid-1980s, are still strikingly contemporary and more successful than many younger upstarts.

▶ P.126 ▶ THE CITY　　　　　▲

Swiss Re

The latest lofty addition to the City skyline, Norman Foster's unusual cone-shaped affair is popularly known as the "erotic gherkin".

▶ P.126 ▶ THE CITY　　　　　▲

Canary Wharf

Loved and hated in equal measure, Cesar Pelli's stainless steel skyscraper is the centrepiece of the Canary Wharf Docklands development.

▶ P.137 ▶ THE TOWER AND DOCKLANDS ▼

Serpentine Gallery pavilions

The annually commissioned summertime tea pavilions have added architectural merit to the green groves of the park.

▶ P.156 ▶ HYDE PARK AND KENSINGTON GARDENS ▲

City Hall (GLA)

Bearing a close resemblance to a giant car headlight, Norman Foster's eco-friendly headquarters for the Greater London Authority occupies a prominent position on the Thames.

▶ P.151 ▶ BANKSIDE AND SOUTHWARK ▼

Millennium Bridge

After a wobbly start, Norman Foster's flashy millennial footbridge, connecting St Paul's Cathedral with the Tate Modern, has proved a hit with locals and tourists alike.

▶ P.146 ▶ BANKSIDE AND SOUTHWARK ▲

Tudor and Stuart London

Much of **Tudor and Stuart London** went up in smoke during the 1666 Great Fire of London, but some gems from the period do survive today. Exuding the flamboyance and exuberance of the period, the grand residences of Hampton Court Palace and Ham House lie well outside the city centre and so were never in peril, but the hammerbeamed Middle Temple Hall and wood-panelled Prince Henry's Room, on the edge of the City, were saved by a matter of a few feet. The Golden Hinde and the Globe Theatre, meanwhile, are meticulous timber-framed reconstructions from London's glorious Elizabethan Renaissance.

Golden Hinde

Seaworthy replica of the dinky timber ship in which Sir Francis Drake circum-navigated the globe.

▸ P.149 ▸ BANKSIDE AND SOUTHWARK ▾

Globe Theatre

Relocated and reconstructed in the 1990s, the Globe gives a fascinating insight into the theatre of Shakespeare's day.

▸ P.148 ▸ BANKSIDE AND SOUTHWARK ▲

Middle Temple Hall

This sixteenth-century lawyers' dining hall boasts a fine hammerbeam roof, wood panelling and a richly carved Elizabethan screen.

▸ P.113 ▸ HOLBORN ◀

Ham House

Seventeenth-century stately home, just up the towpath from Richmond, with one of the finest Stuart interiors in the country.

▸ P.189 ▸ KEW AND RICHMOND ▼

Prince Henry's Room

Hidden gem at the top of Fleet Street, with Jacobean plasterwork and linenfold panelling that miraculously survived the Great Fire.

▸ P.115 ▸ HOLBORN ▲

Hampton Court Palace

Magnificent Tudor palace on which both Cardinal Wolsey and Henry VIII spent a fortune.

▸ P.192 ▸ HAMPTON COURT ▼

Literary and artistic London

London's streets are full of **literary and artistic associations** – from Shakespeare, Dickens and Marx to Orwell, Woolf and Freud. Everywhere you look there's a blue plaque, a statue or a memorial celebrating the city's writers, painters and thinkers. Some have left only memories, others first editions and works of art, and a few have been paid the ultimate homage via the transformation of their former homes into museums.

Keats House

Former home – now shrine – to the ultimate Romantic poet, who fell in love with the girl next door, became consumptive and died in Rome at the age of just 25.

▶ P.175 ▶ HAMPSTEAD AND HIGHGATE

Freud Museum

Fleeing Nazi persecution, the father of psychoanalysis lived out his last months in this well-to-do Hampstead residence.

▶ P.174 ▶ HAMPSTEAD AND HIGHGATE

British Library

Home of artistic literary masterpieces such as the Lindisfarne Gospels, as well as original manuscripts by the likes of James Joyce.

▶ P.103 ▶ BLOOMSBURY ▼

Leighton House

Purpose-built studio and living space of the successful Victorian painter Lord Leighton, chum of the pre-Raphaelites and lover of the exotic.

▶ P.164 ▶ HIGH STREET KENSINGTON TO NOTTING HILL ▲

2 Willow Road

The Hampstead abode of Hungarian modernist architect Ernö Goldfinger is filled with avant-garde artworks by such greats as Max Ernst, Marcel Duchamp, Man Ray and Henry Moore.

▶ P.175 ▶ HAMPSTEAD AND HIGHGATE ▼

Handel House Museum

Court composer Georg Friedrich Handel spent the best part of his life in this Georgian terraced house, now refurbished as a period set-piece.

▶ P.88 ▶ PICCADILLY AND MAYFAIR ▲

Afternoon tea

One of London's most accessible indulgent rituals is taking **afternoon tea** in a luxury hotel. At a cost of around £25 a head, this is no quick cuppa, but a high-cholesterol feast that kicks off with sandwiches, moves on to scones slathered with clotted cream and jam, and finishes up with assorted cakes, all washed down with innumerable pots of tea.

Ritz

The Palm Court here has been a favourite spot to take tea since the hotel first wowed Edwardian society in 1906.

▸ P.72 ▸ TRAFALGAR SQUARE AND WHITEHALL ▲

Savoy

Superb Art Deco hotel, originally managed by César Ritz, and where Guccio Gucci started out as a dishwasher.

▸ P.72 ▸ TRAFALGAR SQUARE AND WHITEHALL ▲

Dorchester

Wildly over-the-top gilded and mirrored
Hollywood decor is the Dorchester's
hallmark.

▸ **P.72** ▸ **TRAFALGAR SQUARE
AND WHITEHALL** ▾

Claridge's

Tasteful and terribly English Art Deco hotel
that's perfect for a champagne tea.

▸ **P.72** ▸ **TRAFALGAR SQUARE
AND WHITEHALL** ▲

Lanesborough

Exclusive and very plush venue in a
converted hospital on Hyde Park Corner,
where tea is served in the glass-roofed
conservatory.

▸ **P.72** ▸ **TRAFALGAR SQUARE
AND WHITEHALL** ▾

Places

Places

Trafalgar Square and Whitehall

Despite the scruffy urban pigeons and the traffic noise, **Trafalgar Square** is still one of London's grandest architectural set-pieces, and as such is prime tourist territory. Most folk head here for the National Gallery, at the top of the square, then linger by the fountains before wandering down the unusually broad avenue of **Whitehall** en route to the Houses of Parliament and Westminster Abbey. Whitehall itself is synonymous with the faceless, pinstriped bureaucracy who run the various governmental ministries located here, but it's also the venue for the most elaborate Changing of the Guard, which usually attracts a small crowd of onlookers.

Trafalgar Square

As one of the few large public squares in London, Trafalgar Square has been a focus for political demonstrations since it was laid out in the 1820s. Most days, however, it's crowds of pigeons that you're more likely to encounter, as they wheel around the square hoping some unsuspecting visitor will feed them (it's now, in fact, illegal to do so, as they've been declared a nuisance). Along with its fountains, the square's central focal point is the deeply patriotic **Nelson's Column**, which stands 170ft high and is topped by a 17ft statue of the one-eyed, one-armed admiral who defeated the French at Trafalgar. Nelson himself is actually quite hard to see – not so the giant bronze lions at the base of the column, which provide a popular photo opportunity.

National Gallery

Trafalgar Square ☏020/7747 2885, ⊛www.nationalgallery.org.uk. Daily 10am–6pm, Wed till 9pm. Free.

Despite housing more than 2300 paintings, the main virtue of the National Gallery is not so much the collection's size, but its range, depth and sheer quality. A quick tally of the **Italian** masterpieces, for example, includes works by Uccello, Botticelli, Mantegna, Piero della Francesca, Veronese, Titian, Raphael, Michelangelo and Caravaggio. From **Spain**

▲ FOUNTAINS, TRAFALGAR SQUARE

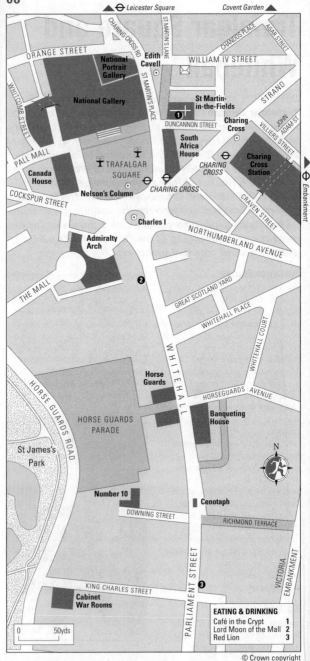

Leicester Square

Covent Garden

ORANGE STREET

CHARING CROSS RD

ST MARTIN'S LANE

CHANDOS PLACE

AGAR STREET

Edith Cavell

WILLIAM IV STREET

National Portrait Gallery

STRAND

National Gallery

ST MARTIN'S PLACE

St Martin-in-the-Fields

JOHN ADAM ST

VILLIERS STREET

WHITCOMB STREET

DUNCANNON STREET

Charing Cross

South Africa House

Charing Cross

PALL MALL

TRAFALGAR SQUARE

Charing Cross Station

Canada House

CHARING CROSS

Embankment

Nelson's Column

COCKSPUR STREET

CRAVEN STREET

Charles I

NORTHUMBERLAND AVENUE

Admiralty Arch

THE MALL

GREAT SCOTLAND YARD

WHITEHALL PLACE

WHITEHALL COURT

Horse Guards

WHITEHALL

HORSEGUARDS AVENUE

Banqueting House

HORSE GUARDS PARADE

HORSE GUARDS ROAD

St James's Park

N

Number 10

Cenotaph

DOWNING STREET

RICHMOND TERRACE

VICTORIA EMBANKMENT

KING CHARLES STREET

PARLIAMENT STREET

Cabinet War Rooms

0   50yds

EATING & DRINKING
Café in the Crypt   1
Lord Moon of the Mall   2
Red Lion   3

© Crown copyright

there are dazzling pieces by El Greco, Velázquez and Goya; from the **Low Countries**, van Eyck, Memlinc and Rubens, and an array of Rembrandt paintings that features some of his most searching portraits. Poussin, Claude, Watteau and the only Jacques-Louis David paintings in the country are the early highlights of a **French** contingent that has a particularly strong showing of Cézanne and the Impressionists. **British** art is also well represented, with important works by Hogarth, Gainsborough, Stubbs and Turner, though for twentieth-century British art – and many more Turners – you'll need to move on to Tate Britain on Millbank (see p.77).

To view the collection chronologically, begin with the **Sainsbury Wing**, the softly-softly, postmodern 1980s adjunct which is linked to – and playfully imitates – the original Neoclassical building. However, as the National has more than a thousand paintings on permanent display, you'll need real stamina to see everything in one day, so if time is tight your best bet is to home in on your areas of special interest, having picked up a gallery plan at one of the information desks. There's also a Gallery Guide Soundtrack, with a brief audio commentary on a large selection of the paintings on display; it's available free of charge, though you're asked for a "voluntary contribution". Another possibility is to join up with one of the excellent, free **guided tours** (daily 11.30am & 2.30pm, plus Wed 6.30 pm), which set off from the Sainsbury Wing foyer.

National Portrait Gallery

St Martin's Place ☎020/7306 0055, ⊛www.npg.org.uk. Daily 10am–6pm, Thurs & Fri till 9pm. Free. Founded in 1856 to house uplifting depictions of the good and the great, the National Portrait Gallery has some fine individual works. However, many of the studies are of less interest than their subjects, and the overall impression is of an overstuffed shrine to famous Brits rather than a museum offering any insight into the history of portraiture. Nevertheless, it is fascinating to trace who has been deemed worthy of admiration at any moment: aristocrats and artists in previous centuries, warmongers and imperialists in the early decades of the twentieth century, writers and

▼ UCCELLO'S *BATTLE OF SAN ROMANO*, NATIONAL GALLERY

▲ BRUNEL PORTRAIT, NPG

poets in the 1930s and 1940s, and latterly, retired footballers, politicians and film and pop stars. If you want some biographical background on many of the pictures, avail yourself of the NPG's Soundguide; it's free of charge, though you're strongly invited to give a "voluntary contribution" of £3.

The gallery's **special exhibitions** (for which there's often an entrance charge) are well worth seeing – the photography shows, in particular, are usually excellent.

St Martin-in-the-Fields

Duncannon St ⊛ www.stmartin-in-the -fields.org. Mon–Sat 10am–8pm, Sun noon–8pm. Something of a blueprint for eighteenth-century churches across the Empire, St Martin-in-the-Fields is fronted by a magnificent Corinthian portico and topped by an elaborate, and distinctly unclassical, tower and steeple. Completed in 1726, the interior is purposefully simple, though the Italian plasterwork on the barrel vaulting is exceptionally rich; it's best appreciated while listening to one of the church's free **lunchtime concerts** or ticketed, candle-lit evening performances (call ☏020/7839 8362 for timings and information). As well as a licensed café, the crypt holds a shop, a gallery and a good, old-fashioned **brass-rubbing centre** (Mon–Sat 10am–6pm, Sun noon–6pm).

Whitehall

During the sixteenth and seventeenth centuries Whitehall was synonymous with royalty, serving as the permanent residence of England's kings and queens. The original Whitehall Palace was confiscated and greatly extended by Henry VIII after a fire at Westminster forced him to find alternative accommodation, and it was here that he celebrated his marriage to Anne Boleyn in 1533 – and where he died fourteen years later. From the sixteenth century onwards, nearly all the key governmental ministries and offices migrated here, rehousing themselves on an ever-increasing scale. The royalty, meanwhile, moved out to St James's after a fire destroyed most of Whitehall Palace in 1698.

The statues dotted about Whitehall today recall the days when this street stood at the centre of an empire on which the sun never set, while just beyond the Downing Street gates, in the middle of the road, stands Edwin Lutyens' **Cenotaph**, commemorating the dead of both world wars. Eschewing any kind of Christian imagery, the plain monument is inscribed simply with the words "The Glorious Dead" and remains the focus of the country's Remembrance

Sunday ceremony, held here in early November.

Banqueting House

Whitehall ⊛www.hrp.org.uk. Mon–Sat 10am–5pm. £4. One of the few sections of Whitehall Palace to escape the 1698 fire was the Banqueting House, one of the first Palladian buildings to be built in England. The one room open to the public has no original furnishings, but is well worth seeing for the superlative **Rubens ceiling paintings** commissioned by Charles I in the 1630s, depicting the union of England and Scotland, the peaceful reign of his father, James I, and finally his apotheosis. Charles himself walked through the room for the last time in 1649, when he stepped onto the executioner's scaffold from one of its windows.

Horse Guards

Whitehall ⊛www.army.mod.uk /ceremonialandheritage. Outside this modest building (once the old palace guard house) two mounted sentries of the **Queen's Household Cavalry** and two horseless colleagues, all in ceremonial uniform, are posted daily from 10am to 4pm. With nothing in particular to guard nowadays, the sentries are basically here for the tourists, though they are under orders not to smile. Try to coincide your visit with the Changing of the Guard (Mon–Sat 11am, Sun 10am), when a squad of twelve mounted troops arrive in full livery. The main action takes place in the parade ground at the rear of the building overlooking Horse Guards' Parade, which you can reach through the archway.

10 Downing Street

⊛www.number-10.gov.uk. Since the days of Margaret Thatcher, London's most famous address has been hidden behind wrought-iron security gates. A pretty plain, seventeenth-century terraced house, no. 10 has been home to every British prime minister since it was presented to Robert Walpole, Britain's first PM, by George II in 1732.

Cabinet War Rooms

King Charles St ⊛www.iwm.org.uk /cabinet. Daily: April–Sept 9.30am–6pm; Oct–March 10am–6pm. £7.50. In 1938, in anticipation of Nazi air raids, the basements of the civil service buildings on the south side of King Charles Street were converted into the Cabinet War Rooms. From here, Winston Churchill directed operations and held cabinet meetings for the duration of World War II. By the end of the conflict, the warren had expanded to cover more than six acres, including a hospital, canteen and shooting

▼ NAVE OF ST-MARTIN-IN-THE-FIELDS

▲ SOUTH AFRICA HOUSE, TRAFALGAR SQUARE

range, as well as cramped sleeping quarters and a series of tunnels fanning out from the complex to outlying government ministries. The rooms have been left pretty much as they were when they were finally abandoned on VJ Day 1945, and make for an atmospheric underground trot through wartime London. The museum's free acoustophone commentary helps bring the place to life, and includes various eyewitness accounts by folk who worked there.

Cafés

Café in the Crypt

St Martin-in-the-Fields, Duncannon St. Mon–Wed 10am–8pm, Thurs–Sat 10am–11pm, Sun noon–8pm. Offering self-service comfort food (including plenty of veggie choices), and with a handy location, this is an ideal spot to fill up before hitting the West End.

Pubs

Lord Moon of the Mall

16 Whitehall. Huge, high-ceilinged former bank, now a popular Wetherspoon's pub serving decent grub and real ales.

Red Lion

48 Parliament St. Old-fashioned late-Victorian pub popular with politicians, who can be called to parliamentary votes by a division bell in the bar.

Afternoon tea

The classic English **afternoon tea** – assorted sandwiches, scones and cream, cakes and tarts and, of course, lashings of tea – is available all over London, but is best sampled at one of the capital's top hotels; a selection of the best venues are picked out below. Book ahead, and leave your jeans and trainers at home – most hotels will expect men to wear a jacket of some sort, though only *The Ritz* insists on jacket and tie. Expect to pay around £25 per person.

Claridge's Brook St ☏020/7629 8860, ⍟www.savoy-group.co.uk. Daily 3–5.30pm.

The Dorchester 54 Park Lane ☏020/7629 8888, ⍟www.dorchesterhotel.com. Daily 3–6pm.

Lanesborough Hyde Park Corner ☏020/7259 5599, ⍟www.lanesborough.com. Daily 3.30–6pm.

The Ritz Piccadilly ☏020/7493 8181, ⍟www.theritzhotel.co.uk. Daily 1.30, 3.30 & 5.30pm.

The Savoy Strand ☏020/7836 4343, ⍟www.savoy-group.co.uk. Daily 3–5.30pm.

Westminster

Political, religious and regal power has emanated from **Westminster** for almost a millennium. It was King Edward the Confessor who first established this spot as London's royal and ecclesiastical power base, building his palace and abbey some three miles upstream from the City of London in the eleventh century, and the embryonic English parliament met in the abbey from the fourteenth century onwards.

Westminster remains home to the Houses of Parliament today, and as such it's a popular tourist spot, with visitors drawn here by Big Ben, one of the city's most familiar landmarks, and Westminster Abbey, London's most spectacular church. A short walk upriver, Tate Britain houses the most comprehensive collection of British art in the country.

Houses of Parliament

Parliament Square ☎ 020/7219 4272, ⊛ www.parliament.uk. Also known as the Palace of Westminster, the Houses of Parliament are one of London's best-known monuments and the ultimate symbol of a nation once confident of its place at the centre of the world. The city's finest example of Victorian Gothic Revival, the complex is distinguished above all by the ornate, gilded clock tower popularly known as **Big Ben**, after the thirteen-ton main bell that strikes the hour (and is broadcast across the airwaves by the BBC).

The original medieval palace burnt to the ground in 1834, but Westminster Hall survived, and its huge oak hammerbeam roof, and sheer scale – 240ft by 60ft – make it one of the most magnificent pieces of secular medieval architecture in Europe (you get a glimpse of it en route to the public galleries).

To watch the proceedings in either the House of Commons or the Lords, simply join the queue for the public galleries (known as Strangers' Galleries) outside St Stephen's Gate. The public are let in slowly (from 4pm Mon, 1pm Tues–Thurs, 10am Fri); the security checks are very tight, and the whole procedure can take an hour or more. If you want to avoid the queues, turn up an hour or

▲ BIG BEN

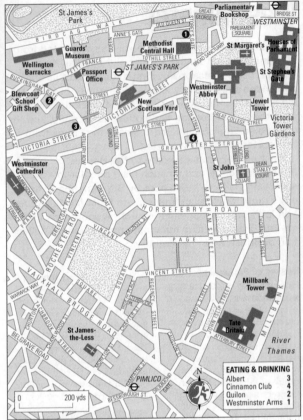

St James's Park
BIRDCAGE WALK
GREAT GEORGE ST
Parliamentary Bookshop
WESTMINSTER
BRIDGE ST
PARLIAMENT SQUARE
OLD QUEEN ST
ANNE'S GATE
QUEEN ANNE'S GATE
TOTHILL STREET
BROAD SANCTUARY
1
Methodist Central Hall
St Margaret's
Houses of Parliament
Guards' Museum
Wellington Barracks
Passport Office
ST JAMES'S PARK
BUCKINGHAM GATE
PETTY FRANCE
Westminster Abbey
St Stephen's Gate
Blewcoat School Gift Shop
2
CAXTON STREET
New Scotland Yard
GREAT SMITH STREET
Jewel Tower
Victoria Tower Gardens
BROADWAY
VICTORIA STREET
3
OLD PYE STREET
GREAT COLLEGE STREET
BUCKINGHAM GATE
ARTILLERY ROW
STRUTTON GROUND
4
GREAT PETER STREET
St John
MARSHAM STREET
SMITH SQUARE
DEAN STANLEY COURT
LORD NORTH ST
MILLBANK
VICTORIA STREET
Westminster Cathedral
AMBROSDEN AVENUE
FRANCIS STREET
GREYCOAT ST
GREENCOAT PLACE
H O R S E F E R R Y   R O A D
ROCHESTER ROW
VINCENT
MARSHAM STREET
P A G E   S T R E E T
THORNEY STREET
VAUXHALL BRIDGE ROAD
VINCENT SQUARE
REGENCY STREET
VINCENT STREET
Millbank Tower
MILLBANK
BELGRAVE ROAD
WARWICK WAY
CHARLWOOD STREET
St James-the-Less
MORETON STREET
VINCENT
TACHBROOK STREET
Tate Britain
ATTERBURY STREET
River Thames
PIMLICO
DRUMMOND GATE
BESSBOROUGH ST
N

EATING & DRINKING	
Albert	3
Cinnamon Club	4
Quilon	2
Westminster Arms	1

0   200 yds

© Crown copyright

more later, when the crowds have usually thinned; phone ☎020/7219 4272 to check the place isn't closed for the holidays.

To see **Question Time** (Mon 2.30–3.30pm, Tues–Thurs 11.30am–12.30pm), when the House is at its most raucous and entertaining, you really need to book a ticket several weeks in advance from your local MP if you're a resident UK citizen, or your home country's embassy (see p.217) in London if you're not. If you're here in late

▲ TAXI LIGHT, PARLIAMENT SQUARE

summer, you can also see Parliament by way of a **guided tour** (Aug & Sept Mon, Tues, Fri & Sat 9.15am–4.30pm, Wed & Thurs 1.15–4.30pm; £7; booking line ☏0870/906 3773), in which visitors get to walk through the two chambers, see some of the state rooms reserved for the Queen, and admire Westminster Hall. It's a good idea to book in advance, or you can simply head for the ticket office on Abingdon Green, opposite Victoria Tower and its adjacent gardens.

Jewel Tower

Abingdon St. Daily: April–Sept 10am–6pm; Oct 10am–5pm; Nov–March 10am–4pm. £1.60. The Jewel Tower is another remnant of the medieval palace. It formed the southwestern corner of the original exterior fortifications (there's a bit of moat left, too), and was constructed in around 1365 by Edward III as a giant strongbox for the crown jewels. These days, it houses an excellent exhibition on the history of parliament – worth checking out before you visit the Houses of Parliament.

St Margaret's Church

Parliament Square ☒westminster-abbey .org/stmargarets. Mon–Fri 9.30am–3.45pm, Sat 9.30am–1.45pm, Sun 2–5pm. Free. Sitting in the shadow of Westminster Abbey, St Margaret's has been the unofficial parliamentary church since the entire Commons tipped up here in 1614 to unmask religious Dissenters among the MPs. The present building dates back to 1523, and its most noteworthy furnishing is the colourful Flemish stained-glass window above the altar, which commemorates the marriage of Henry VIII and Catherine of Aragon (depicted in the bottom left- and right-hand corners).

Westminster Abbey

Parliament Square ☒www .westminster-abbey.org. Mon, Tues, Thurs & Fri 9.30am–3.45pm, Wed 9.30am–7pm, Sat 9.30am–1.45pm. £7.50. The venue for every coronation since William the Conqueror, and the site of just about all royal burials in the five hundred years from Henry III to George II, Westminster Abbey embodies much of England's history. There are scores of memorials to the nation's most famous citizens, too, and the interior is crammed with reliefs and statues.

The abbey's most dazzling architectural set-piece, however, is the **Lady Chapel**, added by Henry VII in 1503 as his future resting place. With its intricately carved vaulting and fan-shaped gilded pendants, the chapel represents the final spectacular gasp of the English Perpendicular style. The sacred heart of the building, though, is the Shrine of Edward the Confessor, which you can enter only as part of a **guided tour** of the abbey (April–Oct Mon–Fri 10am, 10.30am, 11am, 2pm, 2.30pm & 3pm, Sat 10am, 10.30am & 11am; Nov–March Mon–Fri 10am, 11am, 2pm, & 3pm, Sat 10am, 10.30am & 11am), for which you have to stump up an extra £3. The general entry fee does, however, allow you to inspect Edward I's Coronation Chair, a decrepit oak throne dating from around 1300 that's still used for coronations, as well as the **Poets' Corner** in the south transept. The first occupant, Geoffrey Chaucer, was buried here in 1400 merely because he lived nearby, but from the eighteenth century onwards, this area became an artistic Pantheon, with memorials to, among others, John Dryden, Samuel Johnson, Robert Browning, Lord Tennyson, Charles Dickens, Rudyard Kipling, Thomas Hardy and William Shakespeare, whose dandyish figure is set into the east wall. From the south transept, you can view the central sanctuary, site of the coronations, and the wonderful Cosmati floor mosaic, constructed in the thirteenth century by Italian craftsmen, and often covered by a carpet to protect it.

Doors in the south choir aisle lead to the Great Cloisters, at the eastern end of which lies the octagonal **Chapter House** (daily: April–Sept 9.30am–5pm; Oct 10am–5pm; Nov–March 10am–4pm; £1), where the House of Commons met from 1257, with its remarkable thirteenth-century decorative paving-tiles and wall-paintings. Chapter House tickets include entry to the **Abbey Museum** (daily 10.30am–4pm), filled with

▲ MARTIN LUTHER KING STATUE, WESTMINSTER ABBEY

generations of bald royal death masks and wax effigies. If you visit the Cloisters from Tuesday to Thursday, make your way to the little-known **College Garden** (Tues–Thurs: April–Sept 10am–6pm; Oct–March 10am–4pm; free), a 900-year-old stretch of green which now provides a quiet retreat; brass band concerts take place in July and August between 12.30 and 2pm.

It's only after exploring the cloisters that you get to see the **nave** itself: narrow, light and, at over a hundred feet in height, by far the tallest in the country; you exit via the west door.

Westminster Cathedral

Victoria St ⊕ www.rcdow.org.uk. Mon–Fri & Sun 7am–7pm, Sat 8am–7pm. Free. Begun in 1895, the stripy neo-Byzantine, Roman Catholic Westminster Cathedral is one of London's most surprising churches, as well as one of the last – and the wildest – monuments to the Victorian era. Constructed from more than twelve million terracotta-coloured bricks and decorated with hoops of Portland stone, it culminates in a magnificent 274ft tapered campanile, served by a lift (April–Nov 9.30am–12.30pm & 1–5pm; Dec–March Thurs–Sun same hours; £2). The interior is only half finished, so to get an idea of what the place should eventually look like, explore the series of side chapels whose rich, multicoloured decor makes use of over one hundred different types of marble from around the world. Be sure, too, to check out the low-relief Stations of the Cross, sculpted by Eric Gill during World War I.

▲ STATIONS OF THE CROSS, WESTMINSTER CATHEDRAL

Tate Britain

Millbank ☎020/7887 8008,
🌐www.tate.org.uk. Daily 10am–5.50pm.
Free. A purpose-built gallery
founded in 1897 with money
from Henry Tate, inventor of the
sugar cube, Tate Britain is now
devoted exclusively to British art.
As well as displaying works from
1500 to the present, the gallery
also showcases contemporary
British artists and continues to
sponsor the Turner Prize, the
country's most prestigious
modern-art award.

The paintings are rehung
more or less annually, but always
include a fair selection of works
by British artists such as
Hogarth, Constable,
Gainsborough, Reynolds and
Blake, plus foreign painters like
van Dyck who spent much of
their career over here. The ever-
popular Pre-Raphaelites are
always well represented, as are
established twentieth-century
greats including Stanley Spencer
and Francis Bacon alongside
living artists such as David
Hockney and Lucien Freud.
Lastly, don't miss the Tate's
outstanding collection of works
by J.M.W. Turner, displayed in
the Clore Gallery.

Shops

Blewcoats School Gift Shop

23 Caxton St ☎020/7222 2877,
🌐www.nationaltrust.org.uk/giftshop.
Closed Sat & Sun. National Trust
gift shop in a pretty little
Georgian schoolhouse, selling
toiletries, tapestries, waterproof
hats, preserves and books
ranging from gardening to
architecture.

Parliamentary Bookshop

12 Bridge St ☎020/7219 3890. Closed
Sat & Sun. Pick up copies of
Hansard (the word-for-word
account of parliament), plus the
government's white and green
papers.

Tate Britain Gift Shop

Millbank ☎020/7887 8876,
🌐www.tate.org.uk. Lots of art
posters, from Constable to
Turner Prize nonsense, plus
loads of funky, arty accessories.

▲ WILLIAM BLAKE'S *NEWTON*, TATE BRITAIN

Restaurants

Cinnamon Club

Great Smith St ☎020/7222 2555,
🖳www.cinnamonclub.com. Closed Sat
lunch & Sun eve. Very smart – and
expensive – Indian restaurant
housed in a former library; the
power breakfasts are particularly
popular with politicians.

Quilon

41 Buckingham Gate ☎020/7821
1899. Closed Sun. Another very
swish, elegant and expensive
Indian restaurant specializing in
Keralan cuisine – lots of fish,
seafood, fresh peppercorns and
coconut.

Pubs

Albert

52 Victoria St. Roomy High
Victorian pub, with big bay
windows, glass partitions and a
beautiful original ceiling and
carved wooden bar.

Westminster Arms

9 Storey's Gate. A real
parliamentary pub, wall-to-wall
with MPs, and with a division
bell in the bar.

St James's

An exclusive little enclave sandwiched between St James's Park and Piccadilly, **St James's** was laid out in the 1670s close to the royal seat of St James's Palace. Regal and aristocratic residences overlook nearby Green Park and the stately avenue of The Mall, gentlemen's clubs cluster along Pall Mall and St James's Street, while jacket-and-tie restaurants and expense-account gentlemen's outfitters line Jermyn Street. Hardly surprising, then, that most Londoners rarely stray into this area. Plenty of folk, however, frequent St James's Park, with large numbers heading for the Queen's chief residence, Buckingham Palace, and the adjacent Queen's Gallery and Royal Mews.

The Mall

The tree-lined sweep of The Mall – London's nearest equivalent of a Parisian boulevard – was laid out in the first decade of the twentieth century as a memorial to Queen Victoria. These days, it's best to try and visit on a Sunday, when it's closed to traffic. The bombastic Admiralty Arch was erected to mark the eastern entrance to The Mall, just off Trafalgar Square, while at the other end, in front of Buckingham Palace, stands the ludicrously overblown Victoria Memorial, Edward VII's overblown tribute to his mother.

St James's Park

Ⓦwww.royalparks.gov.uk. The south side of The Mall gives on to St James's Park, the oldest of London's royal parks, having been drained and enclosed for hunting purposes by Henry VIII. It was landscaped by Nash in the 1820s, and today its tree-lined lake is a favourite picnic spot for Whitehall's civil servants. Pelicans chill out at the eastern end (feeding takes place daily at 3pm), and there are exotic ducks, swans and geese aplenty. From the bridge across the lake there's also a fine view over to Westminster and the jumble of domes and pinnacles along Whitehall, with the London Eye observation wheel peeking over it all.

▲ CARLTON HOUSE TERRACE

Guards' Museum

Birdcage Walk ⊛ www.armymuseums .org.uk. Daily 10am–4pm. £2. The Neoclassical facade of the Wellington Barracks, built in 1833 and fronted by a parade ground, runs along the south side of St James's Park. In a bunker opposite the barracks' modern chapel, the Guards' Museum, endeavours to explain the complicated evolution of the Queen's Household Regiments, and provide a potted military history since the Civil War. Among the exhibits are the guards' glorious scarlet and blue uniforms, a lock of Wellington's hair and a whole load of war booty, from Dervish prayer mats plundered from Sudan in 1898 to items taken from an Iraqi POW during the Gulf War. The museum also displays (and sells) an impressive array of toy soldiers.

Buckingham Palace

Buckingham Gate ⊛ www.royal.gov.uk. Aug & Sept daily 9.30am–4.30pm. Advance booking on ☎ 020/766 7300. £12.50. The graceless colossus of

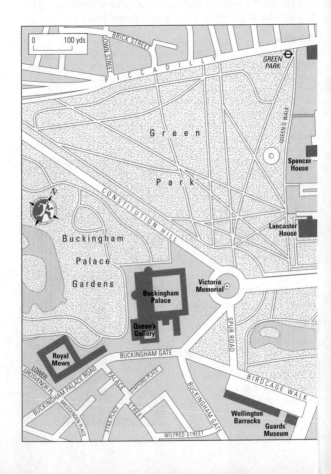

Buckingham Palace, popularly known as "Buck House", has served as the monarch's permanent London residence only since the accession of Victoria (if the Queen is at home, the Royal Standard flies from the roof of the palace). Bought by George III in 1762, the building was overhauled by Nash in the late 1820s, and again by Aston Webb in time for George V's coronation in 1913, producing a Neoclassical monolith that's about as bland as it's possible to be.

For two months of the year, the hallowed portals are grudgingly nudged open to the public; timed tickets are sold from the marquee-like box office in Green Park at the western end of The Mall. The interior, however, is a bit of an anticlimax: of the palace's 660 rooms, you're permitted to see around twenty, and there's little sign of life as the Queen decamps to Scotland every summer. For the other ten months of the year there's little to do here, as the palace is closed

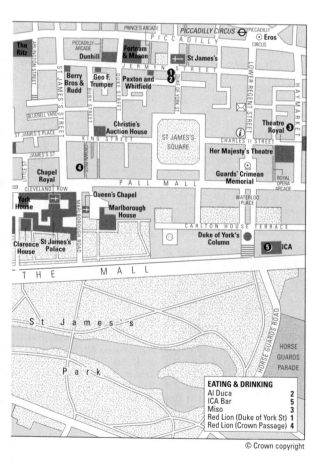

© Crown copyright

EATING & DRINKING	
Al Duca	2
ICA Bar	5
Miso	3
Red Lion (Duke of York St)	1
Red Lion (Crown Passage)	4

to visitors – not that this deters the crowds who mill around the railings and gather in some force to watch the **Changing of the Guard** (see p.71).

Queen's Gallery

Buckingham Gate ֎www.royal.gov .uk. Daily 10am–5.30pm. £6.50. The public can also visit the changing exhibitions at the Queen's Gallery. These are drawn from the Royal Collection, the vast array of artworks snapped up by the royal family which is three times larger than that at the National Gallery. Among the thousands of works the curators have to choose from are some incredible masterpieces by Michelangelo, Reynolds, Gainsborough, Vermeer, van Dyck, Rubens, Rembrandt and Canaletto, as well as numerous Fabergé eggs and heaps of Sèvres china.

Royal Mews

Buckingham Palace Rd ֎www.royal .gov.uk. Aug & Sept daily 10am–5pm; Oct–July Mon–Thurs & Fri–Sat 11am–4pm. £5.50. There's more pageantry on show at the Nash-built Royal Mews. The horses can be viewed in their luxury stables, along with an exhibition of equine accoutrements, but it's the royal carriages that are the main attraction. The most ornate is the Gold State Coach made for George III in 1762, smothered in 22-carat gilding and weighing four tons, its axles supporting four life-size figures. The Mews also houses the Royal Family's gleaming fleet of five Rolls Royce Phantoms and three Daimlers.

St James's Palace

Marlborough Rd ֎www.royal.gov.uk. Originally built by Henry VIII for Anne Boleyn, St James's Palace became the principal royal residence when Whitehall Palace burnt to the ground in 1698 (the court moved down the road to Buckingham Palace under Queen Victoria). The imposing red-brick gate-tower that forms the main entrance, and the Chapel Royal, are all that remain of the original Tudor palace. The rambling complex is off-limits to the public, though you can attend services at the Chapel Royal (Oct to Good Friday Sun 8.30am & 11.15am), venue for numerous royal weddings, and the Neoclassical Queen's Chapel (Easter–July Sun 8.30am & 11.15am). Until recently, the palace was used as a bachelor pad by Prince Charles (֎www.princeofwales .gov.uk) until he moved next door to Clarence House.

Clarence House

Stable Yard Rd ֎www.royal.gov.uk. Aug to mid-Oct daily 9.30am–6pm. £5.50. Built by John Nash for the future William IV, Clarence House is best known as the former home of the late Queen Mum. It now serves as Prince Charles's chief London residence, and a handful of

▲ QUEEN ALEXANDRA MEMORIAL, MARLBOROUGH ROAD

▲ ST JAMES'S PARK

rooms were opened to the public for the first time in the summer of 2003. Visits are by guided tour only, and, apart from a peek behind the scenes in a royal palace, the main draw is the selection of paintings by the likes of Walter Sickert and Augustus John.

Spencer House

St James's Place ⓦ www .spencerhouse.co.uk. Feb–July & Sept–Dec Sun 10.30am–5.45pm. £6. Most of St James's palatial residences are closed to the public, but one happy exception is Spencer House, a superb Palladian mansion erected in the 1750s. The ancestral home of the late Princess Diana, it was last lived in by the family in 1927, and is currently leased to the Rothschilds. Inside, guides take you on an hour-long tour through nine of the state rooms. The Great Room features a stunning coved and coffered ceiling in green, white and gold, while the adjacent Painted Room is a feast of

Neoclassicism, decorated with murals in the "Pompeian manner". The most outrageous decor, though, is to be found in Lord Spencer's Room, with its astonishing gilded palm-tree columns.

Shops

Berry Bros & Rudd

3 St James's St ☏ 020/7396 9600, ⓦ www.bbr.com. Closed Sun. This well-stocked, 300-year-old establishment houses a huge range of fine wines, and the friendly and helpful staff know pretty much everything there is to know on the subject.

Dunhill

48 Jermyn St ☏ 020/7499 9566, ⓦ www.whitespot.co.uk. Closed Sun. An enormous range of pipes and cigars on the first floor, and a small museum of old Dunhill gadgets and accessories on the ground floor.

Geo F. Trumper

20 Jermyn St ☏ 020/7734 1370, ⓦ www.trumpers.com. Closed Sun. Founded in 1875, this impeccably discreet "Gentlemen's Perfumer" is *the* barber of choice, with a shaving school that will teach you how to execute the perfect wet shave.

Paxton & Whitfield

93 Jermyn St ☏ 020/7930 0259, ⓦ www.paxtonandwhitfield.co.uk. Closed Sun. Quintessentially English, 200-year-old cheese shop offering a very traditional range of British and European varieties, plus a good range of wine and port.

▲ PLANE TREES IN GREEN PARK

Restaurants

Al Duca

4–5 Duke of York St ☎020/7839 3090, ⊛www.alduca-restaurant.co.uk. High quality, sophisticated Italian food, slick service and good set menus: lunches start at just under £20; dinner at just over.

Miso

66 Haymarket ☎020/7930 4800. Huge helpings of eastern, wok-fried and soupy noodle and rice dishes that will fill your belly for under £10.

Pubs and bars

ICA

94 The Mall ⊛www.ica.org.uk. You have to be a member to drink at the *ICA Bar* – but anyone can join on the door (Mon–Fri £1.50; Sat & Sun £2.50). It's a cool drinking venue, with a *noir* dress code observed by the arty crowd and staff, and sweaty DJ nights at the weekends.

Red Lion

23 Crown Passage. Closed Sun. Hidden away in a passageway off Pall Mall, this tiny, wood-panelled local attracts a smart besuited clientele, who fill up on sandwiches and quaff real ale before moving on to somewhere more upmarket.

Red Lion

2 Duke of York St. Closed Sun. Genuine old Victorian gin palace run by the Nicholson's chain, with elegant etched mirrors, polished wood and a great ceiling.

Piccadilly and Mayfair

Forming the border between St James's and Mayfair, traffic-clogged Piccadilly is no longer the fashionable promenade it once was. However, a whiff of exclusivity still pervades the streets of Mayfair, particularly Bond Street and its tributaries, where designer clothes emporia jostle for space with jewellers, bespoke tailors and fine art dealers. Most Londoners, however, stick to Regent and Oxford streets on the fringes of Mayfair, home to the flagship branches of the country's most popular chain stores. It's here that Londoners are referring to when they talk of "going shopping up the West End".

Piccadilly Circus

Anonymous and congested it may be, but for many Londoners, Piccadilly Circus is the nearest their city comes to having a centre. Originally laid out in 1812 and now a major traffic bottleneck, it's by no means a picturesque place, and is probably best seen at night when the spread of vast illuminated signs (a feature since the Edwardian era) provide a touch of Las Vegas dazzle, and when the human traffic is at its most frenetic. Somewhat inexplicably, Piccadilly Circus attracts a huge number of tourists, who come here to sit on the steps of the central fountain, topped by an aluminium statue popularly known as **Eros**. Despite the bow and arrow, it depicts not the god of love but the Angel of Christian Charity, and was erected to commemorate the Earl of Shaftesbury, a Bible-thumping social reformer who campaigned against child labour.

Regent Street

ⓦwww.regent-street.co.uk. Drawn up by John Nash in 1812 as both a luxury shopping street and a new, wide triumphal approach to Regent's Park, Regent Street was the city's first real attempt at dealing with traffic congestion. At the same time, it helped clear away a large swath of slums, and create a tangible borderline to shore up fashionable Mayfair against the chaotic maze of Soho. Even today, it's still possible to admire the stately intentions of Nash's plan, particularly evident in the Quadrant, the street's partially

▼ EROS, PICCADILLY CIRCUS

arcaded, curved section which swerves westwards from Piccadilly Circus. In the nineteenth century, however, the increased purchasing power of the city's middle classes brought the tone of the street "down", and heavyweight stores catering for the masses now predominate.

Piccadilly

Piccadilly apparently got its name from the ruffs or "pickadills" worn by the dandies who promenaded along this wide boulevard in the late seventeenth century. Despite its fashionable pedigree, and the presence of the *Ritz Hotel* halfway along, it's no place for promenading in its current state,

with traffic careering up and down it nose to tail day and night. Infinitely more pleasant places to window-shop are the various nineteenth-century arcades here, originally built to protect shoppers from the mud and horse-dung on the streets, but now equally useful for escaping exhaust fumes.

Burlington Arcade

⊛ www.burlington-arcade.co.uk. Mon–Sat 9am–6pm. Awash with mahogany-fronted jewellers and gentlemen's outfitters, Burlington is Piccadilly's longest and most expensive nineteenth-century arcade. It was built in 1819 for Lord Cavendish, then owner of neighbouring

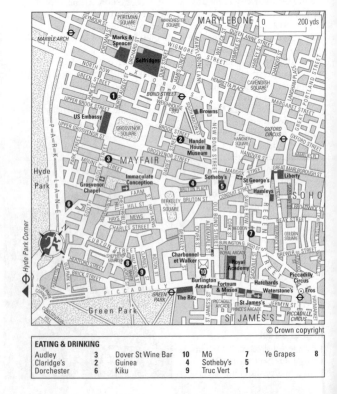

© Crown copyright

EATING & DRINKING							
Audley	3	Dover St Wine Bar	10	Mô	7	Ye Grapes	8
Claridge's	2	Guinea	4	Sotheby's	5		
Dorchester	6	Kiku	9	Truc Vert	1		

▲ BURLINGTON ARCADE

its exhibitions tend to be crowd-pleasers, interspersed with the occasional controversial show guaranteed to grab the headlines. However, the Academy is best known for the **Summer Exhibition**, which opens in June and remains an essential stop on the social calendar of upper middle-class England. Anyone can enter paintings in any style, and the lucky winners get hung, in rather close proximity, and sold. Supposed gravitas is added by the RA "Academicians", who are allowed to display six of their own works – no matter how awful. The result is a bewildering display, which gets annually panned by the critics.

Bond Street and around

While Oxford Street, Regent Street and Piccadilly have all gone downmarket, Bond Street has carefully maintained its exclusivity. It is, in fact, two streets rolled into one: the southern half, laid out in the 1680s, is known as Old Bond Street; its northern extension, which followed less than fifty years later, is New Bond Street. Both are pretty unassuming architecturally, but the shops that line them – and those of neighbouring Conduit Street and South Molton Street – are among the flashiest in London, dominated by perfumeries, jewellers and designer clothing emporia such as Versace, Gucci and Yves Saint-Laurent.

In addition to fashion, Bond Street is also renowned for its auction houses, the oldest of which is **Sotheby's**, at no. 34–35 (ⓦwww.sothebys.com). Despite a price-fixing scandal in 2002 that resulted in the imprisonment of one of its former chairmen and a £12

Burlington House, to prevent commoners throwing rubbish into his garden. Upholding Regency decorum, it is still illegal to whistle, sing, hum, hurry, carry large packages or open umbrellas on this small stretch – the arcade's beadles (known as Burlington Berties), in their Edwardian frock-coats and gold-braided top hats, take the prevention of such criminality very seriously.

Royal Academy

ⓦwww.royalacademy.org.uk. Daily 10am–6pm, Fri till 10pm. £4–9 depending on the exhibition. The Royal Academy of Arts (RA) occupies the enormous Burlington House, one of the few survivors of the aristocratic mansions that once lined Piccadilly. The country's first-ever formal art school, the Academy was founded in 1768 by a group of English painters including Thomas Gainsborough and Joshua Reynolds, the first president, whose statue now stands in the main courtyard, palette in hand. The college has always had a conservative reputation for its teaching, and million fine, business is still booming. The viewing galleries (free) are open to the public, as are the auctions themselves. Bond Street's **art galleries** are another favourite place for the wealthy to offload their heirlooms; for contemporary art, head for neighbouring Cork Street. Both sets of galleries have impeccably presented and somewhat intimidating staff, but if you're interested, walk in and look around. They're only shops, after all.

Handel House Museum

25 Brook St ⊛ www.handelhouse.org. Tues–Sat 10am–6pm, Thurs till 8pm, Sun noon–6pm. £4.50. The German-born composer Georg Friedrich Händel (1685–1759) spent the best part of his life in London, producing all his best-known work at what's now the Handel House Museum. The composer used the ground floor as a sort of shop where subscribers could buy scores, while the first floor was employed as a rehearsal room. Although containing few original artefacts, the house has been painstakingly restored, and further atmosphere is provided by music students who come to practise on the house's harpsichords. More formal performances take place on Thursday evenings from 6pm (£5, includes museum admission). Access to the house is via the chic cobbled yard at the back.

Oxford Street

⊛ www.oxfordstreet.co.uk. The old Roman road to Oxford has been London's main shopping mecca for the last hundred years. Today, despite successive recessions and sky-high rents, this aesthetically unremarkable two-mile hotchpotch of shops is still one of the world's busiest streets. East of Oxford Circus, it forms the northern border of Soho; to the west, the one great landmark is Selfridges, a huge Edwardian pile fronted by giant Ionic columns, with the Queen of Time riding the ship of commerce and supporting an Art Deco clock above the main entrance. The store was opened in 1909 by Chicago millionaire Gordon Selfridge, who flaunted its 130 departments under the slogan, "Why not spend a day at Selfridges?"; he was later pensioned off after running into trouble with the Inland Revenue.

Shops

Browns

23–27 & 50 South Molton St ☎ 020/7514 0052, ⊛ www .brownsfashion.com. London's largest range of designer wear, with big international names under the same roof as more cutting-edge, up-and-coming designers, and catering equally well for women as for men.

Charbonnel et Walker

1 Royal Arcade, 28 Old Bond St ☎ 020/7491 0939, ⊛ www.charbonnel .co.uk. Closed Sun. Established in 1875, this is where Her Majesty binges on chocolate, which comes presented in the most exquisite wrapping.

Fortnum & Mason

181 Piccadilly ☎ 020/7743 8040, ⊛ www.fortnumandmason.com. Beautiful and eccentric store offering gorgeously presented and pricey food; also specializes in designer clothes, furniture and stationery.

Hamleys

188–196 Regent St ☎ 0870/333 2455,

▲ ART DECO FACADE, SELFRIDGES

ⓦwww.hamleys.com. Possibly the world's largest toy shop, and certainly a feast for the eyes of most small children, with lots of gadget demonstrations going on in its six floors of mayhem.

Hatchards

187 Piccadilly ☎020/7439 9921, ⓦwww.hatchards.co.uk. The Queen's official bookseller, Hatchards holds its own when it comes to quality fiction, royal biography and history.

Liberty

210–220 Regent St ☎020/7734 1234, ⓦwww.liberty.co.uk. A fabulous, partly mock-Tudor emporium of luxury. Best known for its fabrics, though it is, in fact, a full-blown department store.

Marks & Spencer

458 Oxford St ☎020/7935 7954, ⓦwww.marksandspencer.co.uk. The largest London branch of this British institution offers a huge range of own-brand clothes, food, homeware and furnishings.

Selfridges

400 Oxford St ☎0870/837 7377, ⓦwww.selfridges.com. London's first great department store, and still one of its best: a huge, airy mecca of clothes, food and furnishings.

Waterstone's

203–206 Piccadilly ☎020/7851 2400, ⓦwww.waterstones.co.uk. This flagship bookstore – Europe's largest – occupies the former Simpson's department store building and boasts a café, bar, gallery and events rooms as well as five floors of books.

Cafés

Mô

25 Heddon St. Closed Sun. Serving reasonably priced and delicious snacks, this is London's ultimate Arabic pastiche café, with tables and hookahs spilling out onto the pavement of a quiet little Mayfair alleyway.

Sotheby's

34–35 New Bond St ⓦwww.sothebys.com. Closed Sat & Sun. Sotheby's café is by no means cheap, but the lunches are exquisitely prepared, and the excellent afternoon teas are a fraction of the price of the nearby hotels.

Restaurants

Kiku

17 Half Moon St ☎020/7499 4208. "Kiku" translates as pricey, but for top-quality sushi and sashimi, this place doesn't charge the earth. Take a seat at the traditional sushi bar and wonder at the dexterity of the knife man.

Truc Vert

42 North Audley St ☎020/7491 9988. Very upmarket takeaway deli (quiche, salads, rotisserie chicken, patés, cakes and pastries) incorporating a small restaurant. The menu changes daily; you can even assemble your own after-dinner cheese platter and pay by weight. Corkage is £4.50.

Pubs and bars

Audley

41 Mount St. A grand Mayfair pub, with its original Victorian burgundy lincrusta ceiling, chandeliers and clocks.

Claridge's

49 Brook St ☎www.savoy-group.com. The bar here has a tasteful Art Deco feel, with terribly English waiters and splendid cocktails from £8 each.

Dorchester

63 Park Lane ☎www.dorchesterhotel .com. Wildly over-the-top gilded, mirrored Hollywood decor, big booths to ease into, and jolly good cocktails at just under £10 a hit.

Dover Street Wine Bar

8–9 Dover St. Enjoyable central brasserie hosting blues, R&B, jazz and soul bands every night until 3am.

Guinea

30 Bruton Place. Closed Sun. Tiny, old-fashioned, flower-strewn mews pub, serving good Young's bitter and excellent steak-and-kidney pies.

Ye Grapes

16 Shepherd Market. Busy Victorian free house, with a good selection of real ales and an open fire – a great local in the heart of Mayfair.

▲ CAFÉ CULTURE OFF OXFORD STREET

Marylebone

Marylebone may not have quite the pedigree and snob value of Mayfair, but it's still a wealthy and aspirational area. Built in the eighteenth century, its mesh of smart Georgian streets and squares survives more or less intact today, and compared to the brashness of nearby Oxford Street, the backstreets of Marylebone are a pleasure to wander, especially the chi-chi, village-like quarter around the High Street. In fact, the area only really gets busy and touristy around the north end of Baker Street, home of the fictional detective Sherlock Holmes, and one of London's biggest visitor attractions, Madame Tussaud's waxworks' extravaganza.

Wallace Collection

Hertford House, Manchester Square
⊛ www.wallacecollection.org. Mon–Sat 10am–5pm, Sun noon–5pm. Free.
Housed in a miniature eighteenth-century French chateau, the Wallace Collection is best known for its eighteenth-century French paintings (especially Watteau); look out, too, for Franz Hals' *Laughing Cavalier*, Titian's *Perseus and Andromeda*, Velázquez's *Lady with a Fan* and Rembrandt's

EATING & DRINKING
Barley Mow — 3
Fairuz — 7
La Galette — 2
Golden Hind — 9
Match — 10
O'Conor Don — 8
Patisserie Valerie at Sagne — 5
Paul — 6
Phoenix Palace — 1
The Providores — 4

© Crown copyright

affectionate portrait of his teenage son, Titus.

The inner courtyard is now a modern, rather formal, glass-roofed café, but at heart, the Wallace Collection remains an old-fashioned place, with exhibits piled high in glass cabinets, paintings covering every inch of wall space and a bloody great armoury. If you're here for the paintings, you'll find the best works in the **Great Gallery**.

RIBA

66 Portland Place ⓦ www.architecture.com. Mon–Fri 10am–6pm, Sat 9am–5pm. Free. With its sleek 1930s Portland-stone facade, the Royal Institute of British Architects (RIBA) headquarters is easily the finest building on Portland Place. Inside, the main staircase remains a wonderful period piece, with etched glass balustrades, walnut veneer and two large columns of black marble rising up on either side. You can view the interior en route to the institute's often thought-provoking first-floor architectural exhibitions (free)

and to its café, or if you visit for one of the Tuesday-evening lectures (£6–10) held here. The excellent ground-floor bookshop is also worth a browse.

Madame Tussaud's and the Planetarium

Marylebone Rd ☎ 0870/400 3000. Mon–Fri 10am–5.30pm, Sat & Sun 9am–5.30pm; school holidays daily 9am–5.30pm. £14.95; Sat & Sun in peak season £16.95. The wax models at Madame Tussaud's (ⓦ www.madame-tussauds.com) have been pulling in the crowds ever since the good lady arrived in London in 1802 bearing the sculpted heads of guillotined aristocrats. The entrance fee might be extortionate, the likenesses occasionally dubious and the automated dummies inept, but you can still rely on finding London's biggest queues here – to avoid joining them, book your ticket over the phone or online in advance. After star-spotting at the Garden Party and trawling through the irredeemably tasteless Chamber of Horrors,

▼ ETCHED BALUSTRADES, RIBA

▲ ST MARYLEBONE'S CHURCH SPIRE

the Tussaud's finale is a manic five-minute "ride" through the history of London in a miniaturized taxi cab.

For an extra £2.45 you can visit the adjoining London **Planetarium** (⍙www.london-planetarium.com) for a thirty-minute high-tech zip through the universe projected onto a giant dome and accompanied by a cosmic astro-babble commentary.

Sherlock Holmes Museum

239 Baker St ⍙www.sherlock-holmes.co.uk. Daily 9.30am–6pm. £6. Sherlock Holmes's fictional address was 221b Baker Street, hence the number on the door of the Sherlock Holmes Museum. Stuffed full of Victoriana and life-size models of characters from the books, it's an atmospheric and very competent exercise in period reconstruction. You can stroll in and out of the rooms, and don a deerstalker to have your picture taken by the fireside, looking like the great detective himself, but there's no attempt to impart any insights (or even too many basic facts) about Holmes or Doyle.

Cafés

Golden Hind

73 Marylebone Lane. Closed Sun. Founded in 1914, Marylebone's heritage fish and chip restaurant serves classic cod and chips alongside fancier fare. Eat here or take away.

Patisserie Valerie at Sagne

105 Marylebone High St ⍙www.patisserie-valerie.co.uk. Founded as Swiss-run *Maison Sagne* in the 1920s, and preserving its wonderful period decor, the café is now run by Soho's fab patisserie makers, and is one of Marylebone's finest.

Paul

116 Marylebone High St. Upmarket, seriously French boulangerie with a small wood-panelled café at the back. Before launching into the exquisite patisserie, try one of the chewy fougasses, quiches or tarts.

▲ PATISSERIE VALERIE CAKES

Restaurants

Fairuz

3 Blandford St ☏ 020/7486 8182. One of London's more accessible Middle Eastern restaurants, with an epic list of mezze, delicate and fragrant charcoal grills and one or two oven-baked dishes. Get here early to secure one of the nook-and-crannyish, tent-like tables.

La Galette

56 Paddington St ☏ 020/7935 1554, ⊛ www.lagalette.com. Bright, modern pancake place, where the hors d'oeuvres are very simple and very French, and the savoury and sweet buckwheat galettes generous; be sure to sample the range of Breton ciders, too. Breakfast is available between 10am and 4pm.

Phoenix Palace

3–5 Glentworth St ☏ 020/7486 3515. The menu here stretches off into the farthest corners of Chinese chefly imagination, and it's worth a careful read. Better still, the cooking is good and the portions large.

The Providores

109 Marylebone High St ☏ 020/7935 6175, ⊛ www.theprovidores.co.uk. Outstanding fusion restaurant split into two distinct areas: snacky *Tapa Bar* downstairs and full-on restaurant upstairs. On either level the food, which may sound like an untidy assemblage on paper, is original and wholly satisfying.

▲ O'CONOR DON

Pubs and bars

Barley Mow

8 Dorset St. Closed Sun. Beautiful old pub, tucked away in the backstreets of Marylebone, with lots of hidden nooks and even some completely enclosed little booths for total privacy.

Match Bar

38 Margaret St ⊛ www.matchbar.com. Closed Sun. Smart, cool cocktail-driven bar with lots of retro brown leatherette loungers and bottled beers.

O'Conor Don

88 Marylebone Lane. Closed Sat & Sun. A stripped-bare, stout-loving pub that's a cut above the average, with excellent Guinness, a pleasantly easy-going pace and Irish food on offer.

Soho

One of London's most diverse, busy and characterful areas, **Soho** is very much the heart of the West End. It's been the city's premier red-light district for centuries, and retains an unorthodox and slightly raffish air that's unique for central London. Conventional sights are few and far between, yet it's a great area to wander through, even if you just take in the lively fruit and vegetable market on Berwick Street; whatever the hour, however, there's always something going on. Most folk head here to visit one of the many cinemas or theatres, or to grab a bite to eat or a drink at the incredible variety of cafés, restaurants and bars. Soho is also a very upfront gay mecca, with bars and cafés concentrated around the Old Compton Street area.

Leicester Square

By night, when the big cinemas and nightclubs are doing brisk business and the buskers are entertaining passers-by, Leicester Square is one of the most crowded places in London; on a Friday or Saturday night, it can seem as if half the youth of the city's suburbs have congregated here, supplemented by a vast number of tourists. By day, queues form for theatre and concert deals at the square's half-price ticket booth, while clubbers hand out flyers to likely looking punters.

It wasn't until the mid-nineteenth century that the square began to emerge as an entertainment zone, with accommodation houses (for prostitutes and their clients) and music halls such as the grandiose Empire and the Hippodrome (just off the square), edifices which survive today as cinemas and discos. Cinema moved in during the 1930s – a golden age evoked by the sleek black lines of the Odeon on the east side – and maintains its grip on the area. The Empire is the favourite for big red-carpet premieres and, in a rather half-hearted imitation of the Hollywood tradition, there are even handprints-of-the-stars indented into the pavement of the square's southwestern corner.

Chinatown

A self-contained jumble of shops, cafés and restaurants, Chinatown is one of London's most distinct and popular ethnic enclaves. Centred

▲ ODEON CINEMA, LEICESTER SQUARE

© Crown copyright

EATING & DRINKING

Alphabet	12	China City	20	Lab	15	Red Veg	3
Bar Italia	14	Chowki	19	Mildred's	10	The Social	1
Beatroot	13	Dog & Duck	9	Mr Kong	21	Spiga	11
Busaba Eathai	8	The Edge	4	Patisserie Valerie	17	The Toucan	6
Candy Bar	7	Freedom	16	Pizza Express	5		
Centrale	18	Kopi-Tiam	22	Rasa Samudra	2		

around **Gerrard Street**, it's a tiny area of no more than three or four blocks, thick with the aromas of Chinese cooking and peppered with ersatz touches. Few of London's 70,000 Chinese actually live in Chinatown, but it nonetheless remains a focus for the community: a place to

do business or the weekly shopping, celebrate a wedding, or just meet up for meals – particularly on Sundays, when the restaurants overflow with Chinese families tucking into *dim sum*. Most Londoners come to Chinatown simply to eat – easy and inexpensive enough to do. Cantonese cuisine

▲ CHINATOWN

predominates, and you're unlikely to be disappointed wherever you go.

Charing Cross Road

Charing Cross Road, which marks Soho's eastern border, boasts the highest concentration of bookshops anywhere in London. One of the first to open here, in 1906, was Foyles at no. 119 – De Valera, George Bernard Shaw, Walt Disney and Conan Doyle were all once regular customers. You'll find more of Charing Cross Road's original character at the string of specialist and secondhand bookshops south of Cambridge Circus. One of the nicest places for specialist and antiquarian book-browsing is Cecil Court, the southernmost pedestrianized alleyway between Charing Cross Road and St Martin's Lane.

Photographers' Gallery

5 & 8 Great Newport St ⊛www.photonet.org.uk. Mon–Sat 11am–6pm, Sun noon–6pm. Free. Established in 1971 as the first of its kind in London, the Photographers' Gallery hosts excellent temporary photographic exhibitions, often featuring leading contemporary photographers, that are invariably worth a browse. Note that the gallery has exhibition spaces at two separate addresses, with a peaceful café at no. 5 and a good bookshop at no. 8.

Old Compton Street

If Soho has a main drag, it has to be Old Compton Street. The corner shops, peep shows, boutiques and trendy cafés here are typical of the area and a good barometer of the latest Soho fads. Soho has been a permanent fixture on the **gay**

scene for much of the twentieth century, but nowadays, it's not just gay bars, clubs and cafés jostling for position on Old Compton Street: there's a gay-run houseshare agency, a financial advice outfit and, even more convenient, a gay taxi service.

Shops

Agent Provocateur

6 Broadwick St ☎020/7439 0229, ⊛www.agentprovocateur.com. Upmarket lingerie store for those with an interest in the kitsch, sexy and glamorous.

Daddy Kool

12 Berwick St ☎020/7437 3535, ⊛www.daddykoolrecords.com. Lots of collectable reggae vinyl, most of it classic roots and Studio One, but with some up-to-the-minute ragga, too.

Foyles

113–119 Charing Cross Rd ☎020/7437 5660, ⊛www.foyles .co.uk. Long-established bookstore with a big Silver Moon feminist section, and Ray's Jazz Shop and café on the first floor.

▲ SOHO BY NIGHT

Mr Bongo

44 Poland St ☎020/7287 1887,
⊛www.mrbongo.com. Good for
12" singles, and for hip-hop,
Latin American and Brazilian
CDs.

Prowler Soho

3–7 Brewer St ☎020/7734 4031,
⊛www.prowlerstores.co.uk. A gay
and lesbian household name,
stocking lots of fetish gear and
erotica, plus a great range of
literature, art, postcards and
gifts.

Sister Ray

94 Berwick St ☎020/7287 8385,
⊛www.sisterray.co.uk. Up-to-the
minute indie sounds, plus lots of
electronica and some forays into
the current dance scene. Most
releases available on vinyl as well
as CD.

The Vintage House

42 Old Compton St ☎020/7437 2592,
⊛www.vintagehouse.co.uk. Wines,
brandies and more than seven
hundred whiskies line the
shelves of this family-run
drinker's paradise.

Cafés

Bar Italia

22 Frith St. This tiny café is a
Soho institution, serving coffee,
croissants and sandwiches more
or less around the clock – as it
has been doing since 1949.

Beatroot

92 Berwick St. Great little veggie
café by the market, doling out
delicious cakes plus hot savoury
bakes, stews and salads in boxes
of varying sizes – all for under a
fiver.

Centrale

16 Moor St. Tiny, friendly Italian
café specializing in huge plates
of steaming, garlicky pasta as
well as omelettes, chicken and
chops for around £5. Bring
your own booze; there's a 50p
corkage charge, but don't drink
too much as there are no toilets.

Kopi-Tiam

9 Wardour St. Bright, cheap
Malaysian café serving up
curries, coconut rice, juices and
"herbal soups", all around the
£5 mark.

Patisserie Valerie

44 Old Compton St ⊛www .patisserie-valerie.co.uk. Popular coffee, croissant and cake emporium dating from the 1950s, and attracting a loud-talking, arty, people-watching crowd.

Red Veg

95 Dean St ⊛www.redveg.com. Closed Sun. There's a faint whiff of 1980s Soviet chic about this minimalist veggie junk-food outlet, which doles out a short list of cheap, classic munchie-fodder: veggie burgers, noodles and felafel.

Restaurants

Busaba Eathai

106–110 Wardour St ☎020/7255 8686, ⊛www.busaba.com. Dark, designery and implacably trendy Thai eatery which serves pretty decent food at low prices. The menu veers towards one-pot dishes, and vegetarians are particularly well catered for.

China City

White Bear Yard, 25 Lisle St ☎020/7734 3388. Large, reasonably priced restaurant tucked into a little courtyard; fresh and bright decor, *dim sum* that's up there with the best and service that is typically "Chinatown brusque".

Chowki

2–3 Denman St ☎020/7439 1330. Large, inexpensive Indian restaurant serving authentic homestyle food in stylish surroundings. The menu changes every month in order to feature three different regions of India – the set "regional feast" for around £10 is great value.

Mildred's

45 Lexington St ☎020/7494 1634. Long-established, buzzy veggie restaurant hidden down a backstreet, offering stir-fries, pasta dishes and burgers that are as wholesome, delicious and inexpensive as ever.

Mr Kong

21 Lisle St ☎020/7437 7923. One of Chinatown's finest, with a chef-owner who pioneered modern Cantonese cuisine: order from the "Today's" and "Chef's Specials" menu, and don't miss the mussels in black-bean sauce.

Pizza Express

10 Dean St ☎020/7439 8722. Enjoy a good pizza, then listen to the resident band or highly skilled guest players. There's also a late night session on Saturdays, from 9pm until the early hours of Sunday morning.

Rasa Samudra

5 Charlotte St ☎020/7637 0222. Smart, pricey, fishy south Indian restaurant which produces classy dishes that would be more at home in Mumbai than London.

▲ CHARLES II STATUE, SOHO SQUARE

Spiga

84–86 Wardour St ☎020/7734 3444.
A pleasantly casual but
upmarket Italian affair, with a
lively atmosphere, a serious
wood-fired oven and cool
designer looks.

Pubs and bars

Alphabet

61–63 Beak St ⓦwww
.alphabetbar.com. Closed Sun.
Upstairs is light and spacious
with decadent leather sofas, a
great choice of European beers
and mouthwatering food;
downstairs, the dimmed
coloured lights and car seats
strewn around make for an
altogether seedier atmosphere.

Candy Bar

4 Carlisle St ⓦwww.thecandybar.co
.uk. The crucial, cruisey vibe
makes this the hottest girl-bar in
central London. Daily happy
hour (5–7pm), pool tables, a
quiz on Tuesdays and clubby
nights at the weekends.

Dog & Duck

18 Bateman St. Tiny Soho pub
that retains much of its old
character. Beautiful Victorian
tiling and mosaics, a good range
of real ales and a loyal clientele.

The Edge

11 Soho Square, ⓦwww.edge.uk.com.
Busy, style-conscious and pricey
café/bar spread over several
floors, although this doesn't
seem to stop everyone ending
up on the pavement, especially
in summer. Food daily,
interesting art exhibitions and
DJs most nights.

Freedom

60–66 Wardour St. Hip, busy, late-

opening place, popular with a
straight/gay Soho crowd. Great
juices and healthy food in the
daytime, cocktails and
overpriced beer in the evening.

Lab

12 Old Compton St ⓦwww.lab-bar
.com. Chic, multicoloured
former strip joint that stirs up
some of the best cocktails in
town for a style-conscious
crowd of beautiful Soho-ites.

The Social

5 Little Portland St. Run by the
Heavenly record label (St
Etienne, Beth Orton, Monkey
Mafia), this industrial – and
often bacchanalian – club-bar
and live music venue hosts
emerging pop-rock-folk bands
on varying week nights.

The Toucan

19 Carlisle St. Closed Sun. Small pub
serving excellent Guinness and a
wide range of Irish whiskies,
plus cheap, wholesome and
filling food. So popular it can
get mobbed.

Bloomsbury

Bloomsbury was built over in grid-plan style from the 1660s onwards, and the formal, bourgeois Georgian squares laid out then remain the area's main distinguishing feature. In the twentieth century, Bloomsbury acquired a reputation as the city's most learned quarter, dominated by the dual institutions of the British Museum and London University, and home to many of London's chief book publishers, but perhaps best known for its literary inhabitants, among them T.S. Eliot and Virginia Woolf. Only in its northern fringes does the character of the area change dramatically, becoming steadily more seedy as you near the two big main-line train stations of Euston and King's Cross.

British Museum

Great Russell St ⊚ www.british-museum.ac.uk. Mon–Wed, Sat & Sun 10am–5.30pm, Thurs & Fri 10am–8.30pm. Free. One of the great museums of the world, the British Museum contains an incredible collection of antiquities, prints, drawings and books, all housed under one roof. Begun in 1823, the building itself is the grandest of London's Greek Revival edifices, and its central **Great Court** (Mon–Wed, Sat & Sun 9am–6pm, Thurs & Fri 9am–11pm) now features a remarkable curving glass-and-steel roof designed by Norman Foster. At the Court's centre stands the copper-domed former **Round Reading Room** of the British Library, where Karl Marx penned *Das Kapital*.

The BM's collection of **Roman and Greek antiquities** is unparalleled, and is most famous for the Parthenon sculptures, better known as the Elgin Marbles after the British aristocrat who walked off with the reliefs in 1801. Elsewhere, the **Egyptian collection** is easily the most significant outside Egypt, ranging from monumental sculptures to the ever-popular mummies and their ornate outer caskets. Also on display is the Rosetta Stone, which finally unlocked the secret of Egyptian hieroglyphs. Other highlights include a splendid series of **Assyrian reliefs** from Nineveh, and several extraordinary artefacts from **Mesopotamia** such as the enigmatic Ram in the Thicket (a goat statuette in lapis lazuli and shell) and the remarkable hoard of goldwork known as the Oxus Treasure.

The leathery half-corpse of the 2000-year-old Lindow Man,

▲ BLOOMSBURY GROUP PLAQUE, GORDON SQUARE

▲ ⊖ Goodge St

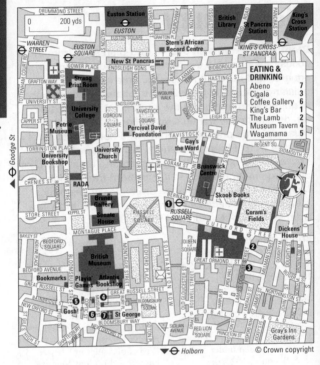

© Crown copyright

discovered in a Cheshire bog, and the Anglo-Saxon treasure from the Sutton Hoo ship burial are among the highlights of the **Prehistoric** and **Romano-British** collection. The **medieval** and **modern** collections, meanwhile, range from the twelfth-century Lewis chessmen carved from walrus ivory, to twentieth-century exhibits such as a copper vase by Frank Lloyd Wright.

Don't miss the museum's expanding **ethnographic collection**, too, including the atmospheric Mexican and North American galleries, plus the new African galleries in the basement. In the north wing of the museum, closest to the back entrance on Montague Place,

there are also fabulous Oriental treasures including ancient Chinese porcelain, ornate snuffboxes, miniature landscapes and a bewildering array of Buddhist and Hindu gods.

London University

ⓦwww.lon.ac.uk. London has more students than any other city in the world (over half a million at the last count), which isn't bad going for a city that only organized its own University in 1826, more than six hundred years after the likes of Oxford and Cambridge. The university started life in Bloomsbury, but it wasn't until after World War I that the institution really began to take over the area.

This piecemeal development means that departments are spread over a wide area, though the main focus is between the 1930s Senate House skyscraper on Malet Street, behind the British Museum, and the Neoclassical University College (UCL; ⊛www.ucl.ac.uk), near the top of Gower Street. UCL is home to London's most famous art school, the Slade, which puts on temporary exhibitions from its collection at the **Strang Print Room**, in the south cloister of the main quadrangle (term-time Wed–Fri 1–5pm; free); call ☎020/7679 2540 to check hours or what's on. Also on display in the south cloisters is the fully-clothed skeleton of philosopher Jeremy Bentham (1748–1832), one of the university's founders, topped by a wax head and wide-brimmed hat.

▲ LONDON UNIVERSITY'S SENATE HOUSE

London University Museums and the Brunei Gallery

On the first floor of London University's D.M.S. Watson building on Malet Place, the **Petrie Museum of Egyptian Archeology** (Tues–Fri 1–5pm, Sat 10am–1pm; free; ⊛www.petrie.ucl.ac.uk) has a couple of rooms jam-packed with antiquities, including the world's oldest dress, an understandably ragged pleated garment worn by an Ancient Egyptian teenager around 3000 BC. Tucked away in the southeast corner of Gordon Square, at no. 53, there's more specialist interest at the **Percival David Foundation of Chinese Art** (Mon–Fri 10.30am–5pm; free; ⊛www.pdfmuseum.org.uk), which boasts two floors of top-notch Chinese ceramics, while the temporary exhibitions of photography and art at the

Brunei Gallery (Mon–Fri 10.30am–5pm; free; ⊛www.soas.ac.uk/gallery), which is part of the School of Oriental and African Studies, are usually well worth visiting; call ☎020/7898 4915 to see what's on.

British Library

96 Euston Rd ☎020/7412 7332, ⊛www.bl.uk. Mon & Wed–Fri 9.30am–6pm, Tues 9.30am–8pm, Sat 9.30am–5pm, Sun 11am–5pm. Free. Opened in 1998 as the country's most expensive public building, it was hardly surprising that the British Library drew fierce criticism from all sides. Certainly, the exterior's red-brick brutalism is horribly out of fashion, and compares unfavourably with its cathedralesque Victorian neighbour, but the interior of the library has met with general approval and the high-tech exhibition galleries are superb.

The library's reading rooms are accessible to its members only, but its exhibition galleries are open to all. These are situated to the left as you enter; straight ahead is the spiritual heart of the BL, a multistorey glass-walled tower housing the vast King's Library, collected by George III and donated to the museum by George IV in 1823; to the side of the King's Library are the pull-out drawers of the philatelic collection.

The first of the three exhibition galleries to head for is the dimly lit John Ritblat Gallery, where a superlative selection of ancient manuscripts, maps, documents and precious books, including the richly illustrated *Lindisfarne Gospels*, are displayed. One of the most appealing innovations is "Turning the Pages", a small room off the main gallery where you can "turn" the pages of selected texts on a computer terminal. The Workshop of Words, Sounds and Images is a hands-on exhibition of more universal appeal, where you can design your own literary publication, while the Pearson Gallery of Living Words puts on excellent temporary exhibitions, for which there is sometimes an admission charge.

St Pancras & King's Cross stations

Euston Rd. Completed in 1876, the former *Midland Grand Hotel*'s majestic sweep of Neo-Gothic lancets, dormers and chimneypots forms the facade of St Pancras Station. In comparison King's Cross Station, opened in 1850, is a mere shed, though it was simple and graceful enough until British Rail added the soon-to-be-demolished modern forecourt. These days, the station is best known as the place from which Harry Potter and his wizarding chums leave for school on the *Hogwarts Express* from platform 9¾. The scenes from the film are, in fact, shot between platforms 4 and 5, as 9 and 10 are unphotogenic side-platforms.

Shops

Atlantis Bookshop

49a Museum St ☎020/7405 2120, ⊛www.theatlantisbookshop .com. Splendid occult-oriented place, with the perfect ambience for browsing through books and magazines covering spirituality, psychic phenomena, witchcraft and the like.

Gay's the Word

66 Marchmont St ☎020/7278 7654, ⊛www.gaystheword.co.uk. An extensive collection of lesbian and gay classics, pulps, contemporary fiction and non-fiction, plus cards, calendars and

▲ RUSSELL HOTEL, RUSSELL SQUARE

weekly lesbian discussion groups and readings.

Gosh!

39 Great Russell St ☎020/7636 1011, ⊛www.goshlondon.com. All kinds of comics for all kinds of readers, whether you're casually curious or a serious collector.

Playin' Games

33 Museum St ☎020/7323 3080, ⊛www.playingames.co.uk. Two floors of traditional board games (Scrabble, Cluedo etc), plus backgammon, war games, fantasy games and more.

Skoob Books

10 Brunswick Centre, off Bernard St ☎020/7278 8760, ⊛www.skoob.com. Cut-price current and recent secondhand academic titles, as well as modern fiction, poetry, travel and more. Students get a ten-percent discount.

Stern's African Record Centre

293 Euston Rd ☎020/7387 5550. World famous for its global specialisms, this expert store has an unrivalled stock of African music, and excellent selections from pretty much everywhere else in the world, too.

Cafés

Coffee Gallery

23 Museum St. Excellent small café serving mouthwatering Italian sandwiches, and a few more substantial dishes at lunchtime. Get there early to grab a seat.

Restaurants

Abeno

47 Museum St ☎020/7405 3211. Japanese restaurant specializing in open kitchen *okonomi-yaki*, which is something like a sloppy pizza crossed with a solid omelette, then layered with all manner of odds and ends – all for around £10.

Cigala

54 Lamb's Conduit St ☎020/7405 1717, ⊛www.cigala.co.uk. Simple dishes, strong flavours, fresh ingredients and real passion are evident at this Iberian restaurant, where a paella will set you back around £15.

Wagamama

4 Streatham St ☎020/7836 3330, ⊛www.wagamama.com. Much copied since, this was the pioneer of austere, minimalist, canteen-style noodle bars, which serves filling main meals for under £10.

Pubs and bars

King's Bar

Great Russell Hotel, Russell Square. The magnificent high ceilings and wood panelling of this Victorian hotel bar provide a great place in which to luxuriate. It's also a lot less posh – and more fun – than most hotel bars, and you get free bowls of nibbles.

The Lamb

94 Lamb's Conduit St. Pleasant Young's pub with a marvellously well-preserved Victorian interior of mirrors, old wood and "snob" screens.

Museum Tavern

49 Great Russell St. Right opposite the main entrance to the British Museum, this large and characterful old pub was where Marx took a break from writing *Das Capital* over the road in the BM.

Covent Garden

Covent Garden's transformation from a fruit, vegetable and flower market into a fashion-conscious shopping quarter was one of the most miraculous developments of the 1980s. Some three centuries ago the piazza served as the great playground (and red-light district) of eighteenth-century London. The Royal Opera House, alongside the area's buskers and numerous theatres, are survivors in this tradition, but in addition, there are now year-round stalls selling everything from antiques to Union Jack T-shirts, as well as numerous unusual shops, the occasional funfair and an annual Christmas market. Nearby, the old warehouses around Neal Street boast some of the most fashionable shops in the West End, selling everything from shoes to skateboards.

Covent Garden Piazza

ⓦ www.coventgardenmarket.co.uk.
London's oldest planned square, laid out in the 1630s by Inigo Jones, Covent Garden Piazza was initially a great success – its novelty value alone ensured a rich and aristocratic clientele for the surrounding properties. Over the next century, though, the tone of the place fell as the fruit and vegetable market expanded, and theatres and coffee houses began to take over the peripheral buildings. Eventually, a large covered market was constructed in the middle of the square, but when the flower market closed in 1974, it was very nearly demolished to make way for an office development. Instead, the elegant Victorian market hall and its largely pedestrianized, cobbled piazza were restored to house shops, restaurants and arts-and-crafts stalls. Boosted by high-quality buskers and street entertainers, the piazza is now one of London's major tourist attractions, its success prompting a wholesale gentrification of the streets all around.

St Paul's Church

Covent Garden Piazza
ⓦ www.actorschurch.org. The only remaining parts of the original piazza are the two rebuilt sections of arcading on the north side, and St Paul's Church on the west side. The proximity of so many theatres has earned it the nickname of the "Actors' Church", and it's filled with memorials to international thespians from Boris Karloff to Gracie Fields. The space in front of the church's Tuscan portico –

▲ COVENT GARDEN BICYCLE TAXIS

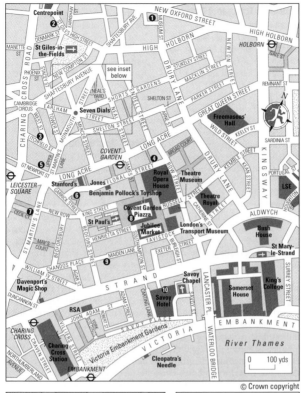

© Crown copyright

EATING & DRINKING (main map)

AKA	1	Lamb & Flag	6
American Bar	10	Porterhouse	9
Café des Amis	4	Punch & Judy	8
First Out	2	Salisbury	7
The Ivy	3	Zoomslide Café	5

(inset map)

Belgo Centraal	18
The Bünker	17
Detroit	15
Food for Thought	16
Mode	11
Monmouth Coffee Company	12
Rock & Sole Plaice	14
World Food Café	13

where Eliza Doolittle was discovered selling violets by Henry Higgins in George Bernard Shaw's *Pygmalion* – is now a legalized venue for buskers and street performers, who must audition for a slot

months in advance. Round the back, the churchyard provides a tranquil respite from the activity outside – access is from King Street, Henrietta Street or Bedford Street.

London's Transport Museum

Covent Garden Piazza
ⓦ www.ltmuseum.co.uk. Mon–Thurs, Sat & Sun 10am–6pm, Fri 11am–6pm. £5.95. Covent Garden's former flower market hall now serves as a retirement home for the old buses, trains and trams of London's Transport Museum. The ever-popular collection also has enough interactive fun – touch-screen computers, vehicles to climb on and the odd costumed conductor – to keep most children amused. There's usually a good smattering of stylish maps and posters on display, too, and you can buy reproductions, plus countless other tube, bus and tram paraphernalia, at the shop on the way out.

Theatre Museum

Russell St ⓣ 020/7943 4700, ⓦ www.theatremuseum.org. Tues–Sun 10am–6pm. Free. Also housed in the old flower market hall, the Theatre Museum displays three centuries of memorabilia from the Western performing arts. The corridors of glass cases cluttered with props, programmes and costumes are not especially

▲ TRAMS, LONDON'S TRANSPORT MUSEUM

exciting, but the special exhibitions and long-term "temporary" shows tend to be a lot more fun, and usually have a performance, workshop or hands-on element to them. The museum also runs a booking service for West End shows and has an unusually good selection of cards and posters.

Royal Opera House

Bow St ⓣ 020/7304 4000, ⓦ www.royaloperahouse.org. The arcading in the northeast side of the piazza was rebuilt in the late 1990s as part of the multi-million pound redevelopment of the Royal Opera House, whose main Neoclassical facade, dating from 1811, opens onto Bow Street (which you can reach via a passageway in the corner of the arcading). As part of the redevelopment, the market's spectacular wrought-iron Floral Hall (daily 10am–3pm) was transformed into the opera house's new first-floor foyer; both this and the glorious terrace overlooking the piazza, beyond the *Amphitheatre* bar/restaurant, are open to the public. Backstage tours of the opera house take place from Monday to Saturday (10.30am, 12.30 & 2.30pm; £7).

Strand

Once famous for its riverside mansions, and later its music halls, the **Strand** is a shadow of its former self today, characterized more by the young homeless who shelter in the shop doorways at night. On the south side of the Strand, a blind side street – where the traffic drives on the right – leads to the *Savoy*, built in 1889 and still London's grandest hotel. César Ritz was the original manager, Guccio Gucci started out as a dishwasher here, and the list of illustrious guests is endless.

Bush House

Strand ◍ www.bbc.co.uk/worldservice. Home of the BBC's World Service since 1940, Bush House was actually built by the American speculator Irving T. Bush, whose planned trade centre flopped in the 1930s. The giant figures on the north facade and the inscription, "To the Eternal Friendship of English-speaking Nations", thus refer to the friendship between the US and Britain, and are not, as many people assume, the declaratory manifesto of the current occupants.

Victoria Embankment

Built between 1868 and 1874, the Victoria Embankment was the inspiration of French engineer Joseph Bazalgette, whose project simultaneously relieved congestion along the Strand, provided an extension to the underground railway and sewage systems, and created a new stretch of parkland with a riverside walk – no longer much fun due to the volume of traffic that barrels along it, though it does afford some good views over the water. London's oldest monument, Cleopatra's Needle, languishes little-noticed on the Thames side of the embankment. The 60-foot-high, 180-ton stick of granite in fact has nothing to do with Cleopatra – it's one of a pair originally erected in Heliopolis in 1475 BC (the other one is in New York's Central Park).

Somerset House

Victoria Embankment ◍ www .somerset-house.org.uk. Courtyard and terrace daily 10am–11pm, interior daily

▲ SOMERSET HOUSE COURTYARD FOUNTAINS

10am–6pm. Free. Sole survivor of the grand edifices which once lined this stretch of the riverfront, Somerset House's four wings enclose an elegant and surprisingly large courtyard. From March to October, a wonderful 55-jet fountain spouts straight from the courtyard's cobbles; in winter, an ice rink is set up in its place. The monumental Palladian building itself was begun in 1776 by William Chambers as a purpose-built governmental office development, but now also houses a series of museums and galleries.

The south wing, overlooking the Thames, is home to the **Hermitage Rooms** (£5; ☎020/7845 4600, ◍www.hermitagerooms.com), featuring changing displays of anything from paintings to Fabergé eggs drawn from St Petersburg's Hermitage Museum, and the magnificent **Gilbert Collection** (£5; ◍www.gilbert-collection.org.uk), displaying decorative artworks from European silver and gold to micro-mosaics, clocks, portrait miniatures and snuffboxes.

In the north wing are the **Courtauld Institute galleries** (£5, free Mon 10am–2pm; ⓦwww.courtauld.ac.uk), chiefly known for their dazzling collection of Impressionist and Post-Impressionist paintings. Among the most celebrated works are a small-scale version of Manet's nostalgic *Bar at the Folies-Bergère*, Renoir's *La Loge*, and Degas's *Two Dancers*, plus a whole heap of Cézanne's canvases, including one of his series of *Card Players*. The Courtauld also boasts a fine selection of works by the likes of Rubens, van Dyck, Tiepolo and Cranach the Elder, as well as twentieth-century paintings and sculptures by, among others, Kandinksy, Matisse, Dufy, Derain, Rodin and Henry Moore.

Shops

Benjamin Pollocks' Toyshop

44 The Market, Covent Garden ☎020/7379 7866, ⓦwww.pollocks-coventgarden.co.uk. Beautiful, old-fashioned toys, for grown-ups as well as children: toy theatres, glove puppets, jack-in-the-boxes and so on.

Birkenstock

37 Neal St ☎020/7240 2783, ⓦwww.birkenstock.co.uk. Comfortable, classic and very fashionable clogs, sandals and shoes in leather, suede, nubuk and vegan styles.

Davenport's Magic Shop

7 Charing Cross Tube Arcade, Strand ☎020/7836 0408, ⓦwww.davenportsmagic.co.uk. The world's oldest family-run magic business, stocking a huge array of marvellous tricks for amateurs and professionals.

Duffer of St George

29 Shorts Gardens ☎020/7379 4660, ⓦwww.thedufferofstgeorge.com. Covetable own-label boys' casuals and streetwear, plus range of other hip designers in the land of jeans, shoes, jackets and so on.

Koh Samui

65 Monmouth St ☎020/7240 4280. The leading promoter of young British designers (and some big-name foreigners too), this one-stop boutique offers a highly selective range of mens' and womenswear with an elegant, eclectic and urban feel.

Neal's Yard Dairy

17 Shorts Gardens ☎020/7240 5700. London's finest cheese shop, with a huge selection of quality cheeses from around the British Isles, as well as a few exceptionally good ones from further afield. You can taste before you buy.

Neal's Yard Remedies

15 Neal's Yard ☎020/7379 7662, ⓦwww.nealsyardremedies.com. Fabulously scented, beautifully presented, entirely efficacious herbal cosmetics, toiletries remedies.

Stanford's Map and Travel Bookshop

12–14 Long Acre ☎020/7836 1321, ⓦwww.stanfords.co.uk. The world's largest specialist travel bookshop, stocking pretty much any map of anywhere, plus a huge range of guides and travel literature.

Cafés

Food for Thought

31 Neal St. Long-established but minuscule bargain veggie restaurant and takeaway counter – the tasty and filling menu

▲ ALFRESCO LUNCH, NEAL'S YARD

changes twice daily, and includes vegan and wheat-free options. Expect to queue, and don't expect to linger at peak times.

Monmouth Coffee Company

27 Monmouth St. Closed Sun. Cramped wooden booths and daily newspapers on hand evoke an eighteenth-century coffee house atmosphere – pick and mix your coffee from a fine selection.

Rock & Sole Plaice

47 Endell St. A rare survivor: a no-nonsense, traditional fish and chip shop in central London. Take away, eat inside or opt for one of the pavement tables.

World Food Café

14 Neal's Yard ⓦ www.worldfoodcafe .com. Closed Sun. First-floor veggie café that comes into its own in summer, when the windows are flung open and you can gaze down upon trendy humanity as you tuck into pricey but tasty dishes from all corners of the globe.

Zoomslide Café

5 Great Newport St. Situated in the middle of one of the Photographers' Gallery exhibition spaces, this is a wonderfully inexpensive and peaceful haven serving soups, sandwiches, salads and cakes.

Restaurants

Belgo Centraal

50 Earlham St ⓣ 020/7813 2233, ⓦ www.belgo-restaurants.com. Massive metal-minimalist cavern serving excellent kilo buckets of moules marinière, with frites and mayonnaise, washed down with Belgian beers and waffles for dessert. The lunchtime specials, for around £6, are a bargain for central London.

Café des Amis

11–14 Hanover Place, off Long Acre ⓣ 020/7379 3444, ⓦ www .cafedesamis.co.uk. Closed Sun. Modern, clean and bright French restaurant whose menu darts from influence to influence: salmon terrine with guacamole meets confit of halibut and pumpkin gnocchi. The pre- and post-theatre set menus are a real bargain.

The Ivy

1 West St ⓣ 020/7836 4751, ⓦ www.caprice-holdings.co.uk. Expensive, Regency-style restaurant built in 1928 that's long been a theatreland and society favourite. The only problem is getting a table; either book months ahead or go for the bargain £19 three-course weekend lunch, with valet parking thrown in.

Pubs and bars

AKA

18 West Central St ⓦ www.the-end .co.uk. Minimalist club bar, with a chrome balcony overlooking

the main floor, and a well-stocked bar which dispenses good food.

American Bar

The Savoy, Strand ⊛ www.the-savoy .com. Closed Sun. Utterly gorgeous Art Deco bar that's famous for its cocktails (a snip at £10 a throw). Dress code is jacket and tie, or at least very smart. A pianist plays Mon–Sat 7–11pm.

Detroit

35 Earlham St ⊛ www.detroit-bar.com. Cavernous underground venue with an open-plan bar area, secluded Gaudíesque booths, a huge range of spirits and excellent cocktails. DJs take over at the weekends.

First Out

52 St Giles High St ⊛ www.firstoutcafebar.com. The West End's original gay café/bar: upstairs is airy and non-smoking, downstairs dark and foggy. On Friday's there's a busy pre-club warm-up session for women; gay men are welcome as guests.

Bünker Bier Hall

41 Earlham St ⊛ www.bunkerbar.com. Busy, brick-vaulted basement bar with wrought-iron pillars, lots of brushed steel and pricey, strong brews, most made on the premises.

Lamb & Flag

33 Rose St. Busy, tiny and highly atmospheric pub, hidden away down an alley between Garrick Street and Floral Street. John Dryden was attacked here in 1679 after scurrilous verses had been written about one of Charles II's mistresses (by someone else as it turned out).

▲ SEVEN DIALS SUNDIALS

Porterhouse

21–22 Maiden Lane ⊛ www.porterhousebrewco.com. Loud, buzzing micro-brewery which has eschewed Victoriana for lots of exposed wood and copper pipes. Plenty of own-brewed stouts, ales and lagers to choose from, and lots of suits to rub shoulders with.

Punch & Judy

40 The Market. Horribly mobbed and loud, but boasting an unbeatable location with a very popular balcony overlooking Covent Garden Piazza.

Salisbury

90 St Martin's Lane. One of the most superbly preserved Victorian pubs in London – and certainly the most central – with cut, etched and engraved windows, bronze statues, red-velvet seating and a fine lincrusta ceiling.

Holborn

Holborn (pronounced "Hoe-bun") is a fascinating area to explore. Strategically placed between the royal and political centre of Westminster and the financial might of the City, this wedge of land became the hub of the English legal system in the early thirteenth century. Hostels, known as Inns of Court, were established where lawyers could eat, sleep and study English Common Law; even today, in order to qualify, every aspiring barrister must study at one of the Inns, whose archaic, cobbled precincts dominate the area and exude the rarefied atmosphere of an Oxbridge college.

Temple

Temple is the largest and most complex of the Inns of Court, and is made up of two Inns: Middle Temple (ⓦwww .middletemple.org.uk) and Inner Temple (ⓦwww.innertemple .org.uk). A few very old buildings survive here, but the overall scene is dominated by neo-Georgian reconstructions that followed the devastation of the Blitz. Still, the maze of courtyards and passageways is fun to explore – especially after dark, when Temple is gas-lit.

Medieval students ate, attended lectures and slept in the **Middle Temple Hall** (Mon–Fri 10am–noon & 3–4pm; free), still the Inn's main dining room. Constructed in the 1560s, the hall provided the setting for many great Elizabethan masques and plays – probably including Shakespeare's *Twelfth Night*, which is believed to have been premiered here in 1602. The hall is worth a visit for its fine hammerbeam roof, wooden panelling and decorative Elizabethan screen.

The two Temple Inns share use of the complex's oldest building, **Temple Church** (Wed–Sun 11am–4pm; ⓦwww.templechurch.com), built in 1185 by the Knights Templar. An oblong chancel was added in the thirteenth century, and the whole building was damaged in the Blitz, but the original round church – modelled on the Holy Sepulchre in Jerusalem – still stands, with its striking Purbeck-marble piers, recumbent marble effigies of knights, and tortured grotesques grimacing in the spandrels of the blind arcading.

Royal Courts of Justice

Strand ☎020/7947 6000, ⓦwww.courtservice.gov.uk. Mon–Fri 8.30am–4.30pm. Free. Home to the Court of Appeal and the High Court, the Royal Courts of Justice are where England's most important civil cases are tried. Appeals and libel suits are heard here – countless pop and soap stars have battled it out with the tabloid press, while appeals have led to freedom for those wrongfully imprisoned, such as the high-profile Birmingham Six and Guilford Four. The fifty-odd courtrooms are open to the public, though you have to go through stringent security checks first (strictly no cameras allowed).

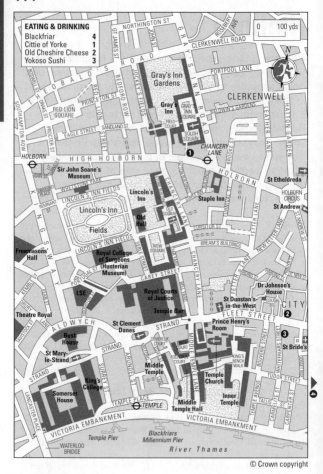

EATING & DRINKING
Blackfriar	4
Cittie of Yorke	1
Old Cheshire Cheese	2
Yokoso Sushi	3

© Crown copyright

Fleet Street

In 1500, one Wynkyn de Worde, a pupil of William Caxton, moved the Caxton presses from Westminster to Fleet Street, in order to be close to the Inns of Court (lawyers were among his best customers) and to the clergy of St Paul's, who comprised the largest literate group in the city. Britain's first daily newspapers were published here, and by the nineteenth century, all the major national and provincial dailies had their offices and printing presses in the Fleet Street district. Since the 1980s, all but a handful of the press headquarters that once dominated this part of town have relocated to the Docklands and elsewhere. Nonetheless, Fleet Street still offers one of the grandest approaches to the City, thanks to the view across to Ludgate Hill and beyond to St Paul's Cathedral.

Prince Henry's Room

17 Fleet St ⊛www.cityoflondon
.gov.uk/phr. Mon–Sat 11am–2pm. Free.
The first floor of this fine
Jacobean house, with its
distinctive timber-framed bay
windows, now contains material
relating to the diarist Samuel
Pepys (1633–1703), who was
born in nearby Salisbury Court
and baptized at St Bride's. Even
if you've no interest in Pepys, the
wooden-panelled room itself is
worth a look – it contains one of
the finest Jacobean plasterwork
ceilings in London, and a lot of
original stained glass.

St Bride's

Fleet St ⊛www.stbrides.com. Mon–Sat
9am–5pm. Free. To get a sense of
old-style Fleet Street, head for
the so-called "journalists' and
printers' cathedral", the church
of St Bride's, which boasts
Christopher Wren's tallest and
most exquisite spire (said to be
the inspiration for the tiered
wedding cake). The crypt
contains a little museum of
Fleet Street history, with
information on the *Daily
Courant* and the *Universal Daily
Register*, which later became *The*

Times and which then claimed
to be "the faithful recorder of
every species of intelligence . . .
circulated for a particular set of
readers only".

Dr Johnson's House

17 Gough Square ⊛www.drjh.dircon
.co.uk. May–Sept Mon–Sat
11am–5.30pm; Oct–April Mon–Sat
11am–5pm. £4. Despite
appearances, Dr Johnson's House
is the only authentic seventeenth-
century building on Gough
Square. It was here the great
savant, writer and lexicographer
lived from 1747 to 1759 whilst
compiling the 41,000 entries for
the first dictionary of the English
language. The grey-panelled
rooms of the house are peppered
with period furniture and lined
with portraits and etchings,
including one of Johnson's black
servant Francis Barber. Two first-
edition copies of the great
Dictionary are on display, while
the open-plan attic, in which
Johnson and his six helpers put
the tome together, is now lined
with explanatory panels on
lexicography.

Lincoln's Inn

Lincoln's Inn Fields/Chancery Lane
☎020/7405 1393, ⊛www.lincolnsinn
.org.uk. Mon–Fri 9am–6pm. Free.
Lincoln's Inn was the first –
and in many ways is the
prettiest – of the Inns of Court,
having miraculously escaped
the ravages of the Blitz; famous
alumni include Thomas More,
Oliver Cromwell and Margaret
Thatcher. The main entrance is
the diamond-patterned, red-
brick Tudor gateway on
Chancery Lane, adjacent to
which is the early seventeenth-
century chapel (Mon–Fri
noon–2pm), with its unusual
fan-vaulted open undercroft
and, on the first floor, a late

▲ ST BRIDE'S SPIRE

Gothic nave, hit by a Zeppelin in World War I and much restored since. The Inn's fifteenth-century Old Hall (open by appointment), where Dickens set the case Jarndyce versus Jarndyce in *Bleak House*, features a fine timber roof, linenfold panelling and an elaborate, early Jacobean screen.

Hunterian Museum

Royal College of Surgeons, Lincoln's Inn Fields ® www.rcseng.ac.uk. Mon–Fri 10am–5pm. Free. The unique specimen collection of the surgeon-scientist John Hunter (1728–93), the Hunterian Museum first opened in 1813, was repaired following damage during the Blitz, and is currently in the process of being totally rebuilt. Since most of the exhibits are jars of pickled skeletons and body pieces, it's certainly not a museum for the squeamish. Also on view are the skeletons of the Irish giant, O'Brien (1761–83), who was seven feet ten inches tall, and the Sicilian midget Caroline Crachami (1815–24), who was just one foot ten and a half inches when she died at the age of 9.

Sir John Soane's Museum

Lincoln's Inn Fields ® www.soane.org. Tues–Sat 10am–5pm, candle-lit first Tues of the month 6–9pm. Free. The chief architect of the Bank of England, Sir John Soane (1753–1837) was an avid collector who designed this house not only as a home and office, but also as a place to stash his large assortment of art and antiquities; opened up as a museum, it's now one of London's best-kept secrets. Arranged much as it was in his lifetime, the ingeniously planned house has an informal, treasure-hunt atmosphere, with surprises in every alcove. The star exhibits

are Hogarth's satirical *Election* series and his merciless morality tale *The Rake's Progress*, as well as the alabaster sarcophagus of Seti I. At 2.30pm every Saturday, a fascinating, hour-long guided tour (£3) takes you round the museum and the enormous research library next door, which contains architectural drawings, books and exquisitely detailed architectural models in cork and wood.

Cafés

Yokoso Sushi

40 Whitefriars St. Closed Sat & Sun. Top-notch sushi place serving really fresh fish at very affordable prices; dishes are mostly under £3 and set meals under £10.

Pubs and bars

Blackfriar

174 Queen Victoria St. Closed Sat & Sun. Gorgeous, utterly original pub, with Art Nouveau marble friezes of boozy monks and a wonderful highly decorated alcove, all dating from 1905.

Cittie of Yorke

22 High Holborn. One of London's most venerable pubs, with a vaulted cellar bar, wood panelling, cheap Sam Smith's beer and a grand quasi-medieval wine hall, whose cosy cubicles were once the preserve of lawyers and their clients.

Old Cheshire Cheese

Wine Office Court, 145 Fleet St. Closed Sun eve. A famous seventeenth-century watering hole, with real fires and several snug, dark-panelled bars. Popular with tourists, but by no means exclusively so.

Clerkenwell

A typical London mix of Georgian and Victorian town-houses, housing estates, loft conversions and art studios, Clerkenwell has been transformed over the last decade or so. On the edge of London's financial sector, this formerly workaday district – famous for lockmaking, clockmaking, printing and jewellery – is now a fashionable, residential enclave for portfolio-carrying designers and media types. Well off the conventional tourist trail, there's only a smattering of minor sights here, but the area's main highlight is its abundance of trendy restaurants, bars and clubs.

Old Bailey

Newgate St ◉ www.cjsonline.org. Mon–Fri 10.30am–1pm & 2–4pm. Free. The Central Criminal Court, more popularly known as the Old Bailey, was built on the site of the notoriously harsh Newgate Prison, where folk used to come to watch public hangings. The current, rather pompous Edwardian building is distinguished by its green dome, surmounted by a gilded statue of Justice, unusually depicted without blindfold, holding her sword and scales. The Old Bailey is now the venue for all the country's most serious criminal court cases; you can watch the proceedings from the visitors' gallery, but note that bags, cameras, mobiles, personal stereos and food and drink are not allowed in, and there is no cloakroom.

St Bartholomew-the-Great

Cloth Fair ◉ www.greatstbarts.com. Tues–Fri 8.30am–5pm, Sat 10.30am–1.30pm, Sun 8.30am–1pm & 2.30–8pm; mid-Nov to mid-Feb closes 4pm Mon–Fri. Free. Begun in 1123, St Bartholomew-the-Great is London's oldest and most exquisite parish church. Its half-timbered Tudor gatehouse on Little Britain Street incorporates a thirteenth-century arch that once formed the entrance to the nave; above, a wooden statue of St Bartholomew stands holding the knife with which he was flayed. One side of the medieval cloisters survives to the south, immediately to the right as you enter the church. The rest is a confusion of elements, including portions of the transepts and, most impressively, the chancel, where stout Norman pillars separate the main body of the church from

▲ JUSTICE ATOP THE OLD BAILEY

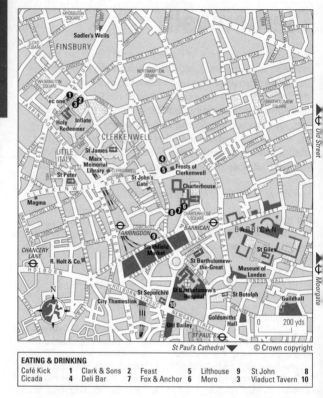

St Paul's Cathedral ▼   © Crown copyright

EATING & DRINKING								
Café Kick	1	Clark & Sons	2	Feast	5	Lifthouse	9	St John	8
Cicada	4	Deli Bar	7	Fox & Anchor	6	Moro	3	Viaduct Tavern	10

the ambulatory. There are various pre-Fire monuments to admire, the most prominent being the tomb of Rahere, court jester to Henry I, which shelters under a fifteenth-century canopy north of the main altar.

Smithfield

Blood and guts were regularly spilled at Smithfield long before today's meat market was legally sanctioned here in the seventeenth century. For more than three centuries it was a popular venue for public executions: the Scottish hero, William Wallace, was hanged, disembowelled and beheaded

here in 1305, and the Bishop of Rochester's cook was boiled alive in 1531, but the local speciality was burnings, which reached a peak in the mid-sixteenth century during the reign of "Bloody" Mary, when hundreds of Protestants were burned at the stake for their beliefs. These days, Smithfield is dominated by its **meat market**, housed in a colourful and ornate Victorian market hall on Charterhouse Street; if you want to see it in action, get here early – the activity starts around 4am and is all over by 9am or 10am. The compensation for getting up at this ungodly hour are the early licensing laws, which mean you can get a hearty breakfast and an early morning pint from the local pubs.

Museum of London

London Wall, Barbican ☎020/7600 3699, ⊛www.museumoflondon.org.uk. Mon–Sat 10am–5.50pm, Sun noon–5.50pm. Free. Despite London's long pedigree, very few of its ancient structures are still standing. However, numerous Roman, Saxon and Elizabethan remains have been discovered during the City's various rebuildings, and many of these finds are now displayed at the Museum of London. The permanent exhibition provides an educational trot through London's past from prehistory to the present day, hence the large number of school groups who pass through. Displays are imaginatively set out, though only the new prehistory gallery has much in the way of hands-on stuff. Specific exhibits to look out for include the Bucklersbury Roman mosaic; the sarcophagus, coffin and

skeleton of a wealthy Roman woman found in Spitalfields; and the Lord Mayor's heavily gilded coach (still used for state occasions). The real strength of the museum, though, lies in the excellent temporary exhibitions, lectures, walks and videos it organizes throughout the year.

Barbican

The City's only large residential complex is the Barbican, a monumental concrete ghetto built over the heavily bombed Cripplegate area. The zone's solitary prewar building is the heavily restored sixteenth-century church of **St Giles Cripplegate** (Mon–Fri 11am–4pm), situated across from the infamously user-repellent **Barbican Arts Centre** (☎020/7638 8891, ⊛www.barbican.org.uk) on Silk Street, London's supposed answer to Paris's Pompidou Centre which was formally opened in 1982. The complex, which is traffic-free, serves as home to the London Symphony Orchestra and the capital's chapter of the Royal Shakespeare Company, and stages regular free gigs in the foyer area.

Marx Memorial Library

37a Clerkenwell Green ⊛www.marxlibrary.net. Mon, Tues & Thurs 1–6pm, Wed 1–8pm, Sat 10am–1pm. Free. Housed in a former Welsh Charity School, the Marx Memorial Library was where Lenin edited seventeen editions of the Bolshevik paper *Iskra* in 1902–03. The library was founded in 1933 in response to the book burnings taking place in Nazi Germany, and the poky little back room where Lenin worked is

▲ ST BARTHOLOMEW GATEHOUSE

maintained as it was then, as a kind of shrine – even the original lino survives. You're free to view the Lenin Room, where there's an original copy of *Iskra*, and the workerist *Hastings Mural* from 1935, but to consult the unrivalled collection of books and pamphlets on the labour movement you need to become a library member.

Exmouth Market

⊛www.exmouth-market.com. Exmouth Market is at the epicentre of newly fashionable Clerkenwell. The old market proper has been reduced to a raggle-taggle of tatty stalls, but the rest of the street has been colonized by modish new shops, bars and restaurants (plus the inevitable Starbucks). The only striking building is the Roman Catholic church of the **Holy Redeemer**, which boasts an unusual Italianate campanile; the groin-vaulted interior is lined with big composite pillars, and a large baldachin occupies centre stage, but it's otherwise lightly decorated for a Catholic church.

Shops

ec one

41 Exmouth Market ☎020/7713 6185, ⊛www.econe.co.uk. Stunning contemporary jewellery by a whole host of top designers: everything from simple perspex necklaces to very expensive diamond rings.

Frosts of Clerkenwell

60–62 Clerkenwell Rd ☎020/7253 0315, ⊛www.frostsofclerkenwell .co.uk. Closed Sat & Sun. One of the few clock and watch places left in an area once famous for them: choose from antique

grandfather clocks to second-hand wristwatches.

Inflate

28 Exmouth Market ☎020/7713 9096, ⊛www.inflate.co.uk. Closed Sat & Sun. Temple for all things plastic and inflatable, from postcards (yes, really) and piggy banks to an entire office.

R. Holt & Co

98 Hatton Garden ☎020/7405 5286, ⊛www.rholt.co.uk. Closed Sat & Sun. Choose your stone from the thousands in stock, and get a bespoke ring, necklace or pendant made up.

Cafés

Clark & Sons

46 Exmouth Market. Closed Sun. Exmouth Market has changed beyond recognition, but this genuine pie-and-mash shop – the most central one in the capital – is still going strong.

Deli Bar

117 Charterhouse St. Closed Sun. Doorstop focaccia sandwiches, a great salad bar and a relaxed vibe are the main draws of this two-tier place: café/bar upstairs, takeaway deli downstairs.

Feast

86 St John St ⊛www.feastwraps.com. Closed Sat & Sun. Delicious tortilla-wrapped sandwiches made to order; take away or eat in at this small, designer-ish Clerkenwell café.

Restaurants

Cicada

132 St John St ☎020/7608 1550, ⊛www.cicada.nu. Closed Sun. Part bar, part restaurant, *Cicada* offers

▲ VIADUCT TAVERN BAR

an unusual Thai-based menu that ranges from fishy *tom yum* to ginger noodles or sushi.

Moro

34–36 Exmouth Market ☎020/7833 8336. Closed Sat lunch & Sun. Modern, rather stark place serving food from Spain, Portugal and North Africa, much of it cooked in a wood-fired oven.

St John

26 St John St ☎020/7251 0848, ⓦwww.stjohnrestaurant.co.uk. Closed Sat lunch & Sun. Minimalist former smokehouse that's now a decidedly old-fashioned English restaurant specializing in offal. The cooking is of a very high standard. Booking essential.

Pubs and bars

Café Kick

43 Exmouth Market ⓦwww.cafekick.co.uk. Stylish take on a smoky French-style café/bar in the heart of fashionable Exmouth Market, with three busy table-football games to complete the retro theme.

Fox & Anchor

115 Charterhouse St. Closed Sat & Sun. Handsome Smithfield Market pub that's famous for its early opening hours and huge breakfasts (served 7–10am).

Lifthouse

85 Charterhouse St ⓦwww.lifthouse .co.uk. Three-floored New York style complex with a restaurant, cocktail bar and club space that gets especially lively on Friday and Saturday nights.

Viaduct Tavern

126 Newgate St. Glorious Victorian gin palace, built in 1869 opposite what was then Newgate Prison and is now the Old Bailey. The walls are beautifully decorated with oils of faded ladies representing Commerce, Agriculture and the Arts.

The City

The City is where London began, and its boundaries today are only slightly larger than those in Roman and medieval times. However, you'll find few visible leftovers of London's early days, since four-fifths of it burned down in the Great Fire of 1666. With the notable exception of St Paul's Cathedral and Wren's numerous smaller churches, what you see now is mostly the product of the Victorian construction boom, postwar reconstruction and the office-building frenzy of the 1980s. The

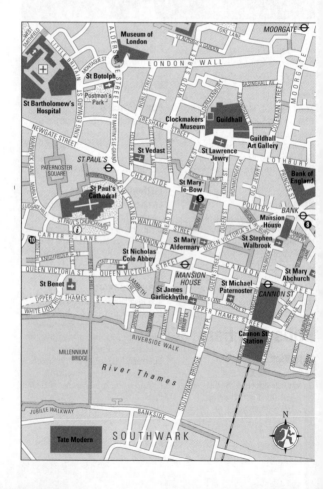

majority of Londoners lived and worked in or around the City up until the eighteenth century – nowadays, however, over a million commuters spend the best part of Monday to Friday here, but only a few thousand actually live here. It's best to try and visit during the week, since many pubs, restaurants and even some tube stations and tourist sights close down at the weekend.

St Paul's Cathedral

Ludgate Hill ⊛ www.stpauls.co.uk. Mon–Sat 8.30am–5pm. £6. Designed by Christopher Wren and completed in 1711, St Paul's remains a dominating presence in the City despite the encroaching tower blocks. Topped by an enormous lead-covered dome that's second in

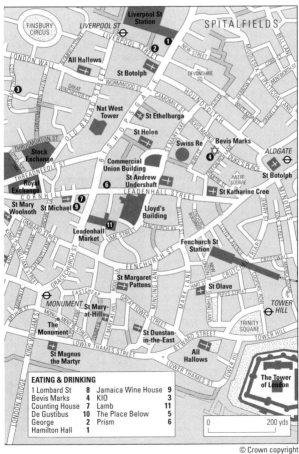

EATING & DRINKING

1 Lombard St	8	Jamaica Wine House	9
Bevis Marks	4	KIO	3
Counting House	7	Lamb	11
De Gustibus	10	The Place Below	5
George	2	Prism	6
Hamilton Hall	1		

0   200 yds

size only to St Peter's in Rome, its showpiece west facade is particularly magnificent, and is most impressive at night when bathed in sea-green arc lights. However compared to its great rival, Westminster Abbey, St Paul's is a soulless but perfectly calculated architectural set piece, a burial place for captains rather than kings.

The best place to appreciate the building's glory is from beneath the **dome**, adorned (against Wren's wishes) by trompe l'oeil frescoes. The most richly decorated section of the cathedral is the **chancel**, where the late Victorian mosaics of birds, fish, animals and greenery are particularly spectacular. The intricately carved oak and lime-wood choir stalls, and the imposing organ case, are the work of Wren's master carver, Grinling Gibbons.

Beginning in the south aisle, a series of stairs lead to the dome's three galleries, the first of which is the internal **Whispering Gallery**, so called because of its acoustic properties – words whispered to the wall on one side are distinctly audible over one hundred feet away on the other, though you often can't hear much above the hubbub. Of the two exterior galleries, the best views are from the tiny **Golden Gallery**, below the golden ball and cross which top the cathedral.

Although the nave is crammed full of overblown monuments to military types, burials in St Paul's are confined to the crypt, reputedly the largest in Europe. The whitewashed walls and bright lighting, however, make this one of London's least atmospheric mausoleums, but **Artists' Corner** here does boast as many painters and

architects as Westminster Abbey has poets, including Christopher Wren himself. The star tombs, though, are those of Nelson and Wellington, both occupying centre stage and both with more fanciful monuments upstairs.

It's well worth attending one of the cathedral's **services**, if only to hear the ethereal choir, who perform during most evensongs (Mon–Sat 5pm), and on Sundays at 10am, 11.30am and 3.15pm.

Guildhall

Aldermanbury Street ⊛ www .cityoflondon.gov.uk. May–Sept daily 10am–5pm; Oct–April Mon–Sat 10am–5pm. Free. Situated at the geographical centre of the City, Guildhall has been the area's administrative seat for over eight hundred years. It remains the headquarters of the Corporation of London, the City's governing body, which still uses it for many formal civic occasions. Architecturally, however, it's not

▲ MAGOG STATUE, GUILDHALL

quite the beauty it once was, having been badly damaged in both the Great Fire and the Blitz, and scarred by the addition of a grotesque 1970s concrete cloister and wing. Nonetheless, the Great Hall, basically a postwar reconstruction of the fifteenth-century original, is worth a brief look, as is the **Clockmakers' Museum** (Mon–Fri 9.30am–4.30pm; free), a collection of over six hundred timepieces, including one of the clocks that won John Harrison the Longitude prize. Also worth a visit is the purpose-built **Guildhall Art Gallery** (Mon–Sat 10am–5pm, Sun noon–4pm; £2.50), which contains one or two exceptional works, such as Rossetti's *La Ghirlandata* and Holman Hunt's *The Eve of St Agnes*, plus a massive painting depicting the 1782 Siege of Gibraltar, commissioned by the Corporation. In the basement, you can view the remains of a Roman amphitheatre, dating from around 120 AD, which was discovered during the gallery's construction.

Bank of England

Threadneedle St www.bankofengland.co.uk. Mon–Fri 10am–5pm. Free. Established in 1694 by William III to raise funds for the war against France, the Bank of England stores the gold reserves of seventy or so central banks from around the world in its vaults. All that remains of the original building, on which John Soane spent the best part of his career (from 1788 onwards), is the windowless, outer curtain wall, which wraps itself round the 3.5-acre island site. However,

you can view a reconstruction of Soane's Bank Stock Office, with its characteristic domed skylight, in the museum, which has its entrance on Bartholomew Lane. The permanent exhibition here includes a model of Soane's bank and a Victorian-style diorama of the night in 1780 when the bank was attacked by rioters. Sadly most of the gold bars are fakes, but there are specimens of every note issued by the Royal Mint over the centuries.

City churches

www.cityoflondonchurches.com.
The City is crowded with churches – well over forty at the last count, the majority built or rebuilt by Wren after the Great Fire. Those particularly worth seeking out include **St Stephen Walbrook** (Mon–Thurs 10am–4pm, Fri 10am–3pm), on Walbrook, Wren's most spectacular church after St Paul's, with sixteen Corinthian columns arranged in clusters around a central coffered dome, and exquisite dark-wood furnishings by Grinling Gibbons. On King William Street, **St Mary Woolnoth** (Mon–Fri 7.45am–5pm) is a typically idiosyncratic creation of Nicholas Hawksmoor, one of Wren's pupils, featuring an ingenious lantern lit by semicircular clerestory windows, and a striking altar canopy held up by barley-sugar columns. The interior of Wren's **St Mary Abchurch** (Mon–Thurs 10am–2pm), on Abchurch Lane, is dominated by an unusual and vast dome fresco, painted by a local parishioner and lit by oval lunettes, while the superlative lime-wood reredos is again by Gibbons.

Lloyd's Building and Swiss Re

East of Bank, and beyond Bishopsgate, on Lime Street, stands Richard Rogers' glitzy **Lloyd's Building**, completed in 1984. A startling array of glass and blue steel pipes – a vertical version of Rogers' own Pompidou Centre – this is easily the most popular of the modern City buildings, at least with the general public. Its closest rival, to the north on St Mary Axe, is Norman Foster's giant new 590ft-tall building for **Swiss Re**, known to Londoners as the "erotic gherkin".

Note that neither building is open to the public.

Leadenhall Market

Leadenhall St. Mon–Fri 11am–2pm. The picturesque cobbles and richly painted, graceful Victorian cast-ironwork of Leadenhall Market date from 1881. Inside, the traders cater mostly for the lunchtime City crowd, their barrows laden with exotic seafood and game, fine wines, champagne and caviar.

Bevis Marks Synagogue

Bevis Marks. Guided tours Mon–Wed & Fri noon, Sun 11.15am. £2. Hidden away in a little courtyard behind a modern red-brick office block, the Bevis Marks Synagogue was built in 1701 by Sephardic Jews who had fled the Inquisition in Spain and Portugal. It's the country's oldest surviving synagogue, and the roomy, rich interior gives an idea of just how wealthy the worshippers were at the time. The Sephardic community has now dispersed across London and the congregation has dwindled, but the magnificent array of chandeliers ensure that it's a popular venue for candle-lit Jewish weddings.

Monument

Monument St. Daily 10am–6pm. £1.50. The Monument was designed by Wren to commemorate the Great Fire of 1666. A plain Doric column crowned with spiky gilded flames, it stands 202 feet high, making it the tallest isolated stone column in the world; if it were laid out flat it would touch the bakery where the Fire started, east of Monument. The bas-relief on the base, now in very bad shape, depicts Charles II and the Duke of York in Roman garb conducting the emergency relief operation. The 311 steps to the viewing gallery once guaranteed an incredible view; nowadays it is somewhat dwarfed by the buildings around it.

Cafés

De Gustibus

53–55 Carter Lane ⊛ www.degustibus .co.uk. Closed Sat & Sun. Award-winning bakery that constructs a wide variety of sandwiches, bruschetta, croque monsieur and quiche to eat in (perched on stools) or take away.

▲ LLOYD'S BUILDING ORIGINAL PORTICO

K10

20 Copthall Ave. Closed Sat & Sun. Remarkably good, inexpensive sushi outlet, with a busy takeaway section upstairs, and a *kaiten* (conveyor-belt) dining area downstairs.

The Place Below

St Mary-le-Bow, Cheapside ⓦwww.theplacebelow.co.uk. Closed Sat & Sun. This café serving imaginative vegetarian dishes is something of a find in the midst of the City. Added to that, the wonderful Norman crypt makes for a very pleasant place in which to dine.

Restaurants

1 Lombard Street

1 Lombard St ⓣ020/7929 6611, ⓦwww.1lombardstreet.com. Closed Sat & Sun. Set in a former banking hall, this is a classy, pricey City brasserie with a buzzy circular bar under a suitably imposing glass dome. Straightforward – and expensive – Michelin-starred French fare.

Bevis Marks

Bevis Marks ⓣ020/7283 2220, ⓦwww.bevismarkstherestaurant.com. Closed Fri eve, Sat & Sun. Super-smart restaurant in the glassed-over courtyard outside Bevis Marks Synagogue, serving expensive, modern kosher dishes as well as traditional Jewish fare.

Prism

147 Leadenhall St ⓣ020/7256 3888, ⓦwww.harveynichols.com. Closed Sat & Sun. A very slick expense-account restaurant in another old banking hall, with a fashionably long bar, suave service and a menu comprised of well-judged English

▲ VIEWING PLATFORM, MONUMENT

favourites with modernist influences.

Pubs and bars

The Counting House

50 Cornhill. Closed Sat & Sun. Successful bank conversion, with fantastic high ceilings, a glass dome, chandeliers and a central oval bar. Naturally enough, given the location, it's wall-to-wall suits.

Hamilton Hall

Liverpool Street Station, Liverpool St. Cavernous former hotel ballroom, adorned with gilded nudes and chandeliers and packed-out with City commuters tanking up before the train home.

Jamaica Wine House

St Michael's Alley. Closed Sat & Sun. An old City institution tucked away down a narrow alleyway. Despite the name, this is really just a pub, divided into four large "snugs" by the original high wooden-panelled partitions.

Hoxton and Spitalfields

Until recently, **Hoxton** was an unpleasant amalgam of wholesale clothing and shoe shops, striptease pubs and roaring traffic. But over the last ten years, the area has been colonized by artists, designers and architects and transformed itself into the city's most vibrant artistic enclave, peppered with contemporary art galleries and a whole host of very cool bars and clubs. **Spitalfields**, to the south, lies at the heart of the old East End, once the first port of call for thousands of immigrants over the centuries, and now best known for its Sunday markets and its cheap Bangladeshi curry houses.

Hoxton Square

The geographical focus of Hoxton's so-hip-it-hurts metamorphosis is Hoxton Square, a strange and not altogether happy mixture of light industrial units, supercool bars and artists' studios arranged around a leafy, formal square. Despite the lack of aesthetic charm, the square is now an undisputedly fashionable place to live and work; several leading West End **art galleries** have opened up premises hereabouts, most prominently White Cube (Tues–Sat 10am–6pm; ⓦ www.whitecube.com) at no.

▲ WHITE CUBE GALLERY, HOXTON SQUARE

48, which has been likened to a miniature Tate Modern, partly due to the glass roof that tops the building, and partly because it touts the likes of Damien Hirst, Tracey Emin and various other Turner Prize artists.

Wesley's Chapel & Museum

49 City Rd ⓦ www.wesleyschapel .org.uk. Mon–Sat 10am–4pm. Free. A place of pilgrimage for the world's Methodists, Wesley's Chapel was built in 1777, and heralded the coming of age of the faith founded by John Wesley (1703–91). The interior is uncharacteristically ornate, with powder-pink columns of French jasper and a superb, Adam-style gilded plasterwork ceiling. Predictably enough, the Museum of Methodism in the basement has only a passing reference to the insanely jealous 40-year-old widow Wesley married, and who eventually left him. Wesley himself spent his last two years in Wesley's House, a delightful Georgian place to the right of the main gates. On display inside are his death bed and an early shock-therapy machine he was particularly keen on.

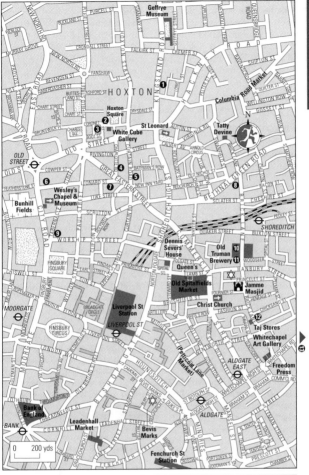

© Crown copyright

EATING & DRINKING							
Brick Lane		Dragon	6	Ktchn	4	Sosho	9
Beigel Bake	8	Home	7	New Tayyab	13	Vibe Bar	10
Café 1001	11	Hoxton Square		The Pool	5	Viet Hoa	1
Café Naz	12	Bar & Kitchen	2	Real Greek	3		

Bunhill Fields

City Rd ⓦ www.cityoflondon.gov.uk.
April–Sept Mon–Fri 7.30am–7pm, Sat
& Sun 9.30am–4pm; Oct–March closes
4pm. Originally used as a plague
pit, Bunhill Fields was the main
burial ground for Dissenters or
Nonconformists (practising
Christians who were not
members of the Church of
England) until 1852. It's no
longer used for burials, but the
flagstone paths and tall trees
make it a popular lunchtime

spot for local workers. The cemetery's three most famous incumbents are commemorated in the central paved area: William Blake's simple monument stands northeast of the obelisk to Daniel Defoe, while opposite lies John Bunyan's recumbent statue.

Petticoat Lane

Middlesex St @www .eastlondonmarkets.com. Sun 9am–2pm. Petticoat Lane (officially named Middlesex Street) may not be one of London's prettiest streets, but it does play host to one of the capital's longest-running Sunday markets, specializing in cheap (and often pretty tacky) clothing. As such, it's resolutely unfashionable, with old-style Cockney traders yelling out prices, others flogging pretty African and Indian fabrics, and lots of stalls selling pungent, partially tanned leather jackets with shoulder pads.

Whitechapel Art Gallery

80–82 Whitechapel High St @020/7522 7888, @www.whitechapel.org. Tues & Thurs–Sun 11am–6pm, Wed 11am–8pm. Free. The East End institution that draws in more outsiders than any other is the Whitechapel Art Gallery, housed in a beautiful crenellated 1899 Arts and Crafts building. The gallery puts on some of London's most innovative exhibitions of contemporary art, as well as hosting the biennial Whitechapel Open, a chance for local artists to get their work shown to a wider audience. The complex also has a pleasant café overlooking Angel Alley, where there's a stainless steel anarchist portrait gallery courtesy of the Freedom Press bookshop (see p.32).

Brick Lane

Brick Lane lies at the heart of London's Bengali community, whose inexpensive curry houses dominate the "Banglatown" (southern) end of the street. The red-brick chimney half way up Brick Lane heralds the **Old Truman Brewery** (@www.trumanbrewery.com), founded in 1666 and the largest in the world at the end of the nineteenth century. It ceased operations in 1989 and is now home to a vast number of young designers, artists, DJs and architects, who've carved out quite a hip niche in this part of Brick Lane. North of the brewery and railway arch, among the cheap leather shops and bagel bakeries, are the streets that serve as the venue for **Brick Lane's Sunday market** of bric-a-brac (@www .eastlondonmarkets.com). There are virtually no stalls on Brick Lane itself; instead head down Cheshire Street, where you'll find everything from bad-quality hardware and cheap CDs to 1970s accessories and military memorabilia; down Sclater Street

▲ BRICK LANE MARKET

and beyond, folk flog what looks like the contents of their cupboards straight off the pavement. All in all, it's a mad and manic affair that's worth a look for the street theatre alone.

Christ Church, Spitalfields

Commercial St @www.christchurchspital-fields.org. Built between 1714 and 1729 to a characteristically bold design by Nicholas Hawksmoor, Christ Church features a huge 225-foot-high broach spire and giant Tuscan portico, raised on steps and shaped like a Venetian window (a central arched opening flanked by two smaller rectangles), a motif repeated in the tower and doors. Inside, there's a forest of giant columned bays, with a lion and a unicorn playing peekaboo on the top of the chancel beam and, opposite, London's largest Georgian organ.

The church hall, next door, was host in 1888 to meetings of the Bryant & May match girls, who personified the Dickensian stereotype of the downtrodden East End girl, and who went on strike against their miserable wages and work conditions.

Old Spitalfields Market

Commercial St @www.oldspitalfields-market.com. Mon–Fri 10am–4pm, Sun 9am–5pm. The capital's premier wholesale fruit and vegetable market until 1991, Old Spitalfields Market now hosts a large, eclectic and fairly sophisticated selection of shops and stalls selling crafts, clothes, food and organic fruit and vegetables. Half the market was recently knocked down to make way for yet more boxy, glassy offices, courtesy of Norman Foster, but the red-brick and green-gabled eastern half of the original building, built in 1893, survives.

Dennis Severs' House

18 Folgate St ☎020/7247 4013, @www.dennissevershouse.co.uk. "Silent Night" Mon: April–Sept 8–11pm; Oct–March 6–9pm; £12. "The Experience" first and third Sun of each month 2–5pm; £8, plus following Mon noon–2pm. £5. Visiting the former home of the late American eccentric Dennis Severs is a bizarre and uncanny theatrical experience, which Severs once described as "passing through a frame into a painting". Visitors are free to explore the candle-lit and log-fired Georgian house unhindered, and are left with the distinct impression that someone has literally just popped out: the house cat prowls, aromas of dinner waft up from the kitchen and the sound of horses' hooves can be heard from the cobbled street outside.

Columbia Road Flower Market

Columbia Rd @www.eastlondonmarkets.com. Sun 8am–1pm. Columbia Road is the city's most popular market for flowers and plants; it's also the liveliest, with the loud and upfront stallholders catering to an increasingly moneyed clientele. As well as seeds, bulbs, potted plants and cut flowers from the stalls, you'll also find every kind of gardening accessory from the chi-chi shops that line the street, and you can keep yourself sustained with bagels, cakes and coffee from the local cafés.

Geffrye Museum

Kingsland Rd @www.geffrye-museum.org.uk. Tues–Sat 10am–5pm, Sun noon–5pm. Free. Set back from the main road in a peaceful little enclave of eighteenth-century ironmongers' almshouses, Hoxton's one conventional tourist sight is the Geffrye Museum, dedicated to furniture

▲ GEFFRYE MUSEUM

design since 1911. A series of period living rooms, ranging from the oak-panelled seventeenth century through refined Georgian and cluttered Victorian, leads to the state-of-the-art New Gallery Extension, housing the excellent twentieth-century section and a pleasant café/restaurant. One of the almshouses has been restored to its original condition and can be visited on the first Saturday of the month (£2).

Shops

Freedom Press

Angel Alley ☎020/7247 9249. Closed Sun. Upholding a long East End tradition of radical politics, this small anarchist bookshop is packed with everything from Bakhunin to Chomsky.

Queens

Shop 111B, Gate 14, Old Spitalfields Market ☎020/7426 0017. Closed Sat. Pink, high-camp shop specializing in kitsch gifts – just the place to pick up a pair of fairy wings or a gay teddy.

Tatty Devine

236 Brick Lane ☎020/7739 9009, ⊛www.tattydevine.com. Funky shop which stocks (and exhibits) wacky, tacky T-shirts and accessories by young designers: tape measure belts, safety-pin brooches and perspex earrings.

Cafés

Brick Lane Beigel Bake

159 Brick Lane. Classic 24hr takeaway bagel shop in the heart of the East End – unbelievably cheap, even for fillings such as smoked salmon with cream cheese.

Café 1001

1 Dray's Lane. Tucked in by the side of the Truman Brewery, this smoky café has a beaten-up studenty look, with lots of sofas to crash in. Mainstays are simple, filling sandwiches and delicious cakes.

Ktchn

35 Charlotte Rd. Closed Sat & Sun. Tiny, consonant-free Shoreditch

café with just four stools, serving delicious, freshly prepared upmarket lunch options: big soups, grilled tuna, rare-roast beef, exotic salads and great pastries.

Restaurants

Café Naz
46–48 Brick Lane ☎020/7247 0234, ⊛www.cafenaz.co.uk. This self-proclaimed "contemporary Bangladeshi" restaurant, with its open-plan kitchen, cuts an imposing modern figure on Brick Lane. The menu has all the standards (plus plenty of baltis), and the prices are keen.

New Tayyab
83 Fieldgate St ☎020/7247 9543, ⊛www.tayyabs.co.uk. Smart, minimalist place serving straightforward Pakistani fare: good, freshly cooked and served without pretension. Prices have remained low, booking is essential and service is speedy and slick.

Real Greek
15 Hoxton Market ☎020/7739 8212, ⊛www.therealgreek.co.uk. Closed Sun. A world away from your average London Greek-Cypriot joint, with a lofty, busy *mezedopoliou*, where you can order a few meze (for around £5), and a more formal restaurant offering authentic Greek main courses. Set lunches and early dinners (before 7pm) are under £15. Service is excellent.

Viet Hoa Café
72 Kingsland Rd ☎020/7729 8293. Large, light and airy Vietnamese café in a street now heaving with similar places. Try one of the splendid "meals in a bowl", or the noodle dishes with everything from spring rolls to tofu.

Pubs and bars

Dragon
5 Leonard St. This discreetly signed, clubby pub with bare-brick walls and crumbling leather sofas attracts a bohemian mix of locals and pre-clubbers most nights.

Home
100–106 Leonard St ⊛www.homebar .co.uk. Closed Sun. Hoxton's original club-bar continues to attract a hip, friendly crowd. No DJs, but plenty of comfy leather sofas and good vibes.

Hoxton Square Bar and Kitchen
2–4 Hoxton Square. Blade Runner-esque concrete bar that attracts artists, writers and wannabes with its mix of modern European food, kitsch-to-club soundtracks, worn leather sofas and temporary painting and photography exhibitions. Best in the summer, when the drinking spills into the square in a carnival-like spirit.

The Pool
104–108 Curtain Rd. Popular two-floored bar with pool tables, big bean bags and weekend DJs playing a mix of upfront house and garage.

Sosho
2a Tabernacle St ⊛sosho3am.com. Closed Sun. Very trendy club-bar, with good cocktails and decent food; the ambience is chilled until the very popular DJs kick in at 8.30pm (Wed–Sat). Cover charge at weekends.

Vibe Bar
Old Truman Brewery, 91–95 Brick Lane ⊛www.vibe-bar.co.uk. Trendy bar in the old brewery with free Internet access, good lounging sofas and DJs in the evenings.

The Tower and Docklands

One of the city's main tourist attractions, the **Tower of London** was the site of some of the goriest events in the nation's history, and is somewhere all visitors should try and get to see. Immediately to the east are the remains of what was the largest enclosed **cargo-dock** system in the world, built in the nineteenth century to cope with the huge volume of goods shipped in along the Thames from all over the Empire. No one thought the area could be rejuvenated when the docks closed in the 1960s, but over the last twenty years, warehouses have been converted into luxury flats, waterside penthouse apartments have been built and a huge high-rise office development has sprung up around Canary Wharf.

Docklands Light Railway

The best way to visit Docklands is to take the **Docklands Light Railway** or DLR (℡ 020/7363 9700, ⓦ www .tfl.gov.uk/dlr), whose driverless trains run on overhead tracks, and give out great views over the cityscape. DLR trains set off from Bank tube, or from Tower Gateway, close to Tower Hill tube and the Tower of London.

Tower of London

ⓦ www.hrp.org.uk. March–Oct Mon–Sat 9am–6pm, Sun 10am–6pm; Nov–Feb Mon & Sun 10am–5pm, Tues–Sat 9am–5pm. £13.50. One of the most perfectly preserved medieval fortresses in the country, the Tower of London sits beside the Thames surrounded by a wide, dry moat. Chiefly famous as a place of imprisonment and death, it has been used variously as a royal residence, armoury,

▲ DOCKLANDS LIGHT RAILWAY

mint, menagerie, observatory and – a function it still serves – a safe-deposit box for the Crown Jewels. Before you set off to explore the complex, you should take one of the free guided tours, given every thirty minutes or so by one of the Tower's Beefeaters (officially known as Yeoman Warders). As well as giving a good introduction to the Tower's history, these ex-servicemen relish hamming up the gory stories.

Visitors today enter the Tower along Water Lane, but in times gone by most prisoners were delivered through Traitors' Gate, on the waterfront. The nearby Bloody Tower saw the murders of 12-year-old Edward V and his 10-year-old brother, and was used to imprison Walter Ralegh on three separate occasions, including a thirteen-year stretch.

The White Tower, at the centre of the complex, is the original "Tower", begun in 1076 and now home to displays from the Royal Armouries. Even if you've no interest in military paraphernalia, you should at least pay a visit to the Chapel of St John on the second floor; a beautiful Norman structure completed in 1080, it's the oldest intact church building in London. To the west of the White Tower is the execution spot on Tower Green where seven highly-placed but unlucky individuals were beheaded, among them Anne Boleyn and her cousin Catherine Howard (Henry VIII's second and fifth wives).

The **Crown Jewels**, of course, are the major reason so many people flock to the Tower, but the moving walkways which take you past the loot are disappointingly swift, allowing you just 28

▲ TOWER OF LONDON RAVEN

seconds' viewing during peak periods. The oldest piece of regalia is the twelfth-century Anointing Spoon, but the vast majority of exhibits postdate the Commonwealth (1649–60), when many of the royal riches were melted down for coinage or sold off. Among the jewels are the three largest cut diamonds in the world, including the legendary Koh-i-Noor, set into the Queen Mother's Crown in 1937.

Tower Bridge

ⓦ www.towerbridge.org.uk. Tower Bridge ranks with Big Ben as the most famous of all London landmarks. Completed in 1894, its neo-Gothic towers are clad in Cornish granite and Portland stone, but conceal a steel frame which, at the time, represented a considerable engineering achievement, allowing a road crossing that could be raised to give tall ships access to the upper reaches of the Thames. The raising of the bascules (from the French for "see-saw") remains an impressive sight – phone ahead to find out when the bridge is opening (ⓣ020/7940 3984). It's free to walk across the bridge, but you must pay to gain access to the elevated walkways (daily 9.30am–6pm; £4.50) linking

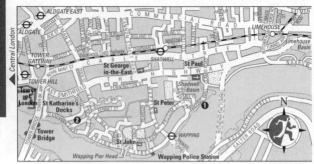

the summits of the towers –
closed from 1909 to 1982 due
to their popularity with
prostitutes and the suicidal. The
views are pretty good and you
get to visit the Engine Room
on the south side of the bridge,
where you can see the giant,
and now defunct, coal-fired
boilers and play some interactive
engineering games.

St Katharine's Docks

⊛www.stkaths.co.uk. Built in the
late 1820s to relieve the
congestion on the River
Thames, St Katharine's Docks
were originally surrounded by
high walls to protect the
warehouses used to store luxury
goods – ivory, spices, carpets
and cigars – shipped in from all
over the Empire. Nowadays, the
docks are used as an upmarket
marina, and the old warehouses
house shops, pubs and
restaurants that get a lot of
passing trade thanks to the close
proximity of the Tower. More
appealing, however, are the old
swing bridges over the basins
(including a Telford footbridge
from 1828), the boats
themselves (you'll often see
beautiful old sailing ships and
Dutch barges), and the
attractive Ivory House
warehouse, with its clock tower,
at the centre of the three
basins.

▲ TOWER BRIDGE

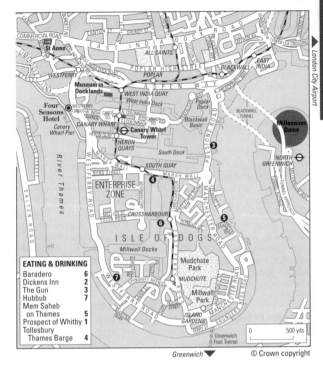

London City Airport

EATING & DRINKING

Baradero	6
Dickens Inn	2
The Gun	3
Hubbub	7
Mem Saheb on Thames	5
Prospect of Whitby	1
Tollesbury Thames Barge	4

Greenwich ▼   © Crown copyright

Wapping High Street

If you arrive on **Wapping High Street** expecting the usual parade of shops, you're in for a surprise. Traditionally, the business of Wapping took place on the river; thus tall brick-built warehouses, most now tastefully converted into expensive flats, line the Thames side of the street, while to the north, in a stark contrast typical of Docklands, lie the district's less salubrious council estates. Halfway along the High Street is Wapping Pier Head, the former entrance to the London Docks, flanked by grand, curvaceous Regency terraces. Further east, a couple of preserved overhead gangways cross the High Street just before Wapping Police Station, headquarters of the world's oldest uniformed police force, the marine police, founded in the 1790s.

Canary Wharf

ⓦ www.canarywharf.com. The geographical and ideological heart of the new Docklands is Canary Wharf, previously a destination for rum and mahogany, later tomatoes and bananas (from the Canary Islands – hence the name). Now a pedestrian-friendly business district, this is the one New Docklands area that you can happily stroll around, taking in the modern architecture and landscaping, looking out for some of the tongue-in-cheek sculptures, and perhaps having a drink overlooking one of the old wharves.

The Millennium Dome

Clearly visible from Greenwich's riverside and park, the **Dome** is the archetypal millennial cock-up. Architecturally, it's eye-catching enough: over half a mile in circumference and 160ft in height, it's the world's largest dome, held up by a dozen, 300ft-tall yellow steel masts. But it's best known for the £800 million of taxpayers' money that was poured into it, much of it to pay for the millennium exhibition and show, which cost £20 a head, was panned by the critics and dismantled after one year. Apart from a few one-off events, the Dome has remained (expensively) empty since then, and its future is as yet undecided.

Canary Wharf's name is, of course, synonymous with Cesar Pelli's landmark tower, officially known as One Canada Square. Britain's tallest building and the first skyscraper anywhere to be clad in stainless steel, it's an undeniably impressive sight, both close up and from a distance – its flashing pyramid-shaped pinnacle is a feature of the horizon at numerous points in London.

Museum in Docklands

West India Quay, Hertsemere Rd
@www.museumindocklands.org.uk.
Daily 10am–6pm. £5. The last surviving Georgian warehouses of the West India Docks lie on the far side of a floodlit floating bridge at West India Quay. Amidst the dockside bars and restaurants, you'll find Warehouse No. 1, built in 1803 for storing rum, sugar, molasses, coffee and cotton, and now home to the Museum in Docklands. Spread over five floors, the exhibits chart the history of the area from Roman times to the development of Canary Wharf via interactive displays, a period reconstruction of the old docklands and numerous paintings and photographs.

Island Gardens

Manchester Rd. At Island Gardens, the southernmost tip of the Isle of Dogs, the Docklands Light Railway heads under the Thames to Greenwich (see p.180), as does the 1902 Greenwich Foot Tunnel (open 24hr). The gardens themselves are nothing special, but the view is spectacular – this was Christopher Wren's favourite Thames-side spot, from which he could contemplate his masterpieces across the river, the Royal Naval College and the Royal Observatory (see pp.182 & 183).

Cafés

Hubbub

269 Westferry Rd. Within an arts centre in a converted former church, this is a real oasis in the desert of Westferry Road, offering decent fry-ups, sandwiches and a few fancier dishes.

▲ MUSEUM IN DOCKLANDS

▲ MILLENNIUM DOME

Restaurants

Baradero

Turnberry Quay, off Pepper St
☎020/7537 1666. Closed Sat lunch &
Sun. Modern, light and airy, this
is essentially a tapas bar, though
restaurant-quality main courses
are also on offer. Try the simple
pan con tomate or some classic
boquerones (white anchovies),
both under £5 a dish.

Mem Saheb on Thames

65–67 Amsterdam Rd ☎020/7538
3008. Decent Indian restaurant
with a superb view over the
river to the Millennium Dome.
Standard tandoori kebabs, plus
the odd unusual dish like
Rajasthani khargosh (rabbit
and spinach), all for under
£10.

Pubs

Dickens Inn

St Katharine's Way. Very firmly on
the tourist trail, this eighteenth
century timber-framed

warehouse is a remarkable
building (with a great view), and
houses a branch of *Wheeler's* fish
restaurant and a pizzeria as well
as serving lunchtime pub food.

The Gun

27 Cold Harbour. An old dockers'
pub with lots of maritime
memorabilia and – the main
attraction – an unrivalled view
of the Millennium Dome.

Prospect of Whitby

57 Wapping Wall. London's most
famous riverside pub, with a real
feel of the old docklands: a
flagstone floor, a cobbled
courtyard and great views over
the Thames. Courage beer and
surprisingly adventurous pub
food, too.

Tollesbury Thames Barge

Marsh Wall. Closed Sun eve. The
ultimate new Docklands
experience: an old Thames
barge, a pint, and a view of the
Millwall Docks. Wine is the
tipple of choice, but there's also
Harvey's Sussex bitter and cheap
bar snacks.

South Bank and around

The **South Bank** has a lot going for it. As well as the massive waterside arts centre, it's home to a host of tourist attractions including the enormously popular London Eye observation wheel. With most of London sitting on the north bank of the Thames, the views from here are the best on the river, and thanks to the wide, traffic-free riverside boulevard, the whole area can be happily explored on foot. A short walk from the South Bank lie one or two lesser-known but nonetheless absorbing sights such as the Imperial War Museum, which contains the country's only permanent exhibition devoted to the Holocaust.

South Bank Centre

☎020/7960 4242, ⓦwww.sbc.org.uk. The South Bank Centre is home to a whole variety of artistic institutions, the most attractive of which is the **Royal Festival Hall** (RFH; ⓦwww.rfh.org.uk), built in 1951 for the Festival of Britain and one of London's chief concert venues. With its open-plan, multi-level foyer, replete with café and bookshop and often hosting a free gig or exhibition, it's a great place to wander through during the day.

Architecturally, the most depressing part of the South Bank Centre are the grim-grey,

Hungerford Bridge

The best way to approach the South Bank is to walk from Embankment tube across the **Hungerford Bridge**, a majestic, symmetrical double suspension footbridge that runs either side of Hungerford rail-way bridge, dishing out great river views either side, but particularly to the south towards Big Ben.

concrete exteriors of the Queen Elizabeth Hall (QEH) and the more intimate Purcell Room, built in the 1960s to the north of the RFH in an uncompromisingly brutalist 1960s style. Above these two,

▲ SOUTH BANK VIEW FROM HUNGERFORD BRIDGE

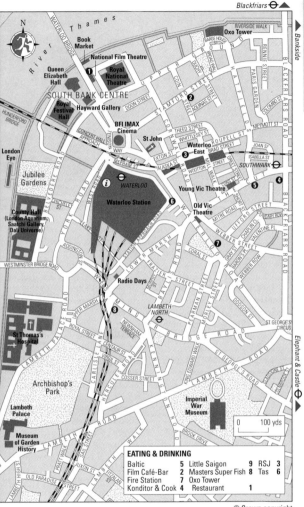

PLACES South Bank and around

0   100 yds

EATING & DRINKING			
Baltic	5	Little Saigon	9	RSJ	3
Film Café-Bar	2	Masters Super Fish	8	Tas	6
Fire Station	7	Oxo Tower			
Konditor & Cook	4	Restaurant	1		

© Crown copyright

with its strange rooftop neon sculpture, sits the **Hayward Gallery** (daily 10am–6pm, Tues & Wed until 8pm; £9 depending upon the exhibition; ⓦ www.hayward.org.uk), one of the city's best venues for large-scale contemporary art exhibitions and retrospectives.

Tucked underneath Waterloo Bridge is the **National Film Theatre** (NFT; ⓦ www.bfi.org.uk/nft), which screens London's most esoteric movies and has a decent café/bar. Behind the NFT, at the southern end of Waterloo Bridge, is the eye-catching glass-drum of the high-tech BFI London IMAX Cinema. Lastly,

▲ ROYAL FESTIVAL HALL, SOUTH BANK

on the east side of Waterloo Bridge, its series of horizontal concrete layers looking suspiciously like a multistorey car park, is the **Royal National Theatre** (☎020/7452 3000, ⓦwww.nt-online.org), popularly known as "the National" or NT. It boasts three separate theatres – a Greek-style arena, a proscenium arch and a flexible studio – and puts on everything from Shakespeare to the latest David Hare.

Oxo Tower

ⓦwww.oxotower.co.uk. Daily until 10pm. The Oxo Tower started life as a power station before being converted into a meat-packing factory for the company that makes Oxo stock cubes – the lettering is spelt out in the windows of the main tower. The building now contains flats, browsable studio-shops for contemporary designers (Tues–Sun 11am–6pm) and an art gallery (daily 11am–6pm; free), whose exhibitions of contemporary photographs, paintings or sculptures are usually intriguing; on the top floor,

there's a very swanky restaurant and brasserie.

You don't need to eat or drink here to enjoy the view from the top: just take the lift to the eighth-floor public viewing gallery.

London Eye

☎0870/5000 600, ⓦwww .ba-londoneye.com. Daily: April–Sept 9.30am–10pm; Oct–March 9am–8pm. £11. London's most prominent recent landmark is the London Eye, the magnificently graceful observation wheel which spins slowly and silently over the Thames. Standing 443ft high, the wheel is the largest ever built, and it's constantly in slow motion – a full-circle "flight" in one of its 32 pods takes around thirty minutes, and lifts you high above the city. At the top, you're at one of the few places (apart from a plane window) from which London looks a manageable size, as you can see right out to where the suburbs slip into the countryside. Ticket prices are outrageously high, though the engineering and the views are awesome; queues can also be very bad at the weekend, so book in advance over the phone or online.

County Hall

The colonnaded crescent of County Hall is the only truly monumental building on the South Bank. Designed to house the now defunct London County Council, it was completed in 1933 and enjoyed its greatest moment of fame as headquarters of the GLC (Greater London Council), which was abolished by Margaret Thatcher in 1986 leaving London as the only European city without an elected authority. In 2000, the former GLC leader Ken Livingstone was elected as Mayor of London, and moved into the new GLA (Greater London Authority) building further downstream (see p.151). County Hall, meanwhile, is now in the hands of a Japanese property company, and currently houses several hotels, restaurants, an amusement arcade and a bizarre clutch of tourist attractions.

London Aquarium

ⓦ www.londonaquarium.co.uk. Daily 10am–6pm or later. £8.75. The most popular attraction in County Hall is the London Aquarium, laid out across three floors of the basement. With some super-large, multi-floor tanks, and everything from dog-face puffers to piranhas, it's pretty much guaranteed to please younger kids. The "Beach", where children can actually stroke the (non-sting) rays, is particularly popular. Though impressive in scale, the aquarium is fairly conservative in design, with no walk-through tanks and only the very briefest of information on any of the fish.

Saatchi Gallery

ⓣ 020/7823 2363, ⓦ www .saatchi-gallery.co.uk. Mon–Thurs & Sun 10am–6pm, Fri & Sat 10am–10pm. £8.50. The Saatchi Gallery of contemporary art occupies the incongruously imposing former council chamber of County Hall. Charles Saatchi, the collector behind the gallery, was, in fact, the man whose advertising for the Conservative government helped topple County Hall's previous incumbents, the GLC. Saatchi's extravagant wallet also helped promote the Young British Artists of the 1980s and 1990s, as he snapped up headline-grabbing works such as Damien Hirst's pickled shark and Tracey Emin's soiled and crumpled bed. The gallery puts on changing exhibitions drawn primarily from Saatchi's vast collection.

Dalí Universe

Riverside Walk ⓦ www.daliuniverse .com. Daily 10am–5.30pm. £8.50. Three giant surrealist sculptures on the river-facing side of County Hall herald the Dalí Universe. Yet while Dalí was undoubtedly an accomplished and prolific artist, you'll be disappointed if you're expecting to see his "greatest hits" here – those are scattered across the globe. Most of the works on display are little-known bronze and glass sculptures, as well as drawings from the many illustrated books which he published, ranging from Ovid to the Marquis de Sade. Aside from these, there's one of the numerous Lobster Telephones, which Edward James commissioned for his London home, a copy of his famous Mae West lips sofa, and the oil painting from the dream sequence in Hitchcock's movie *Spellbound*.

Museum of Garden History

Lambeth Palace Rd ⊛www.cix.co.uk /~museumgh. March to mid-Dec daily 10.30am–5pm. Free, though £2.50 donation suggested. Housed in the deconsecrated Kentish ragstone church of St Mary-at-Lambeth, this unpretentious little museum puts particular emphasis on John Tradescant, gardener to James I and Charles I, who is buried here. The graveyard has been transformed into a small seventeenth-century garden, where two interesting sarcophagi lurk among the foliage: one belongs to Captain Bligh, the commander of the *Bounty* in 1787; the more unusual is Tradescant's memorial, depicting, among other things, a seven-headed griffin and several crocodiles.

▲ DALÍ SCULPTURE, SOUTH BANK

Imperial War Museum

Lambeth Rd ⊛www.iwm.org.uk. Daily 10am–6pm. Free. Housed in a domed building that was once the infamous "Bedlam" lunatic asylum, the Imperial War Museum holds by far the best collection of militaria in the capital. The treatment of the subject matter is impressively wide-ranging and fairly sober, with the main hall's militaristic display offset by the lower-ground-floor array of documents and images attesting to the human damage of war. Entered from the third floor, the harrowing Holocaust Exhibition (not recommended for children under 14) pulls few punches, and has made a valiant attempt to avoid depicting the victims of the Holocaust as nameless masses by focusing on individual cases, interspersing the archive footage with eyewitness accounts from contemporary survivors.

Shops

Book Market

South Bank, beneath Waterloo Bridge. Sat & Sun only. Secondhand book market by the Thames, offering everything from current and recent fiction to obscure psychology textbooks, film theory, modern European poetry and pulp science fiction.

Radio Days

87 Lower Marsh. Fantastic collection of memorabilia and accessories from the 1930s to the 1970s, including shoes, shot-glass collections, cosmetics and vintage magazines. A huge stock of well-kept womens' and mens' clothing from the same period fills the back room.

Cafés

Konditor & Cook

22 Cornwall Rd. Closed Sun. Quality bakery, with a few tables, offering wonderful cakes and biscuits, as well as sandwiches and coffee and tea.

Masters Super Fish

191 Waterloo Rd. Closed Sun. Good, old-fashioned, no-nonsense fish and chip pit stop; eat in or take away.

Restaurants

Little Saigon

139 Westminster Bridge Rd ☎020/7207 9747. Family-run place offering pukka Vietnamese spring rolls, grilled squid-cake and crystal pancakes, all served with a wonderful array of sauces, plus great crispy fried noodles.

Oxo Restaurant

Oxo Tower, Barge House St ☎020/7803 3888, ⓦwww .harveynichols.com. Run by Harvey Nichols, this elegant eighth-floor restaurant offers great views and equally good Modern European cuisine. There's a brasserie (main dishes £10–15) and a restaurant (£15–20).

RSJ

13a Coin St ☎020/7928 4554, ⓦwww.rsj.uk.com. Closed Sun. Regularly high standards of Anglo-French cooking make this a good spot for a meal before or after an evening at a South Bank theatre or concert hall. Set meals for around £16.

Tas

33 The Cut ☎020/7928 3300, ⓦwww.tasrestaurant.com. Welcoming restaurant serving excellent, competitively priced Turkish food. The menu is a monster so most folk go for the set options, starting at three courses for around £8.

Pubs and bars

Baltic

74 Blackfriars Rd ☎020/7928 1111, ⓦwww.balticrestaurant.co.uk. Stark, stylish bar (and restaurant) situated opposite Southwark tube in an old Georgian coachworks, specializing in vodka shots and Baltic snacks.

Film Café-bar

South Bank. The National Film Theatre's bar is the only one on the South Bank riverfront between Westminster and Blackfriars bridges – worth checking out for the views and the congenial crowd.

Fire Station

150 Waterloo Rd. This gloriously red-painted former fire station is a popular place for an after-work pint. The restaurant at the back is good, too – expect modern Britsh dishes (£10–15).

Bankside and Southwark

In Tudor and Stuart London, the chief reason for cross-ing the Thames to **Southwark** was to visit the then-dis-reputable **Bankside** entertainment district around the south end of London Bridge. Four hundred years on, Londoners have rediscovered the area, thanks to wholesale regeneration that has engendered a wealth of new attractions along the riverside between Blackfriars and Tower bridges and beyond – with the charge led by the mighty Tate Modern art gallery. And with a traffic-free, riverside path connecting most of the sights, this is easily one of the most enjoyable areas of London in which to hang out.

Millennium Bridge

The first new bridge to be built across the Thames since Tower Bridge opened in 1894, the sleek, stainless-steel Millennium Bridge is London's sole pedestrian-only crossing. A suspension bridge of innovative design, it famously bounced up and down when it first opened and had to be closed immediately for another two years for repairs. It still wobbles a bit, but most people are too

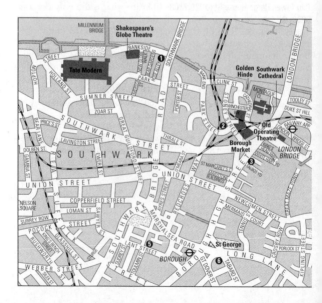

busy enjoying the spectacular
views across to St Paul's
Cathedral and Tate Modern to
notice.

Tate Modern

Bankside ☎020/7887 8008,
⊛www.tate.org.uk. Daily 10am–6pm;
Fri & Sat open until 10pm. Free.
Bankside is dominated by the
austere power station now
transformed by the Swiss duo
Herzog & de Meuron into the
Tate Modern art gallery. The
masterful conversion has left
plenty of the original industrial
feel, while providing
wonderfully light and spacious
galleries to show off the Tate's
vast collection of international
twentieth-century art. The best
way to enter is down the ramp
from the west, so you get the
full effect of the stupendously
large turbine hall, usually used
to display one huge, mind-
blowing installation. Given that
Tate Modern is the world's

> ### Tate to Tate
>
> Tate to Tate **boats** (specially
> designed by Damien Hirst) shuttle
> between Tate Modern and Tate
> Britain via the London Eye every
> forty minutes; journey time is twen-
> ty minutes, and multi-trip tickets,
> valid all day, cost £4.50.

largest modern art gallery, you
need to devote the best part of a
day to do it justice – or be very
selective. It's easy enough to find
your way around the galleries:
pick up a plan (and, for an extra
£1, an audioguide), and take the
escalator to level 3. This, and
level 5, display the permanent
collection; level 4 is used for
fee-paying temporary
exhibitions, and level 7 has a
rooftop café with a great view
over the Thames.

The curators have eschewed
the usual chronological
approach through the "isms",
preferring to group works

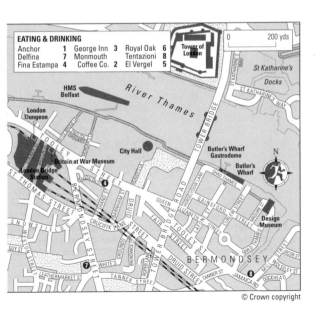

EATING & DRINKING					
Anchor	1	George Inn	3	Royal Oak	6
Delfina	7	Monmouth		Tentazioni	8
Fina Estampa	4	Coffee Co.	2	El Vergel	5

© Crown copyright

▲ TATE MODERN

together thematically: Landscape/Matter/ Environment; Still Life/ Object/Real Life; History/Memory/Society; and Nude/Action/Body. On the whole this works very well, though the early twentieth-century canvases, in their gilded frames, do struggle when made to compete with contemporary installations.

Although the displays change every six months or so, you're still pretty much guaranteed to see at least some works by Monet and Bonnard, Cubist pioneers Picasso and Braque, Surrealists such as Dalí, abstract artists like Mondrian, Bridget Riley and Pollock, and Pop supremos Warhol and Lichtenstein. There are also seminal pieces such as a replica of Duchamp's urinal, entitled *Fountain* and signed "R. Mutt", Yves Klein's totally blue paintings and Carl André's trademark piles of bricks. And such is the space here that several artists get whole rooms to themselves; these include Francis Bacon, whose anguished paintings still have the ability to shock, and Joseph Beuys, with

his shamanistic wax and furs. Mark Rothko's abstract "Seagram Murals", originally destined for a posh restaurant in New York, also have their own shrine-like room in the heart of the collection.

Shakespeare's Globe Theatre

Bankside ☎ 020/7902 1400
✆ www.shakespeares-globe.org. Daily: May–Sept 9am–noon & 12.30–4pm; Oct–April 10am–5pm. £8 Seriously dwarfed by the Tate Modern, the Shakespeare's Globe Theatre is an equally spectacular reconstruction of the polygonal playhouse where most of the Bard's later works were first performed. Sporting the first new thatched roof in central London since the 1666 Great Fire, the theatre puts on plays (mid-Sept to mid-May only) by Shakespeare and his contemporaries, using only natural light and the minimum of scenery. To get to see inside the building, you must either attend a performance, or visit the Globe's pricey but stylish exhibition. It begins by detailing the long campaign by the late American actor Sam Wanamaker to have the Globe rebuilt, but

it's the imaginative hands-on exhibits that really hit the spot. You can have a virtual "play" on medieval instruments such as the crumhorn or sackbut, prepare your own edition of Shakespeare, and feel the thatch, hazelnut-shell and daub used to build the theatre. Visitors to the exhibition also get taken on an informative guided tour round the theatre itself, except in the afternoons during the summer season, when you can only visit the exhibition (for a reduced fee).

Golden Hinde

St Mary Overie Dock, Cathedral St ☎0870/011 8700, ⊛www.goldenhinde .co.uk. Phone for opening hours. £2.75, with guided tour £3.50. An exact replica of the galleon in which Francis Drake sailed around the world from 1577 to 1580, the Golden Hinde was launched in 1973, and circumnavigated the world for some twenty years before eventually settling permanently in Southwark. The ship is surprisingly small and, with a crew of eighty-plus, must have been cramped, to say the least. There's a lack of interpretive panels, so it's worth paying the little bit extra and pre-booking a **tour**. Guides clad in period garb show you the ropes, so to speak, and demonstrate activities such as firing a cannon or using the ship's toilet.

Southwark Cathedral

London Bridge ⊛www.dswark.org /cathedral. Mon–Sat 10am–6pm, Sun 11am–5pm. Free. Built as the medieval Augustinian priory church of St Mary Overie, Southwark Cathedral gained its cathedral status in 1905. Of the original thirteenth-century church, only the choir and retrochoir now remain, separated by a tall and beautiful stone Tudor screen; they're thought to be the oldest Gothic structures left in London. The nave was entirely rebuilt in the nineteenth century, but the cathedral contains numerous interesting monuments, from a thirteenth-century oak effigy of a knight to an early twentieth-century memorial to Shakespeare (his brother is buried here). Above the memorial is a stained-glass window featuring a whole cast of characters from the plays. You can happily skip the new multi-media exhibition (£3) by the bookshop, which whizzes through Southwark's history at breakneck speed.

Borough Market

8 Southwark St ⊛www.boroughmarket .org.uk. Fri noon–6pm, Sat 9am–4pm. There's been a thriving market hereabouts since medieval times. Squeezed beneath the railway arches between the High Street and the cathedral, the present Borough Market is one of the few wholesale fruit and vegetable markets in London still trading under its original Victorian wrought-iron shed. At the weekends, though, it transforms itself into a small foodie haven, and the general public turn up in droves to sample the produce on the gourmet stalls and in the nearby shops.

Old Operating Theatre, Museum and Herb Garret

9a St Thomas's St ⊛www.thegarret .org.uk. Daily 10.30am–5pm. £4. The Old Operating Theatre and Herb Garret is by far the most educational – and strangest – of Southwark's museums, and despite being entirely gore-free, it's as stomach-churning as the

London Dungeon (see below). Visitors climb up to the attic of a former church tower, which houses an old hospital apothecary with displays explaining the painful truth about pre-anaesthetic operations. These took place in the adjacent women's operating theatre, designed in 1821 "in the round", literally like a theatre, so that students (and members of high society) could view the proceedings. The surgeons had to concentrate on speed and accuracy (most amputations took less than a minute), but there was still a thirty-percent mortality rate, with many patients simply dying of shock, and many more from bacterial infection, about which very little was known.

London Dungeon

28–34 Tooley St ⊛ www.thedungeons .com. Daily: March to mid-July & Sep–Oct 10am–5.30pm; mid-July to Aug 9.30am–7.30pm; Nov–Feb 10.30am–5pm. £12.95. Young teenagers and the credulous probably get the most out of the

▲ SHAKESPEARE WINDOW, SOUTHWARK CATHEDRAL

ever-popular London Dungeon. The life-sized waxwork tableaux inside include a man being hung, drawn and quartered and one being boiled alive, while the general hysteria is boosted by actors dressed as top-hatted Victorian vampires pouncing out of the darkness. Visitors are herded into a court room, condemned to the "River of Death" boat ride, and forced to endure the "Jack the Ripper Experience", an exploitative trawl through post-mortem photos and wax mock-ups of the victims, followed by the "Great Fire of London", in which you experience the heat and the smell of the plague-ridden city, before walking through a revolving "tunnel of flames".

Note that you can avoid the inevitable queues by pre-buying tickets online.

Britain at War Museum

64–66 Tooley St ⊛ www.britainatwar .co.uk. Daily: April–Sept 10am–5.30pm; Oct–March 10am–4.30pm. £7.50. For an illuminating insight into London's stiff-upper-lip mentality during the World War II Blitz, head for Winston Churchill's Britain at War, where you'll find hundreds of fascinating wartime artefacts, from ration books to babies' gasmasks. You can sit in darkness in an Anderson shelter, hear the chilling sound of the V1 "doodlebugs" and tune in to contemporary radio broadcasts. The final set-piece is a walk through the chaos of a just-bombed street.

HMS Belfast

Morgan's Lane, Tooley St ⊛ www.iwm .org.uk. Daily: March–Oct 10am–6pm; Nov–Feb 10am–5pm. £6. An 11,550-ton Royal Navy cruiser, armed with six torpedoes and six-inch guns with a range of over fourteen miles, HMS *Belfast* saw action both in the Barents Sea during World War II and in the Korean War, and has been permanently moored on the Thames since being decommissioned in 1971. The most enjoyable aspect of a visit is exploring the *Belfast's* maze of cabins and scrambling up and down the vertiginous ladders of the ship's seven confusing decks, which could accommodate a crew of over nine hundred. If you want to know more about the ship's history, head for the Exhibition Flat in Zone 5; in the adjacent Life at Sea room, you can practise your morse code and knots and listen to accounts of naval life on board.

▲ HMS *BELFAST*

City Hall

The Queen's Walk ⊛ www.london .gov.uk. Mon–Fri 8am–8pm. Free. Bearing a striking resemblance to a giant car headlight, the centrepiece of the redevelopment near Tower Bridge is Norman Foster's startling glass-encased City Hall. Headquarters for the Greater London Authority and the Mayor of London, it's a "green" building that uses a quarter of the energy a high-specification office would normally use. Visitors are welcome to stroll around and watch the London Assembly proceedings from the second floor. On certain weekends, it's also possible to visit "London's Living Room" on the ninth floor, from where there's a great view over the Thames.

Design Museum

Butler's Wharf, 28 Shad Thames ⊛ www.designmuseum.org. Daily 10am–5.45pm. £6. A Bauhaus-like conversion of an old 1950s riverside warehouse, the stylish white edifice of the Design Museum is the perfect showcase for mass-produced industrial design, from classic cars to Tupperware. The museum has nothing on permanent display, but instead hosts a series of temporary exhibitions (up to four at any one time) on important designers, movements or single products.

Shops

Butlers Wharf Gastrodome

36d & 36e Shad Thames. Among the clutch of chi-chi emporia here, look out for the Oil & Spice Shop, stocking a beautifully presented and mouthwatering range of oils, vinegars and spices, and the Pont de la Tour, offering an excellent range of deli fare.

Cafés

El Vergel

8 Lant St ⊛ elvergel.serversure.net. Closed Sat & Sun. Small, very busy

▲ DESIGN MUSEUM

weekday café which does all the usual lunchtime takeaways, as well as Latin American specialities: empanadas, tacos, tostadas and tortillas.

Monmouth Coffee Company

2 Park St. Perfect pit stop in between perusing the Borough Market stalls. This place takes its coffee seriously, as well as offering moist and succulent cakes and pastries.

Restaurants

Delfina Studio Café

50 Bermondsey St ☏020/7357 0244, ⊛www.delfina.org.uk. Closed Sat & Sun. Despite its name, this adjunct to the Delfina art gallery houses a serious (lunchtime-only) restaurant. The cooking is superb: try carrot-chilli blini or Asian braised pigeon for starters (around £5), and rosemary roasted pumpkin or monkfish *stifado* for mains (£10-plus).

Fina Estampa

150 Tooley St ☏020/7403 1342. Closed Sat lunch & Sun. London's only Peruvian restaurant, and very good it is too. The traditional menu emphasizes seafood; starters include marinated white fish with sweet potatoes (£5 and upwards), while mains (£10 or more) range from chicken in coriander to *carapulcra* (dried potatoes, pork, chicken and cassava).

Tentazioni

2 Mill St ☏020/7237 1100, ⊛www.tentazioni.co.uk. Closed Mon & Sat lunch, & Sun. Small, busy Italian restaurant serving high-quality peasant fare with strong, rich flavours. Starters (£8–10) can be turned into main courses (£12–20), or you can try the splendid five-course regional menu (£36).

Pubs

Anchor

34 Park St. Still looking much as it did when it was first built in 1770, with a warren of small wood-panelled rooms and exposed beams, this is a good bet for alfresco drinking by the river.

George Inn

77 Borough High St. London's only surviving coaching inn, dating from the seventeenth century and now owned by the National Trust; expect lots of wonky flooring, half-timbering and a good range of real ales.

Royal Oak

44 Tabard St. Closed Sat & Sun. Beautiful, lovingly restored Victorian pub that eschews jukeboxes and one-armed bandits, and opts simply for serving real ales from Lewes in Sussex.

Hyde Park and Kensington Gardens

Most visitors are amazed at how green and pleasant so much of London's centre is. Hyde Park, together with its westerly extension, Kensington Gardens, covers a distance of two miles from Oxford Street in the north-east to Kensington Palace in the southwest. In between, people jog, swim, fish, sunbathe or mess about in boats on the Serpentine, cross the park on horseback or mountain bike, or view the latest in modern art at the Serpentine Gallery. Princess Diana's home until her death, Kensington Palace sits at the more fashionable end of the park, which gets mobbed on summer weekends with rollerbladers.

Wellington Arch

Hyde Park Corner ⊛www .english-heritage.org.uk. Wed–Sun: April–Sept 10am–6pm; Oct 10am–5pm; Nov–March 10am–4pm. £2.50. Standing in the midst of one of London's busiest traffic interchanges, Wellington Arch was erected in 1828 to commemorate Wellington's victories in the Napoleonic Wars. A standard Neoclassical triumphal arch, it was originally topped by an equestrian statue of the Duke himself, later replaced by Peace driving a four-horse chariot. Inside, you can view an informative exhibition on London's outdoor sculpture and take a lift to the top of the monument, where the exterior balconies offer a bird's-eye view of the swirling traffic.

Wellington Museum, Apsley House

149 Piccadilly ⊛www.apsleyhouse .org.uk. Tues–Sun 11am–5pm. £4.50. The former London residence of the "Iron Duke", Apsley House has housed the Wellington Museum since 1952.

However unless you're a keen fan of the Duke (or the building's architect, Benjamin Wyatt), the highlight here is the art collection, much of which used to belong to the King of Spain. Among the best pieces, displayed in the Waterloo Gallery on the first floor, are works by de Hooch, van Dyck, Velázquez, Goya, Rubens and Murillo. The famous, more than twice life-size, nude statue of Napoleon by Antonio Canova stands at the foot of the main staircase.

▲ ROLLERBLADERS, KENSINGTON GARDENS

Hyde Park and Kensington Gardens

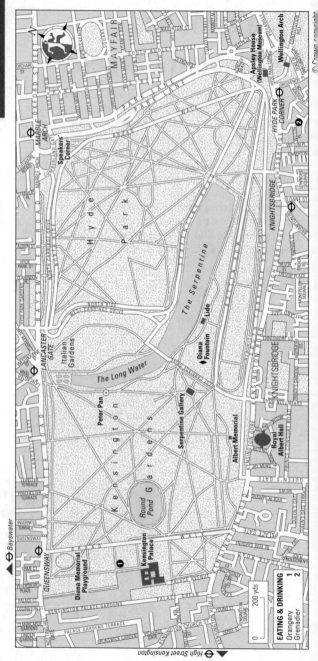

© Crown copyright

EATING & DRINKING
| Orangery | 1 |
| Grenadier | 2 |

0   200 yds

▲ WELLINGTON ARCH

Hyde Park

ⓦ www.royalparks.gov.uk. Daily 5am–midnight. Hangings, muggings, duels and the Great Exhibition of 1851 are just some of the public events that have been staged in Hyde Park, which remains a popular rallying point for political demonstrations. For most of the time, however, the park is simply a lazy leisure ground – a wonderful open space which allows you to lose all sight of the city beyond a few persistent tower blocks.

At the treeless northeastern corner is Marble Arch, erected in 1828 as a triumphal entry to Buckingham Palace but now stranded on a ferociously busy traffic island at the west end of Oxford Street. This is the most historically charged spot in Hyde Park, as it marks the site of Tyburn gallows, the city's main public execution spot until 1783. It's also the location of Speakers' Corner, a peculiarly English Sunday tradition, featuring an assembly of soap-box orators, religious extremists and hecklers.

A more immediately appealing approach is to enter from the southeast around Hyde Park Corner, from which paths lead past pretty flower gardens towards the curvaceous lake of the Serpentine. The lake's popular Lido (June–Aug daily 10am–6pm; £3) is situated on the south bank, and rowboats and pedalos can be rented (March–Oct daily 10am–6.30pm or dusk; £4 per hour) from the boathouse on the north bank.

Kensington Gardens

ⓦ www.royalparks.gov.uk. Daily 6am–dusk. The more tranquil, leafier half of Hyde Park, Kensington Gardens is home to Long Water, the upper section of the Serpentine and by far the prettiest section of the lake. It narrows until it reaches a most unlikely sight in an English park: the Italian Gardens, a group of four fountains laid out symmetrically in front of a pumphouse disguised in the form of an Italianate loggia. The best-loved of Kensington Gardens' outdoor monuments is to Peter Pan, the fictional

▲ PETER PAN STATUE

character who enters London along the Serpentine in the eponymous tale. The book's author, J.M. Barrie, used to walk his dog in Kensington Gardens, and it was here that he met the five pretty, upper-class Llewellyn Davies boys, who wore "blue blouses and bright red tam o'shanters", were the inspiration for the book's "Lost Boys", and whose guardian he eventually became. Paid for by Barrie himself and erected in secret during the night in 1912, the statue depicts Peter presiding over a pedestal crowded with fairies, squirrels, rabbits, birds and mice.

Serpentine Gallery

Kensington Gardens
ⓦ www.serpentinegallery.org. Daily 10am–6pm. Free. The Serpentine Gallery was built as a tearoom in 1908 because the park authorities thought "poorer visitors" might cause trouble if left without refreshments. The building has served as an art gallery since the 1960s, with a reputation for lively, controversial exhibitions; it also annually commissions world-renowned architects to design a temporary pavilion for its summer-only tea-house extension. The results have been adventurous and exciting, ranging from Zaha Hadid's giant marquee to Toyo Ito's partially opaque enclosed box.

Albert Memorial

Kensington Gardens. Erected in 1876, the richly decorated, High Gothic Albert Memorial is as much a hymn to the glorious achievements of Britain as to its subject, Queen Victoria's husband (who died of typhoid in 1861). Recently restored to his former gilded glory, Albert occupies the central canopy, clutching a catalogue for the Great Exhibition that he helped to organize. If you want to learn more about the 169 life-sized depictions of long-gone artists (all men) around the pediment, and the various other allegorical sculptures dotted about the memorial, join one of the weekly **guided tours** (Sun 2 & 3pm; £3.50).

Royal Albert Hall

Kensington Gore ☎020/7589 8212, ⓦ www.royalalberthall.com. The profits of the Great Exhibition were used to buy a large tract of land south of the park, and to build the vast Royal Albert Hall, a splendid iron-and-glass-domed concert hall, with an exterior of red brick, terracotta and marble that became the hallmark of South Kensington architecture. As well as hosting a variety of events throughout the year, from pop concerts to sumo wrestling, the hall is the venue for Europe's most democratic music festival, the Henry Wood Promenade Concerts or **Proms** (see p.215), which take place every night from July to September. The classical concerts are top-class and standing-room tickets go for as little as £3, but the Proms are best known for the flag-waving, patriotic last night.

Kensington Palace

Kensington Gardens ⓦ www .hrp.org.uk. March–Oct daily 10am–6pm; Nov–Feb 10am–5pm. £10.50. Bought by William and Mary in 1689, the modestly proportioned Jacobean brick mansion of Kensington Palace was the chief royal residence for the next fifty years. KP, as it's fondly known in royal circles, is best known today as the place where Princess Diana lived from her marriage until her death in 1997. It was, in fact, the official London residence of both Charles and Di until the couple formally separated and Charles moved to St James's Palace. In the weeks following Diana's death, literally millions of flowers, mementos, poems and gifts were deposited at the gates to the south of the palace.

Diana's former apartments, where various minor royals still live, are closed to the public. Instead, guided tours take in some of the frocks worn by Diana, as well as several of the Queen's, and then the sparsely furnished state apartments. The highlights are the trompe l'oeil ceiling paintings by William Kent, particularly those in the Cupola Room, and the paintings in the King's Gallery by, among others, Tintoretto. En route, you also get to see the tastelessly decorated rooms in which the future Queen Victoria spent her unhappy childhood.

Diana Memorial Playground

Kensington Gardens. As befits a play area dedicated to the memory of the Princess of Wales, this is no ordinary playground, and gets so popular that entry numbers have to be limited in the height of summer. The centrepiece is a sailing ship sunk into sand, which kids can clamber all over; elsewhere there's paving gongs and other groovy playthings. Diana is also due to be commemorated by a giant oval fountain to the south of the Serpentine, scheduled to be unveiled in autumn 2004.

Cafés

The Orangery

Kensington Palace, Kensington Gardens. Very swish café in a brilliant-white orangery, originally built for Queen Anne as a summer dining room, and offering great cakes as well as savoury tarts.

Pubs

Grenadier

18 Wilton Row. Wellington's local (his horse-block survives outside) and his former officers' mess too. The original pewter bar survives, and the Bloody Marys are very special.

▲ ALBERT HALL FACADE

South Kensington, Knightsbridge and Chelsea

London's wealthiest district, the Royal Borough of Kensington and Chelsea is particularly well-to-do in the area south of Hyde Park. Known popularly as the "Tiara Triangle", the moneyed feel here is evident in the flash shops and swanky bars as well as the plush houses and apartments. Aside from the shops around Harrods in **Knightsbridge**, however, the popular tourist attractions lie in **South Kensington**, where three of London's top museums stand side by side.

From the Swinging Sixties and even up to the Punk era, **Chelsea** had a slightly bohemian pedigree; these days, it's just another wealthy west London suburb, famous only as the spiritual home of Sloanes, the sons and daughters of the wealthy, whose most famous specimen was Princess Diana herself.

Natural History Museum

Cromwell Rd ☎020/7942 5000, ⊛www.nhm.ac.uk. Mon–Sat 10am–5.50pm, Sun 11am–5.50pm. Free. With its 675-foot terracotta facade, Alfred Waterhouse's purpose-built mock-Romanesque colossus ensures the Natural History Museum's status as London's most

▲ NATURAL HISTORY MUSEUM

handsome museum. The contents, though, are a bit of a mishmash, with truly imaginative exhibits peppered amongst others little changed since the building opened in 1881. This disparity is the result of a genuine conundrum, though – the collections are as much an important resource for serious zoologists as they are a popular attraction.

The main entrance leads to the **Life Galleries**, whose vast Central Hall is dominated by an 85ft-long plaster cast of a Diplodocus skeleton. To one side, you'll find the Dinosaur gallery, where a team of animatronic deinonychi feast on a half-dead tenontosaurus. Other child-friendly sections include the Creepy-Crawlies Room, which features a live colony of leaf-cutter ants, the Mammals

Hyde Park ▲

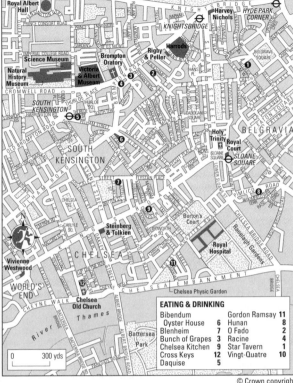

EATING & DRINKING

Bibendum		Gordon Ramsay	11
Oyster House	6	Hunan	8
Blenheim	7	O Fado	2
Bunch of Grapes	3	Racine	4
Chelsea Kitchen	9	Star Tavern	1
Cross Keys	12	Vingt-Quatre	10
Daquise	5		

© Crown copyright

gallery with its life-size model of a blue whale, and the walk-through rainforest in the high-tech Ecology Gallery.

For a visually exciting romp through evolution, head for the **Earth Galleries**; popular sections include the slightly tasteless Kobe earthquake simulator, and the spectacular display of gems and crystals in the Earth's Treasury. Visitors can also sign up for a free 35-minute guided tour (every 30min; book ahead online or on ☎020/7942 6128) of the new **Darwin Centre**, which houses more of the museum's millions of zoological specimens. Tours allow visitors a closer look at the specimens, to see behind the scenes at the labs, and to talk to the museum's scientists.

Science Museum

Exhibition Rd ☎0870/870 4868, ⊛www.sciencemuseum.org.uk. Daily 10am–6pm. Free. The Science Museum is undeniably impressive, filling seven floors with items drawn from every conceivable area of science, including space travel, telecommunications, time measurement, chemistry, computing, photography and medicine. Keen to dispel the enduring image of such museums as boring and full of dusty glass cabinets, the Science Museum has been busy updating its galleries with interactive displays, and puts on daily demonstrations to show that not all science teaching has to be deathly dry.

First off, ask at the information desk in the Power Hall for details of the day's (usually free) events and demonstrations. Most people will want to head for the new four-floor **Wellcome Wing**, geared to appeal to even the most museum-phobic teenager with state-of-the-art interactive computers and an IMAX cinema (tickets £7.50). To get there, go past the info desk and through the Space gallery, with its full-size replica of the Apollo 11 landing craft, to the far side of the Making of the Modern World, a display of iconic inventions from Robert Stephenson's *Rocket* steam train of 1829 to the Ford Model T, the world's first mass-produced car.

In the basement, the hands-on displays of the **Launch Pad**, aimed squarely at kids, remains as popular and enjoyable as ever,

▲ *STEPHENSON'S ROCKET*, SCIENCE MUSEUM

as do the Garden and Things galleries.

Victoria & Albert Museum

Cromwell Rd ☎020 7942 2000, ⊛www.vam.ac.uk. Daily 10am–5.45pm, plus Wed & last Fri of the month until 10pm. Free. In terms of sheer variety and scale, the Victoria and Albert (popularly known as the V&A) is the greatest museum of applied arts in the world. Beautifully but haphazardly displayed across a seven-mile, four-storey maze of halls and corridors, the V&A's treasures are impossible to survey in a single visit. Floor plans from the information desks can help you decide which areas to concentrate on.

The most celebrated of the V&A's exhibits are the **Raphael Cartoons**, seven vast biblical paintings that served as designs for a set of tapestries destined for the Sistine Chapel. Close by, you can view highlights from the UK's largest dress collection, and the world's largest collection of Indian art outside India. In addition, there are galleries devoted to British, Chinese, Islamic, Japanese and Korean art, as well as costume jewellery, glassware, metalwork and photography. Wading through the huge collection of European sculpture, you come to the surreal Plaster Casts gallery, filled with copies of European art's greatest hits, from Michelangelo's *David* to Trajan's Column from the forum in Rome (sawn in half to make it fit). There's even a Twentieth-Century Gallery – everything from Bauhaus furniture to Swatch watches – to rival that of the Design Museum (see p.150).

Over in the **Henry Cole Wing**, meanwhile, there's an entire office interior by Frank

Lloyd Wright, a collection of sixteenth-century portrait miniatures, more Constable paintings than the Tate, and a goodly collection of Rodin sculptures. As if all this were not enough, the V&A's temporary shows are among the best in Britain, ranging over vast areas of art, craft and technology.

▲ INDIAN MINIATURE PAINTING, V&A

Brompton Oratory

Brompton Rd ⊕ www.brompton-oratory .org.uk. London's most flamboyant Roman Catholic church, Brompton Oratory was completed in 1886 and modelled on the Gesù church in Rome. The ornate Italianate interior is filled with gilded mosaics and stuffed with sculpture, much of it genuine Italian Baroque, while the pulpit is a superb piece of Neo-Baroque from the 1930s; note the high cherub count on the tester. And true to its architecture, the church practises "smells and bells" Catholicism, with daily Mass in Latin.

Harrods

87–135 Brompton Rd ⊕ www.harrods.com. Mon–Sat 10am–7pm. London's most famous department store, Harrods started out as a family-run grocery shop in 1849 with a staff of two; the current 1905 terracotta building, owned by the *bête noire* of the Establishment, Mohammed Al Fayed, employs in excess of 3000 staff. Tourists flock here – it's thought to be one of the city's top-ranking tourist attractions – though if you can do without the Harrods carrier bag, you can buy most of what the shop stocks more cheaply elsewhere.

The store does, however, have a few sections that are architectural sights in their own right: on the ground floor, the Food Hall, with its exquisite Arts and Crafts tiling, and the pseudo-hieroglyphs and sphinxes of the Egyptian Hall are particularly striking, while the Egyptian Escalators whisk you to the first floor "luxury washrooms", where you can splash on free perfume. At the base of the escalators is the Diana and Dodi fountain shrine. Here, to the strains of Mahler (and the like), you can contemplate photos of the ill-fated couple, and, preserved in a glass pyramid, a dirty wine-glass used on their last evening along with the engagement ring Dodi allegedly bought for Di the previous day.

Note that Harrods has a draconian dress code: no shorts or vest T-shirts, and backpacks must be carried in the hand.

Holy Trinity Church

Sloane Square. Mon–Sat 8.30am–5.30pm, Sun 8.30am–1.30pm. An architectural masterpiece created in 1890, Holy Trinity is probably the finest Arts and Crafts church in London. The east window is the most glorious of the furnishings, a vast, 48-panel extravaganza designed by Edward Burne-Jones, and the largest ever made by Morris & Co. Holy Trinity is very High Church, filled with the smell of incense and statues of Mary, and even offering confession.

King's Road

Chelsea's main artery, King's Road achieved household fame as the unofficial catwalk of the Swinging Sixties and of the hippie and punk eras. The "Saturday Parade" of fashion victims is not what it used to be, but posey cafés, boutiques (and antiques) are still what King's Road is all about. And the traditional "Chelsea Cruise", when every flash Harry in town parades his customized motor, still takes place at 8.30pm on the last Saturday of the month, though nowadays on the Battersea side of the Chelsea Bridge.

Chelsea Physic Garden

Royal Hospital Rd ⊛ www .chelseaphysicgarden.co.uk. April–Oct Wed noon–5pm, Sun 2–6pm. £4. Hidden from the road by a high wall, Chelsea Physic Garden is a charming little inner-city escape. Founded in 1673, it's the second oldest botanic garden in the country and remains an old-fashioned place, with terse Latinate labels and strictly regimented beds. Pick up a plan, which lists the month's most interesting flowers and shrubs, and try to time your visit with one of the free guided tours (phone ☎020/7352 5646 for times), which will explain the fascinating history of the place.

Shops

Harvey Nichols

109–125 Knightsbridge ☎020/7235 5000, ⊛ www.harveynichols.co.uk. The department store made famous by the TV sitcom *Absolutely Fabulous* continues to stay ahead of the crowd, from its ground-floor cosmetics department to the irresistible goodies in its fifth-floor food hall.

Rigby & Peller

2 Hans Rd ☎020/7589 9293, ⊛ www.rigbyandpeller.com. Closed Sun. Corsetières to HM the Queen, this old-fashioned store stocks a wide range of lingerie and swimwear for all shapes and sizes – take ticket, wait for an assistant and order your very own custom-made bra.

Steinberg & Tolkien

193 King's Rd ☎020/7376 3660. Claims to have London's largest collection of vintage and retro gear and accessories; clothing is displayed by designer, which says a lot for the quality of the stock.

Vivienne Westwood

430 King's Rd ☎020/7352 6551, ⊛ www.viviennewestwood.com. Original outlet of the queen of punk fashion. Her trademark style is madly eccentric English, but there's less flamboyant stuff, too.

Cafés

Chelsea Kitchen

98 King's Rd. A branch of the ubiquitous *Stockpot*, experts in budget Anglo-Italian stomach-fillers in the form of steaks, spag bol and the like.

Daquise

20 Thurloe St. Old-fashioned Polish café serving home-

cooked meals or simple coffee, tea and cakes, depending on the time of day.

Vingt-Quatre

325 Fulham Rd. Although an all-night café, this place is more quality brasserie than greasy spoon – and so are the prices.

Restaurants

Bibendum Oyster House

Michelin House, 81 Fulham Rd ☎020/7589 1480, ⍟www.bibendum .co.uk. This glorious tiled former garage, built in 1911, is one of the best places to eat shellfish in London. Half a dozen oysters start at £7.50, while an entire *plateau de fruits de mer* will set you back nearly £30.

Gordon Ramsay

68–69 Royal Hospital Rd ☎020/7352 4441, ⍟www.gordonramsay.com. Closed Sat & Sun. Gordon Ramsay's Chelsea restaurant is a class act through and through, though you have to book ahead to eat here. Set lunches start at £35; fixed-price à la carte menus start at £65.

Hunan

51 Pimlico Rd ☎020/7730 5712. Closed Sun. Probably England's only restaurant serving Hunan food, a relative of Sichuan cuisine. Most people opt for the £30 "leave-it-to-us feast" which lets the chef, Mr Peng, show what he can do.

O Fado

45–50 Beauchamp Place ☎020/7589 3002. This long-established Portuguese restaurant can get rowdy, what with the live *fado* ballads and the family parties, but that's half the enjoyment. Book in advance.

Racine

239 Brompton Rd ☎020/7584 4477. Familiar, delicious, nostalgic dishes from the glory days of French cooking, and friendly service. Starters are well under £10 and main courses only just over; set lunches hover around £15. Booking is imperative.

Pubs

Blenheim

27 Cale St. Large Georgian pub, with lots of lovely wood, an unusual, inexpensive menu and excellent Badger beers.

Bunch of Grapes

207 Brompton Rd. This popular High Victorian pub, complete with snob screens, is the perfect place for a post-museum pint.

Cross Keys

1 Lawrence St. Tucked away in the centre of wealthy, villagey Chelsea, this is a friendly, snug and popular pub.

Star Tavern

6 Belgrave Mews West. Smart, quiet and convivial two-storey mews pub, with fine Fuller's beers and classy food.

▲ BIBENDUM OYSTER HOUSE

High Street Kensington to Notting Hill

Kensington High Street – better known as High Street Ken – is a busy shopping district with all the major UK chains represented. Cultural diversion is at hand, though, in Holland Park and the exotically decorated Leighton House, tucked away in the peaceful surrounding streets of white stucco mansions. **Notting Hill** and adjoining Bayswater, to the north, were slum areas for many years, with a reputation as dens of vice and crime, but gentrification has changed them immeasurably over the last forty years. Now the area is rammed solid with trendy – but wealthy – media folk, yet retains a strong Moroccan and Portuguese presence, as well as vestiges of the African-Caribbean community who initiated – and still run – Carnival, the city's giant August Bank Holiday street party.

Leighton House

12 Holland Park Rd ⊚www.rbkc .gov.uk/leightonhousemuseum. Mon & Wed–Sun 11am–5.30pm. Free. Leighton House was built by the architect George Aitchison for Frederic Leighton, President of the Royal Academy and the only artist ever to be made a peer (albeit on his deathbed). "It will be opulence, it will be sincerity", the artist opined before construction commenced in the 1860s. The big attraction is its domed Arab Hall. Based on the banqueting hall of a Moorish palace in Palermo, it has a central black marble fountain, and is decorated with Saracen tiles, gilded mosaics and latticework drawn from all over the Islamic world. The other rooms are less spectacular but, in compensation, are hung with excellent paintings by Lord Leighton and his Pre-Raphaelite friends Edward Burne-Jones, Lawrence Alma-Tadema and John Everett Millais. Skylights brighten the upper floor, where evening concerts are held in Leighton's vast studio (call ☎020/7602 3316).

Holland Park

The leafy former grounds of the Jacobean Holland House, now replete with woodland and playing fields, Holland Park also boasts several formal areas, such as the Japanese-style Kyoto

▲ HOLLAND HOUSE, HOLLAND PARK

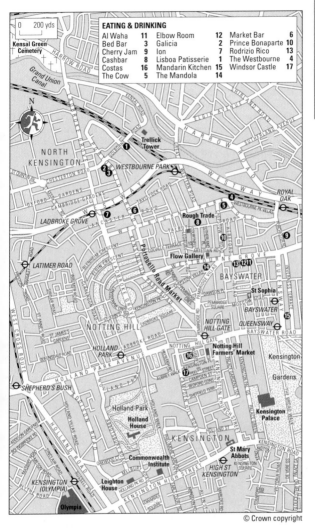

Gardens laid out around the house (only the east wing of which survived the last war). Peppered with modern sculptures, the gardens drift down in terraces to the arcades, Garden Ballroom and Ice House, which have been converted into a café, a restaurant and a contemporary, small-scale art gallery (daily 11am–7pm; free).

Portobello Road Market

Main market Mon–Wed, Fri & Sat 8am–6.30pm, Thurs 8am–1pm; antiques Sat 6am–4pm. Situated in one of the wealthiest, celebrity-saturated parts of town, Portobello Road Market is probably London's trendiest, yet it's always a great spot for a browse and a bargain. Things kick off, at the intersection with Chepstow Road, with junky antique stalls and classier, pricier antique shops. After a brief switch to fruit and veg around the Electric Cinema, the market gets a lot more fun and funky at Portobello Green under the Westway flyover, where the emphasis switches to retro clothes and jewellery, odd trinkets, records and books. The merchandise gets progressively cheaper as the market swings east into Golborne Road, which has its own constellation of bric-a-brac stalls.

Kensal Green Cemetery

Harrow Rd ⊛ www.kensalgreen.co.uk. Opened in 1833, Kensal Green Cemetery was the first of the city's commercial graveyards, and immediately proved itself to be extremely popular – a whole host of luminaries are buried here under some of the most extravagant Gothic tombs in the whole of London. Hemmed in by railway, gasworks and canal, the cemetery is vast, so it makes a lot of sense to join one of the guided tours (£5) that take place every Sunday at 2pm and, on the first and third Sunday of the month, include a visit to the catacombs (bring a torch). Graves of the more famous incumbents – Thackeray, Trollope, Siemens and the Brunels – are less interesting architecturally than those arranged on either side of the Centre Avenue, which leads from the easternmost entrance on Harrow Road. Worth looking out for are Major-General Casement's bier, held up by four grim-looking turbaned Indians; circus manager Andrew Ducrow's conglomeration of beehive, sphinx and angels; and artist William Mulready's neo-Renaissance extravaganza.

Shops

Flow Gallery

1–5 Needham St ☎ 020/7243 0782, ⊛ www.flowgallery.co.uk. Showing the work of mainly British artists, this new enterprise excels in well-crafted goods, such as jewellery, fabrics and sculpture.

Notting Hill Farmers' Market

Kensington Palace car park. Sat 9am–1pm. Fresh fruit, veg, pastries and cakes brought in from farms around London.

Rough Trade

130 Talbot Rd ☎ 020/7229 8541, ⊛ www.roughtrade.com. Indie specialist with knowledgeable, friendly staff and a dizzying

▲ WROUGHT-IRON PORCH NEAR HOLLAND PARK

array of wares, from electronica
to hardcore and beyond.

Cafés

Cashbar

105–107 Talbot Rd. Laid-back,
Cuban-style café just off
Portobello Road, offering all-
day breakfasts, soups, fritters,
burgers and cocktails. Tables
outside in summer.

Costas Fish Restaurant

18 Hillgate St. Closed Mon & Sun.
This old-fashioned Greek-
Cypriot caff offers one of the
best fish-and-chips experiences
in London.

Lisboa Patisserie

57 Golborne Rd. Authentic
Portuguese *pastelaria*, with the
best *pasteis de nata* (custard tarts)
this side of Lisbon – also coffee,
cakes and a friendly
atmosphere.

Restaurants

Al Waha

75 Westbourne Grove ☎020/7229
0806. Arguably London's best
Lebanese restaurant; meze-
obsessed (£5 and under), but
also painstaking in its
preparation of the main-course
dishes (from around £10).

Galicia

323 Portobello Rd ☎020/8969 3539.
Closed Mon. Pleasant Spanish
restaurant without pretension.
The tapas at the bar are
straightforward and good, so it's
no surprise that quite a lot of
customers get no further. Most
dishes are under £10.

Mandarin Kitchen

14–16 Queensway ☎020/7727 9012.

▲ TRELLICK TOWER, GOLBORNE ROAD

Large Chinese fish restaurant
that purports to sell more
lobsters (at around £15 a
pound) than anywhere else in
Britain. Waiters deftly wheel
four-foot diameter table tops
around like giant hoops as they
set up communal tables for
parties of Chinese diners.

The Mandola

139 Westbourne Grove ☎020/7229
4734, ⊛www.mandolacafe.com.
Strikingly delicious "urban
Sudanese" food at sensible
prices – main courses hover
around £10 – served by
extremely laid-back staff. Check
out the spiced coffee to round
off your meal.

Rodrizio Rico

111 Westbourne Grove ☎020/7792
4035. Eat as much as you like for
around £20 at this Brazilian
churrascaria. Carvers come round
and lop off chunks of freshly
grilled, smoky meats from
skewers, while you prime your
plate from the salad bar and hot
buffet.

▲ ALFRESCO DRINKING, WESTBOURNE PARK ROAD

Pubs and bars

Bed Bar

310 Portobello Rd. Moroccan-themed DJ bar, crammed with hedonistic locals standing on the sofas, arms aloft while the DJs spin funky house and Latin-tinged beats.

Cherry Jam

52 Porchester Rd ⊛www.cherryjam .net. Co-owned by Ben Watt (house DJ and half of pop group Everything But The Girl), this smart, intimate basement place mixes a decadent cocktail bar with top-end West London DJs from the broken beat and deep house scenes.

The Cow

89 Westbourne Park Rd. Owned by Tom Conran, son of gastro-magnate Terence, this pub pulls in the beautiful W11 types, thanks to its spectacular food, which includes a daily supply of fresh oysters.

Elbow Room

103 Westbourne Grove ⊛www .elbow-room.co.uk. With its designer decor, purple-felt American pool tables, and better-than-average grilled fast-food and beer, *Elbow Room* has redefined the pool pub.

Ion

161–165 Ladbroke Grove ⊛www.meanfiddler.com. Cool contemporary feel to this Mean Fiddler-run bar situated under the Westway. There's food available on the mezzanine, plus R&B/soul DJs (and queues outside) most nights.

Market Bar

240a Portobello Rd. Self-consciously bohemian pub with gilded mirrors and weird *objets* – all very Notting Hill.

Prince Bonaparte

80 Chepstow Rd. Very popular pared-down, trendy, minimalist pub, with acres of space for sitting and supping while enjoying the bar snacks or the excellent Brit or Med food in the restaurant area.

The Westbourne

101 Westbourne Park Villas. One of a trio of popular bare-boards Notting Hill gastropubs, serving top-notch Brit-Med food.

Windsor Castle

114 Campden Hill Rd. Very pretty, very popular traditional English pub with a great courtyard, that would like to think it's out in the country rather than tucked away in the backstreets.

Regent's Park and Camden

Framed by dazzling Nash-designed, magnolia-stuccoed terraces, and home to London Zoo, Regent's Park is a very civilized and well-maintained spot. Nearby Camden, by contrast, has a scruffy feel to it, despite its many well-to-do residential streets. This is partly due to the chaos and fall-out from the area's perennially popular weekend market, centred around Camden Lock on the Regent's Canal. A warren of stalls with an alternative past still manifest in its quirky wares, street fashion, books, records and ethnic goods, the market remains one of the city's biggest off-beat attractions.

Regent's Park

ⓦ www.royalparks.org.uk. According to John Nash's 1811 masterplan, drawn up for the Prince Regent (later George IV), Regent's Park was to be girded by a continuous belt of terraces, and sprinkled with a total of 56 villas, including a magnificent pleasure palace for the Prince himself. The plan was never fully realized, but enough was built to create something of the idealized garden city that Nash and the Prince Regent envisaged. Pristine, mostly Neoclassical terraces form a near-unbroken horseshoe around the Outer Circle, which marks the park's perimeter along with a handful of handsome villas. Prominent on the skyline is the shiny copper dome and minaret of the **London Central Mosque** at 146 Park Road (ⓦ www.islamic-culturalcentre.co.uk), an entirely appropriate addition to the park given the Prince Regent's taste for the Orient. Non-Muslim visitors are welcome to look in at the information centre, and glimpse inside the hall of worship, which is packed out with a diversity of communities for the lunchtime Friday prayers.

By far the prettiest section of the park is Queen Mary's Gardens, which lie within the central Inner Circle. As well as a pond replete with exotic ducks, and a handsomely landscaped

▲ CHESTER TERRACE ARCHES, REGENT'S PARK

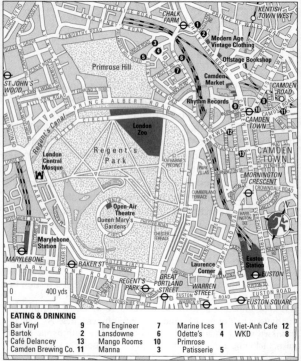

© Crown copyright

EATING & DRINKING

Bar Vinyl	9	The Engineer	7	Marine Ices	1	Viet-Anh Cafe	12
Bartok	2	Lansdowne	6	Odette's	4	WKD	8
Café Delancey	13	Mango Rooms	10	Primrose			
Camden Brewing Co.	11	Manna	3	Patisserie	5		

giant rockery, a large slice of the gardens is taken up with a glorious rose garden, featuring some 400 varieties surrounded by a ring of ramblers. Along the eastern edge of the park, the tree-lined Broad Walk forms a stately approach (much appreciated by rollerbladers) to the park's most popular attraction, London Zoo (see opposite).

Regent's Canal

Completed in 1820, Regent's Canal was constructed as part of a direct link from Birmingham to the newly built London Docks; its seemingly random meandering, from Paddington to the River Thames at Limehouse,

traced the limit of London's northernmost suburbs at the time. Quickly superseded by the railway, the canal never really paid its way as its investors had hoped. By some miracle, however, it escaped being covered over or turned into a rail or road route, and its nine miles, 42 bridges, twelve locks and two tunnels stand as a reminder of London's industrial heyday, and provide an invaluable traffic-free towpath that's great for walking or cycling. The lockless run between Little Venice and Camden Town is the busiest, most attractive stretch, tunnelling through to Lisson Grove, skirting Regent's Park, slicing London

Zoo in two, and passing straight through the heart of Camden Market. It's also the one section that's served year-round by narrowboats offering pleasure cruises (see box), which are without doubt the best way to take in the canal.

London Zoo

Outer Circle, Regent's Park ⓦ www.londonzoo.co.uk. Daily: March–Oct 10am–5.30pm; Nov–Feb 10am–4pm. £13. Over the last decade or so, London Zoo has sought to redefine itself as an eco-conscious place whose prime purpose is to save species under threat of extinction. It's still not the most uplifting spot for animal-lovers, though the enclosures are as humane as any inner-city zoo could make them, and kids usually love the place. Smaller ones are particularly taken with the children's enclosure, where they can handle the animals, and the regular "Animals in Action" live shows where the keepers bring some of their charges out into the open – owls swoop over the audience's heads and lemurs climb up the furniture, but there's no demeaning "performing" involved. The zoo boasts some striking architectural features, too, most notably the modernist, spiral-ramped 1930s concrete penguin pool. Other zoo landmarks include the colossal tetrahedral aluminium-framed tent of the

▲ LONDON CENTRAL MOSQUE

Snowdon Aviary, and the eco-conscious, invertebrate-filled Web of Life.

Camden Market

ⓦ www.camdenlock.net. For all its tourist popularity, Camden Market remains a genuinely offbeat place. The tiny crafts market which began in the cobbled courtyard by the lock has since mushroomed out of all proportion, with everyone trying to grab a piece of the action on both sides of Camden High Street and Chalk Farm Road. More than 150,000 shoppers turn up here each weekend, and some stalls now stay open all week long, alongside a crop of shops, cafés

Regent's Canal by boat

Three companies run **boat trips** on the Regent's Canal between Camden and Little Venice: the narrowboat *Jenny Wren* (☎020/7485 4433), Jason's (☎020/7286 3428, ⓦ www.jasons.co.uk) and the London Waterbus Company (☎020/7482 2660). The latter two run trips all year round, though on weekends only in winter. **Tickets** from all the companies cost £5–6 one-way (and only a little more return), and journey time is fifty minutes one-way.

and bistros. The overabundance of cheap leather, hippy chic, naff jewellery and out-and-out kitsch is compensated for by the sheer variety of what's on offer: everything from bootleg tapes to furniture and mountain bikes, alongside a mass of clubwear and street-fashion stalls, and takeaway food outlets ready to fuel hungry shoppers with wok-fried noodles, bowls of paella, burgers, kebabs, cakes and smoothies.

Shops

Laurence Corner
62–64 Hampstead Rd ☎020/7813 1010. London's oldest and most eccentric army surplus shop, which also stocks catering uniforms, thermals, heavy-duty waterproofs and many kinds of hats.

Modern Age Vintage Clothing
65 Chalk Farm Rd ☎020/7482 3787. Splendid outlet (mostly menswear) for lovers of 1940s and 1950s American-style gear. The best bargains are on the rails outside: inside, the very lovely cashmere and leather coats are a bit pricier.

▲ REGENT'S CANAL, LITTLE VENICE

Offstage Theatre and Cinema Bookshop
37 Chalk Farm Rd ☎020/7485 4996. Excellent, well-stocked shop covering all aspects of stage and screen craft, plus theory, criticism, scripts and biographies.

Rhythm Records
281 Camden High St ☎020/7267 0123. Small, manic shop offering a huge range of indie CDs upstairs (no vinyl), and staff who know exactly what you're asking for. Downstairs is a calmer affair, with rock, folk, soul and R&B vinyl treasures and a pretty hip selection of jazz CDs.

Cafés

Café Delancey
3 Delancey St. Camden's best French-style brasserie, serving coffee, croissants, snacks and full meals.

Marine Ices
8 Haverstock Hill. Splendid and justly famous old-fashioned Italian ice-cream parlour; pizza and pasta are served in the adjacent restaurant.

Primrose Patisserie
136 Regent's Park Rd. Very popular pastel-pink and sky-blue patisserie in fashionable Primrose Hill, offering superb East European cakes and pastries.

Viet-Anh Cafe
41 Parkway ☎020/7284 4082. Authentic, bright, cheerful café run by a friendly and welcoming young Vietnamese couple. Try the prawn sugar-cane sticks, the slurpy noodle soups or the hot lemongrass chicken, all for around a fiver.

▲ CAMDEN MARKET

Restaurants

Mango Rooms

10 Kentish Town Rd ☎020/7482 5065.
Closed Mon. An engaging, laid-
back, Camden-cool Caribbean
place, where the cooking is
consistent and the presentation
first-class. Starters are under £5,
mains around £10.

Manna

4 Erskine Rd ☎020/7722 8028,
🕸www.manna-veg.com. Closed
Mon–Fri lunch, Sat & Sun eve. Old-
fashioned, casual vegetarian
restaurant with 1970s decor,
serving eclectic dishes in large
portions. Starters hover around
£5, while mains breach £10.

Odette's

130 Regent's Park Rd ☎020/7586
5486. Closed Sat lunch & Sun eve.
Charming, picturesque local
restaurant serving well-judged –
though pricey – Modern British
food. Set lunches cost around
£15 – a bargain, since main
courses can easily touch £20.

Pubs and bars

Bar Vinyl

6 Inverness St. This tiny, funky
glass-bricked place is the
archetypal club-bar, with guest
DJs and a record shop downstairs.

Bartok

78–79 Chalk Farm Rd. Sink into one
of the sofas and sup beer or wine,
while listening to classical music
instead of the usual muzak.

Camden Brewing Co.

1 Randolph St. Refurbished old
pub with a boldly colourful
designer interior, comfy sofas,
real fires and good Thai food.

The Engineer

65 Gloucester Ave. Smart, grandiose
Victorian pub in an equally
well-to-do residential area – the
food is exceptional, though
pricey; get a seat early if you're
intending to partake.

Lansdowne

90 Gloucester Ave. Big, bare-boards
minimalist pub with comfy
sofas, in elegant Primrose Hill.
Pricey, tasty food that's a far cry
from most pub grub.

WKD

18 Kentish Town Rd. Laid-back café
and club-bar, where Saturday
daytime features jazz, rare-groove
and hip-hop, and the evenings
are a fusion of soul, reggae and
funky vibes. Open late.

Hampstead and Highgate

The high points of North London, both geographically and aesthetically, the elegant, largely eighteenth-century developments of **Hampstead** and **Highgate** have managed to cling on to their village origins. Of the two, Highgate is slightly sleepier and more aloof, Hampstead busier and buzzier, with high-profile intelligentsia and discerning pop stars among its residents. Both benefit from direct access to one of London's wildest patches of greenery, Hampstead Heath, where you can enjoy stupendous views over London, kite-flying and nude bathing, as well as outdoor concerts and high art in and around the Neoclassical country mansion of Kenwood House.

Fenton House

Windmill Hill ⓦ www.nationaltrust
.org.uk. Mid-March to Oct Wed–Fri
2–5pm, Sat & Sun 11am–5pm. £4.50.
Set grandly behind wrought-iron gates, Fenton House is decorated in impeccable eighteenth-century taste, and houses a collection of European and Oriental ceramics as well as a superb assortment of early musical instruments, bequeathed

▲ FENTON HOUSE GATES

by the building's last private owner, Lady Binning. Among the spinets, virginals and clavichords, look out especially for the early English grand piano, an Unverdorben lute from 1580 (one of only three in the world) and, on the ground floor, a harpsichord from 1612, on which Handel is thought to have played. Experienced keyboard players are sometimes let loose on the instruments during the day. There's very little information in the house, so it's worth buying the briefer of the guides on sale at the entrance, and hiring a tape of music played on the above instruments (£1), to listen to while you walk round. You should also take a stroll in the beautiful formal garden (same hours as house; free), which features some top-class herbaceous borders.

Freud Museum

20 Maresfield Gardens ⓦ www.freud
.org.uk. Wed–Sun noon–5pm. £5.
Hidden away in the leafy streets of south Hampstead, the Freud Museum is one of the most poignant of London's museums. Having lived in Vienna for his

entire adult life, Sigmund Freud was forced to flee the Nazis, and arrived in London during the summer of 1938 as a semi-invalid (he died within a year). The ground-floor study and library look exactly as they did when Freud lived here – the collection of erotic antiquities and the famous couch, sumptuously draped in Persian carpets, were all brought here from Vienna. Upstairs, home movies of family life in Vienna are shown continually, and a small room is dedicated to his daughter, Anna, herself an influential child analyst, who lived in the house until her death in 1982.

2 Willow Road

⊕020/7435 6166, ⊛www .nationaltrust.org.uk. March & Nov Sat noon–5pm; April–Oct Thurs–Sat noon–5pm. £4.50. An unassuming red-brick terraced house built in the 1930s by the Hungarian-born architect Ernö Goldfinger, 2 Willow Road gives a fascinating insight into the modernist mindset. This was a state-of-the-art pad when Goldfinger moved in, and as he changed little during the following sixty years, what you see today is a 1930s avant-garde dwelling preserved in aspic, a house at once both modern and old-fashioned. An added bonus is that the rooms are packed with works of **art** by the likes of Max Ernst, Duchamp, Henry Moore and Man Ray.

Before 3pm, visits are by hour-long guided tour only (noon, 1 & 2pm), for which you must book in advance; after 3pm, the public has unguided, unrestricted access. Incidentally, James Bond's adversary is indeed named after Ernö – Ian Fleming lived close by and had a deep personal dislike of both Goldfinger and his modernist abode.

Keats House

Keats Grove ⊛www.keatshouse .org.uk. Tues–Sun: April–Oct noon–5pm; Nov–March noon–4pm. £3. An elegant, whitewashed Regency double villa, Keats House is a shrine to Hampstead's most lustrous figure. Inspired by the tranquillity of the area and by his passion for girl-next-door Fanny Brawne (whose house is also part of the museum), Keats wrote some of his most famous works here before leaving for Rome, where he died of consumption in 1821 aged just 25. The neat, rather staid interior contains books and letters, Fanny's engagement ring and the four-poster bed in which the poet first coughed up blood, confiding to his companion, Charles Brown, "that drop of blood is my death warrant".

Hampstead Heath

North London's "green lung" Hampstead Heath is the city's most enjoyable public park, and though little of its original heathland remains, there's still a wonderful variety of bucolic scenery in its 800 acres. At the park's southern end are the rolling green pastures of Parliament Hill, north London's premier spot for kite-flying. On either side are numerous ponds, three of which – one for men, one for women and one mixed – you can swim in for free (daily 7am–9pm or dusk). The thickest woodland is to be found in the West Heath, beyond Whitestone Pond, also

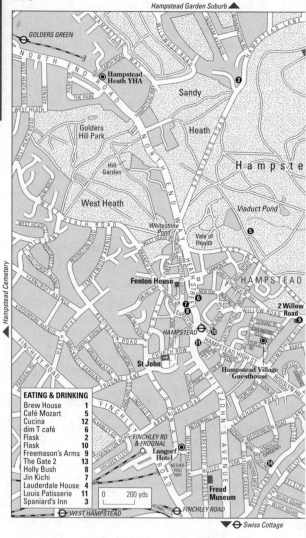

PLACES

Hampstead and Highgate

◀ Hampstead Cemetery

EATING & DRINKING

Brew House	1
Café Mozart	5
Cucina	12
dim T café	6
Flask	2
Flask	10
Freemason's Arms	9
The Gate 2	13
Holly Bush	8
Jin Kichi	7
Lauderdale House	4
Louis Patisserie	11
Spaniard's Inn	3

0 ____ 200 yds

▼ ⊖ Swiss Cottage

the site of the most formal section, Hill Garden, a secretive and romantic little gem with eccentric balustraded terraces and a ruined pergola. Beyond lies Golders Hill Park, where you can gaze at pygmy goats and fallow deer, and inspect the impeccably maintained aviaries,

home to flamingos, cranes and other exotic birds.

Kenwood House

Hampstead Heath. Daily: April–Sept 10am–6pm; Oct 10am–5pm; Nov–March 10am–4pm. Free. The Heath's most celebrated sight is the whitewashed Neoclassical

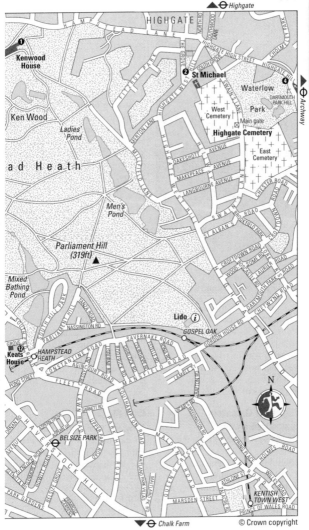

© Crown copyright

mansion Kenwood House, set in its own magnificently landscaped grounds at the high point of the park. The house is home to the **Iveagh Bequest**, a superlative collection of seventeenth- and eighteenth-century art, including a handful of real masterpieces by Vermeer, Rembrandt, Boucher, Gainsborough and Reynolds. Of the period interiors, the most spectacular is Robert Adam's sky-blue and gold library, its book-filled apses separated from the central entertaining area by paired columns.

▲ KITE FLYER, HAMPSTEAD HEATH

The East Cemetery's lack of atmosphere is in part compensated for by the fact that you can wander at will through its maze of circuitous paths. On the other side of Swain's Lane, the overgrown West Cemetery, with its spooky Egyptian Avenue and terraced catacombs, is the ultimate Hammer-horror graveyard. Visitors can only enter by way of a guided tour (March–Nov Mon–Fri noon, 2pm & 4pm; Sat & Sun hourly 11am–4pm; Dec–Feb Sat & Sun hourly 11am–3pm; £3). Among the prominent graves usually visited are those of artist Dante Gabriel Rossetti, and of lesbian novelist Radclyffe Hall.

To the south of the house, a grassy amphitheatre slopes down to a lake, where outdoor classical concerts are held on summer evenings (more info on ☎020/7973 3427, or visit ⓦwww.picnicconcerts.com).

Highgate Cemetery

Swain's Lane ⓦwww .highgate-cemetery.org. Receiving far more visitors than Highgate itself, Highgate Cemetery is London's most famous graveyard. The most illustrious incumbent of the East Cemetery (April–Oct Mon–Fri 10am–5pm, Sat & Sun 11am–5pm; Nov–March closes 4pm; £2) is Karl Marx. Erected by the Communist movement in 1954, his vulgar bronze bust surmounting a granite plinth is a far cry from the unfussy memorial he had requested; close by lies the much simpler grave of the author George Eliot.

Cafés

Brew House

Kenwood House, Hampstead Heath. Full English breakfasts, lunches, cakes and teas served in the old laundry, in the courtyard or on the terrace overlooking the lake.

Café Mozart

17 Swain's Lane. Conveniently located on the southeast side of Hampstead Heath, with a wicked Viennese cake selection and soothing classical music.

dim T café

3 Heath St. Narrow Thai café serving dim sum and noodle dishes, washed down with Chinese tea.

Lauderdale House

Waterlow Park, Highgate Hill. Closed Mon. Lovely café with a terrace overlooking the park, offering full meals and, on summer weekends, outrageous strawberry-and-cream scones.

Louis Patisserie

32 Heath St. Popular and engagingly old-fashioned Hungarian tearooms serving fantastic sticky cakes to a mix of Heath-bound hordes and elderly locals.

Restaurants

Cucina

45a South End Rd ☎020/7435 7814. Closed Sun eve. Brightly painted, fashionable first-floor restaurant where the Modern British menu changes every two weeks or so – it darts about a bit from cuisine to cuisine, but each dish is well presented. Starters cost around £5, mains £10-plus.

The Gate 2

72 Belsize Lane ☎020/7435 7733, ⊛www.gateveg.co.uk. Closed Mon & Tues lunch. Contemporary vegetarian restaurant, serving excellent and original dishes (starters around £5, mains around £10) with intense and satisfying tastes and textures.

Jin Kichi

73 Heath St ☎020/7794 6158. Closed Mon & Tues–Fri lunch. Cramped, rather shabby Japanese restaurant that's nonetheless very busy (book ahead). Sushi is available, but the speciality is deliciously marinated "grilled skewers" (seven for around £10) of anything from asparagus and pork to chicken gizzard.

Pubs

Flask

14 Flask Walk. Located on one of Hampstead's more atmospheric lanes, this convivial local has retained much of its original Victorian interior.

Flask

77 Highgate West Hill. Ideally situated at the heart of Highgate village green, with a rambling, low-ceilinged interior and a summer terrace – as a result, it's very popular.

Freemason's Arms

32 Downshire Hill. Big, smart pub close to the Heath, of interest primarily for its large beer garden and its basement skittle alley.

Holly Bush

22 Holly Mount. A lovely old gas-lit pub, tucked away in the steep backstreets of Hampstead village. Can get a bit too mobbed at weekends.

Spaniard's Inn

Spaniards Rd. Big sixteenth-century coaching inn near to Kenwood and the Heath, frequented over the years by everyone from Dick Turpin to John Keats. Aviary, pergola and roses in the garden.

▲ FLASK PUB, FLASK WALK

Greenwich

Greenwich is one of London's most beguiling spots. Its nautical associations are trumpeted by the likes of the magnificent *Cutty Sark* tea clipper and the National Maritime Museum; its architecture, especially the Old Royal Naval College and the Queen's House, is some of the finest on the river; and its Observatory is renowned throughout the world. With the added attractions of riverside pubs and walks, plus a large and well-maintained park with superb views across the river and to Docklands, and a popular weekend market, you can see why Greenwich is the one place in southeast London that draws large numbers of visitors.

Cutty Sark

King William Walk ⊛ www.cuttysark.org
.uk. Daily 10am–5pm. £4.25. The
Cutty Sark cuts an impressive
figure on the riverfront, its three
square-rigged masts towering
over the centre of Greenwich.
The world's last surviving tea
clipper, built in 1869, it in fact
lasted just eight years in the
China tea trade, and it was as a
wool clipper that it made its
name, returning from Australia
in a record-breaking 72 days.
Inside, there's an exhibition in
the main hold which tells the
ship's fascinating history, from its
inception to its arrival in
Greenwich in 1954.

Greenwich Market

⊛ www.greenwichmarket.net. At the
weekend (particularly on
Sundays), Greenwich Market

pulls in as many visitors as the
rest of the area's attractions
combined. Like Camden, it's a
sprawling, slightly disparate
affair, with three main areas to
head for. In the original covered
Victorian section is the Crafts
Market, which sells twentieth-
century antiques (Thurs & Fri
7.30am–5.30pm), assorted arts
and crafts (Thurs–Sun
9.30am–5.30pm), from spoon
mobiles to mounted exotic
butterflies, and deli food. Nearby
Stockwell Street holds the
Central Market (Sat & Sun
7am–5pm), with a two-floor,
indoor secondhand books
section, plus outdoor stalls and
the indoor Village Market,
stuffed with bric-a-brac – there's
even an adjacent organic food
market on Saturdays. Finally,
there's the Antiques Market

Getting to Greenwich

Greenwich is most quickly reached from central London by **train** from Charing Cross, Waterloo East or London Bridge (every 30min), although taking a **boat** from one of the piers between Westminster and Tower Bridge is more scenic and leisurely (and more expensive). Another possibility is to take the **Docklands Light Railway** (DLR; see p.134) from Bank or Tower Gateway direct to Cutty Sark. For the best view of the Wren buildings, get out at Island Gardens, and then take the Greenwich Foot Tunnel under the Thames.

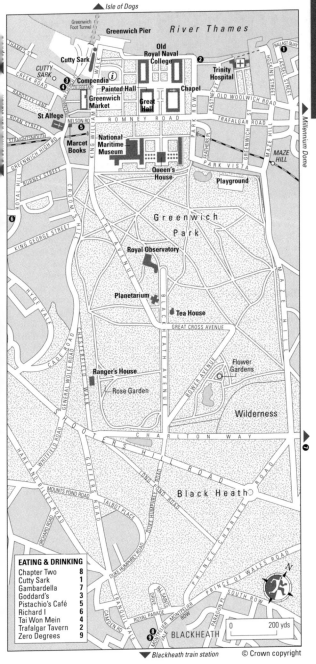

EATING & DRINKING

Chapter Two	8
Cutty Sark	1
Gambardella	7
Goddard's	3
Pistachio's Café	5
Richard I	6
Tai Won Mein	4
Trafalgar Tavern	2
Zero Degrees	9

© Crown copyright

▼ Blackheath train station

▲ GREENWICH MARKET

(Sat & Sun 9am–5pm), off Greenwich High Road, which is really more about collectibles – old comics, pop and sports memorabilia – and junk.

Old Royal Naval College

Romney Rd ⊛ www .greenwichfoundation.org.uk. Daily 10am–5pm. Free. It's entirely appropriate that the Old Royal Naval College is the one London building that makes the most of its riverbank location. Initially intended as a royal palace, Wren's beautifully symmetrical Baroque ensemble was eventually converted into a hospital for disabled seamen in the eighteenth century. From 1873 until 1998 it was home to the Royal Naval College, but now houses the University of Greenwich and the Trinity College of Music.

The two grandest rooms, situated underneath Wren's twin domes, are magnificently opulent and well worth visiting. The Chapel's exquisite pastel-shaded plasterwork and spectacular decorative detailing on the ceiling were designed by James "Athenian" Stuart, after a fire in 1799 destroyed the original interior. The

magnificent Painted Hall features trompe l'oeil fluted pilasters, and James Thornhill's gargantuan allegorical ceiling painting depicting William and Mary handing down Peace and Liberty to Europe, with a vanquished Louis XIV clutching a broken sword below them.

National Maritime Museum and Queen's House

Romney Rd ⊛ www.nmm.ac.uk. Daily 10am–5pm. Free. The excellent National Maritime Museum houses a vast collection of boats and nauticalia, imaginatively displayed in modern, interactive galleries designed to appeal to visitors of all ages. The spectacular glass-roofed, central courtyard houses the museum's largest artefacts, among them the splendid 63ft-long gilded Royal Barge, designed in Rococo style by William Kent for Prince Frederick, the much unloved eldest son of George II.

The themed galleries of the museum proper are superbly designed to appeal to visitors of all ages. In "Explorers", on Level 1, you get to view some of the museum's most highly prized relics, such as Captain Cook's sextant and K1 marine clock, Shackleton's compass, and Captain Scott's furry sleeping bag and sledging goggles. Sponsors P&O get to display their wares in "Passengers", which traces the history of modern passenger liners, and "Cargoes", which concentrates on containerization. On Level 2, there's a large maritime art gallery, a contemporary section on the future of the sea, and a gallery devoted to the legacy of the British Empire, warts and all.

Level 3 boasts two hands-on galleries: "The Bridge", where

you can navigate a catamaran, a paddle steamer and a rowing boat to shore; and "All Hands", where children can have a go at radio transmission, loading miniature cargo, firing a cannon and so forth. Finally, you reach the Nelson Gallery, which contains the museum's vast collection of Nelson-related memorabilia, including Turner's *Battle of Trafalgar, 21st October, 1805*, his largest work and only royal commission.

The **Queen's House** is the focal point of Greenwich's riverside architectural ensemble and an integral part of the Maritime Museum. A bright white Palladian villa flanked by colonnades, it's modest for a royal residence, but as the first Neoclassical building in the country it has enormous significance. Inside, one or two features survive (or have been reinstated) from Stuart times, most notably the cuboid Great Hall, with its Gentileschi fresco, and the beautiful Tulip Staircase, Britain's earliest cantilevered spiral staircase – its name derives from the floral patterning in the wrought-iron balustrade.

Greenwich Park

ⓦwww.royalparks.co.uk. Daily dawn–dusk. A welcome escape from the traffic and crowds, Greenwich Park is a great place to have a picnic or collapse under the shade of one of the giant plane trees. The chief delight, though, is the superb view from the steep hill crowned by the Royal Observatory (see opposite), from which Canary Wharf looms large over Docklands and the Millennium Dome. The park is also celebrated for its rare and ancient trees, its

royal deer enclosure in "The Wilderness" and its semicircular rose garden.

Royal Observatory

Greenwich Park ⓦwww.rog.nmm.ac.uk. Daily: April–Sept 10am–6pm; Oct–March 10am–5pm. Free. Perched on the crest of Greenwich Park's highest hill, the Royal Observatory is housed in a rather dinky Wren-built red-brick building, whose northeastern turret sports a bright-red time-ball that climbs the mast at 12.58pm and drops at 1pm GMT precisely; it was added in 1833 to allow ships on the Thames to set their clocks.

Greenwich's greatest claim to fame, of course, is as the home of Greenwich Mean Time (GMT) and the Prime Meridian. Since 1884, Greenwich has occupied zero longitude – hence the world sets its clocks by GMT. The observatory itself was established in 1675 by Charles II to house the first Astronomer Royal, John Flamsteed, whose chief task was to study the night sky in order to discover an astronomical method of finding the longitude of a ship at sea, the lack of which was causing enormous

▲ TULIP STAIRCASE, QUEEN'S HOUSE

problems for the emerging British Empire. Astronomers continued to work here until the postwar smog forced them to decamp; the old observatory, meanwhile, is now a very popular museum.

The oldest part of the complex is the aforementioned Wren-built Flamsteed House, containing Flamsteed's restored apartments and the Octagon Room, where the king used to show off to his guests. The Chronometer Gallery beyond focuses on the search for the precise measurement of longitude, and displays four of the marine clocks designed by John Harrison, including "H4", which helped win the Longitude Prize in 1763.

In the Meridian Building, you get to see several meridians, including the present-day Greenwich Meridian fixed by the cross hairs in Airy's "Transit Circle", the astronomical instrument that dominates the last room. Things end on a soothing note in the Telescope Dome of the octagonal Great Equatorial Building, home to Britain's largest telescope. In addition, there are regular presentations in the Planetarium (daily 2.30 & 3.30pm; £4), housed in the adjoining South Building.

▲ ROSE GARDEN, GREENWICH PARK

taste was eclectic, ranging from medieval ivory miniatures to Iznik pottery, though he was definitely a man who placed technical virtuosity above artistic merit. Upstairs, the high points of the collection are Memlinc's *Virgin and Child*, a pair of sixteenth-century majolica dishes decorated with mythological scenes for Isabella d'Este; downstairs, take note of the Reynolds portraits and de Hooch interior.

Shops

Compendia

10 Greenwich Market ☎020/8293 6616, ⊛www.compendia.co.uk. Old-fashioned games shop, selling traditional board games from all over the globe, as well as pub favourites like bagatelle, shove ha'penny and skittles.

Marcet Books

23 Nelson Rd ☎020/8853 5408, ⊛www.marcetbooks.co.uk. As befits Greenwich, this is one of a number of bookshops specializing in nautical titles. Good selection of old prints and maps, too, as well as crime novels.

Ranger's House

Chesterfield Walk ⊛www.english-heritage.org.uk. Wed–Sun: April–Sept 10am–6pm; Oct 10am–5pm; Nov, Dec & March 10am–4pm. £4.50. An imposing red-brick Georgian villa, the Ranger's House shelters an art collection amassed by Julius Wernher, the German-born millionaire who made his money by exploiting South Africa's diamond deposits. His

Cafés

Gambardella

48 Vanbrugh Park. Closed Sun. Old-style caff serving filling, comfort food in a beautiful Art Deco interior.

Goddard's

45 Greenwich Church St. Traditional pies (including veggie ones), eels and mash, served in an emerald-green tiled interior.

Pistachio's Café

15 Nelson Rd. Just about the only good sandwich place in the centre of Greenwich; the coffee is excellent, and there are tables in a small garden out back.

Tai Won Mein

39 Greenwich Church St. Good-quality noodle bar that gets very busy at weekends. Choose between rice, soup or various fried noodles all for under a fiver.

Restaurants

Chapter Two

43–45 Montpelier Vale ☎020/8333 2666, ⊛www.chaptersrestaurants .com. Sleek, modern and professionally run, this is a decent local restaurant serving classic, well-thought-out French dishes. Set price dinners cost £17 for two courses, £20 for three, with lunches a couple of pounds cheaper.

Zero Degrees

29–31 Montpelier Vale ☎020/8852 5619, ⊛www .zerodegrees-microbrewery.co.uk. Micro-brewery beers and gourmet pizzas cooked in a wood-fired oven are the rewards at this modern pizzeria.

Pubs

Cutty Sark

Ballast Quay, off Lassell St. The best riverside pub in Greenwich, with friendly staff, an appropriately nautical flavour, a good range of real ales and pub grub served all day.

Richard I

52–54 Royal Hill. Popular local tucked away off the main drag. Good beer and a garden make it an ideal post-market retreat – and if it's too crowded, the *Fox & Hounds* next door is good, too.

Trafalgar Tavern

5 Park Row. A great riverside position and a mention in Dickens' *Our Mutual Friend* have made this Regency-style inn a firm favourite. Good whitebait and other pub snacks.

Kew and Richmond

The wealthy suburbs of **Kew** and **Richmond** like to think of themselves as aloof from the rest of London, and in many ways they are. Both have a distinctly rural feel: Kew, thanks to its outstanding botanic gardens; Richmond, thanks to its picturesque riverside setting. Taking the leafy towpath from Richmond Bridge to one of the nearby stately homes, or soaking in the view from Richmond Park, you'd be forgiven for thinking you were in the countryside. Both Kew and Richmond are an easy tube ride from the centre, but the most pleasant way to reach them is to take one of the boats that plough up the Thames from Westminster.

Syon House and gardens

Twickenham Rd ⓦ www.syonpark .co.uk. House April–Oct Wed, Thurs & Sun 11am–5pm. Gardens daily 10.30am–5.30pm; £3.50. House £3.50, house and gardens £6.95. From its rather plain, castellated exterior, you'd never guess that Syon House boasts London's most opulent eighteenth-century interior. The splendour of Robert Adam's refurbishment is immediately revealed in the pristine Great Hall, an apsed double cube with a screen of Doric columns at one end and classical statuary dotted around

the edges. There are several more Adam-designed rooms to admire, and a smattering of works by van Dyck, Lely, Gainsborough and Reynolds adorn the walls.

While Adam beautified Syon House, Capability Brown laid out its gardens around an artificial lake, surrounding the water with oaks, beeches, limes and cedars. Those with young children will be compelled to make use of the miniature steam train which runs through the park at weekends from April to October, and on Wednesdays during the school holidays.

Butterfly House

Syon Park, Twickenham Rd ⓦ www.butterflies.org.uk. Daily: May–Sept 10am–5pm; Oct–April 10am–4pm. £4.95. Another of Syon's plus-points for kids is its Butterfly House, a small, mesh-covered hothouse where you can walk amid hundreds of exotic butterflies from all over the world, as they flit about the foliage – the giant swallowtails are particularly spectacular. An adjoining room houses a collection of iguanas, millipedes, tarantulas and giant hissing Tanzanian cockroaches.

▲ SYON PARK GATES

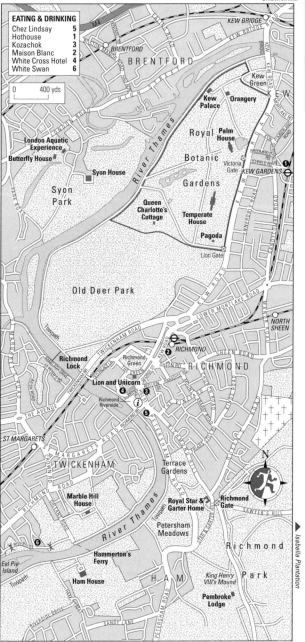

EATING & DRINKING

Chez Lindsay	5
Hothouse	1
Kozachok	3
Maison Blanc	2
White Cross Hotel	4
White Swan	6

0   400 yds

▶ Isabella Plantation

▼ Backhaus

© Crown copyright

London Aquatic Experience

Syon Park, Twickenham Rd
ⓦ www.aquatic-experience.org. Daily:
April–Sept 10am–6pm; Oct–March
10am–5pm. £4. The purpose-built
London Aquatic Experience
displays a mixed range of
creatures from the mysterious
basilisk, which can walk on
water, to the perennially popular
piranhas. There are plenty of
other life-threatening creatures,
too, such as crocodiles, pythons,
boas and even poison-arrow
frogs. Look out, too, for the bird
collection, which includes
macaws, parrots, weaver birds and
some very colourful starlings.

Kew Gardens

ⓦ www.kew.org. Daily 9.30am–7.30pm
or dusk. £6.50. Established in
1759, Kew's Royal Botanic
Gardens have grown from their
original eight acres into a 300-
acre site in which more than
33,000 species are grown in
plantations and glasshouses, a
display that attracts over a
million visitors every year, who
come simply to enjoy the
beautiful landscaped parkland
and steamy palmhouses. There's
always something to see,
whatever the season, but to get
the most out of the place, come
sometime between spring and
autumn, bring a picnic and stay
for the day.

There are four entry points to
the gardens, but the majority of
people arrive at Kew Gardens
tube and train station, a few
minutes' walk east of the
Victoria Gate. Immediately
opposite the Victoria Gate, the
Palm House is by far the most
celebrated of the gardens'
glasshouses, a curvaceous mound
of glass and wrought-iron
designed by Decimus Burton in
the 1840s. Its drippingly humid
atmosphere nurtures most of the

▲ PAGODA, KEW GARDENS

known palm species, while
there's a small but excellent
tropical aquarium in the
basement. South of here is the
largest of the glasshouses, the
Temperate House, which
contains plants from every
continent, including the sixty-
foot Chilean Wine Palm, one of
the largest indoor palms in the
world.

Elsewhere in the park, Kew's
origins as an eighteenth-century
royal pleasure garden are evident
in the numerous follies dotted
about the gardens, the most
conspicuous of which is the
ten-storey, 163-foot-high
Pagoda, visible to the south of
the Temperate House. A sure
way to lose the crowds is to
head for the thickly wooded,
southwestern section of the park
around Queen Charlotte's
Cottage (April–Sept Sat & Sun
10.30am–4pm; free), a tiny

thatched summerhouse built in the 1770s as a royal picnic spot for George III's queen.

Richmond Riverside

Pedestrianized, terraced and redeveloped in the late 1980s, Richmond's riverside is a neo-Georgian pastiche for the most part, and a popular one at that. The real joy of the waterfront, though, is Richmond Bridge, an elegant span of five arches made from Purbeck stone in 1777 and cleverly widened in the 1930s, thus preserving what is London's oldest extant bridge. From April to October you can rent rowing boats from the nearby jetties, or take a boat trip to Hampton Court or Westminster. Alternatively, you can simply head south down the towpath, past the terraced gardens which give out great views over the river. Quite quickly, the towpath leaves the rest of London far behind. On either side are the wooded banks of the Thames; to the left cows graze on Petersham Meadows; beyond lies Ham House (see opposite).

Richmond Park

@www.royalparks.gov.uk. Daily: March–Sept 7am–dusk; Oct–Feb 7.30am–dusk. Free. Richmond's greatest attraction is its enormous park, at the top of Richmond Hill – 2500 acres of undulating grassland and bracken, dotted with coppiced ancient woodland. Eight miles across at its widest point, this is Europe's largest city park, famed for its red and fallow deer, which roam freely, and for its venerable oaks. For the most part untamed, the park does have a couple of deliberately landscaped areas which feature splendid springtime azaleas and rhododendrons; the Isabella Plantation is particularly attractive. For refreshment, head for Pembroke Lodge, a teahouse near King Henry VIII's Mount; this is the park's highest point, affording wonderful views right out to Windsor and back into central London.

Ham House

Ham St @www.nationaltrust.org.uk /hamhouse. April–Oct Mon–Wed, Sat & Sun 1–5pm. £7. Expensively furnished in the seventeenth century but little altered since then, Ham House boasts one of the finest Stuart interiors in the country, from the stupendously ornate Great Staircase to the Long Gallery, featuring six "Court Beauties" by Peter Lely. Elsewhere, there are several fine Verrio ceiling paintings, some exquisite parquet flooring, lavish plasterwork and silverwork as well as paintings by van Dyck and Reynolds. Another bonus are the formal seventeenth-century gardens (Mon–Wed, Sat & Sun 10.30am–6pm; £3), especially the Cherry Garden, with a pungent lavender parterre surrounded by yew hedges and pleached hornbeam

▲ DEER IN RICHMOND PARK

▲ VIEW FROM RICHMOND HILL

arbours. The Orangery, overlooking the original kitchen garden, currently serves as a tearoom.

Marble Hill House

Marble Hill Park, Richmond Rd
ⓦwww.english-heritage.org.uk.
April–Sept daily 10am–6pm; Oct daily 10am–5pm. £3.50. This stuccoed Palladian villa, set in rolling green parkland, was built in 1729 for the Countess of Suffolk, mistress of George II for some twenty years and, conveniently, also a lady-in-waiting to his wife, Queen Caroline (apparently "they hated one another very civilly"). Nothing remains of the original furnishings, and though some period furniture has taken its place the house can feel barren – it's a good idea to get some background via a free audioguide. The principal space is the Great Room, a perfect cube whose coved ceiling carries on up into the top-floor apartments. Copies of van Dyck decorate the walls as they did in Lady Suffolk's day, and a further splash of colour is provided by Panini's Roman landscapes above each of the doors. The other highlight is Lady Suffolk's Bedchamber, which features an Ionic columned recess – a classic Palladian device. You can play minigolf in the grounds, and there are open-air concerts on occasional summer evenings (more info on ☏020/8892 5115, or visit ⓦwww.picnicconcerts.com).

Shops

Backhaus

175 Ashburnham Rd, Richmond
☏020/8948 6040,
ⓦwww.backhaus.co.uk. Top German bakery making authentic cheesecakes, Stollen and to-die-for rye breads, with an adjacent deli selling sausages and cheese.

The Lion & Unicorn

19 King St, Richmond ☏020/8940 0483, ⓦwww.lionunicornbooks.co.uk. Wonderful, busy children's bookshop that regularly

organizes visits by popular children's writers on Saturdays.

Cafés

Hothouse Café

9 Station Parade, Kew. This stylish, inexpensive and congenial café is a great place to fuel up before hitting the botanic gardens. Full English breakfasts, sandwiches and pastries, and an unusually large variety of breads, coffees, teas and juices.

Maison Blanc

27b The Quadrant, Richmond. French patisserie ideal for picking up a picnic of bread and pastries before heading on to the park.

Restaurants

Chez Lindsay

11 Hill Rise, Richmond ☎020/8948 7473. Small, bright and authentic Breton creperie with a loyal local following, offering fixed-price lunchtime menus for just £6. Choose between galettes, crepes or more formal French main courses, including lots of fresh fish and shellfish, and wash it all down with Breton cider.

Kozachok

10 Red Lion St, Richmond ☎020/8948 2366. Closed Mon. Significantly eccentric Ukrainian restaurant decorated with naïve cartoon murals. Warm service, authentic blini (for around £5), *pelmeni*, *shashlik* (for more like £10), and lots of flavoured vodkas.

Pubs

White Cross Hotel

Water Lane, Richmond. With a longer pedigree and more character than its rivals, the *White Cross* has a very popular, large garden overlooking the river.

White Swan

Riverside, Twickenham. Filling pub food, draught beer and a quiet riverside location (except on rugby match days) make this a good halt on any towpath ramble. There's a beer pontoon if you want to get closer to the water.

Hampton Court

Hampton Court Palace is the finest of England's royal abodes and well worth the trip out from central London. A wonderfully imposing, sprawling red-brick ensemble on the banks of the Thames, it was built in 1516 by the upwardly mobile Cardinal Wolsey, Henry VIII's Lord Chancellor, only to be purloined by Henry himself after Wolsey fell from favour. Charles II laid out the gardens, inspired by what he had seen at Versailles, while King William III and Queen Mary II had large sections of the palace remodelled by Wren. With so much to see, both inside and outside the palace, you'd be best off devoting the best part of a day to the place, taking a picnic with you to have in the grounds.

Royal Apartments

ⓦ www.hrp.org.uk. April–Oct Mon 10.15am–6pm, Tues–Sun 9.30am–6pm; Nov–March closes 4.30pm. £11.50.
Arriving by train or boat, you approach the Tudor Great Gatehouse, no longer moated but still very mighty, prickling with turrets, castellations, chimneypots and pinnacles. King Henry lavished more money on Hampton Court than any other palace, yet the only major survival from Tudor times in Henry VIII's State Apartments is his Great Hall, which features a glorious double hammerbeam ceiling. The other highlight is the superbly ornate Chapel Royal, one of the most memorable sights in the whole palace, with its colourful plasterwork vaulting, heavy with pendants of gilded music-making cherubs. The Queen's Apartments (intended for Queen Mary) boast wonderful trompe l'oeil frescoes on the grandiose Queen's Staircase and in the Queen's Drawing Room, where Anne's husband is depicted riding naked and wigless on the back of a "dolphin". The gem of the Georgian Rooms is in fact the Wolsey Closet, a tiny Tudor room that gives a tantalizing glimpse of the splendour of the original palace. The King's Apartments, built at the same time as the Queen's, are even more grand, particularly the militaristic trompe l'oeil paintings on the King's Staircase and the Great Bedchamber, which boasts a superb vertical Gibbons frieze and ceiling paintings by Verrio.

The Renaissance Picture Gallery is chock-full of treasures from the vast Royal Collection including paintings by Tintoretto, Lotto, Titian, Cranach, Bruegel and Holbein.

▲ HAMPTON COURT PALACE GATEHOUSE

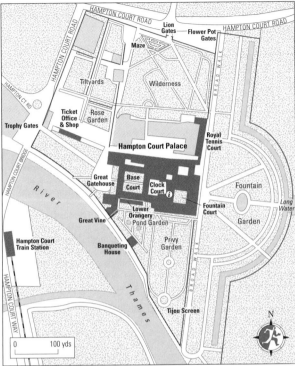

▲ Bushy Park

© Crown copyright

Last, but not least, are the earthy and evocative Tudor Kitchens, large sections of which have survived to this day and have been restored and embellished with historical reconstructions. To make the most of this route, you really do need to use the

Getting to and around the palace

Trains from Waterloo take around half an hour to reach Hampton Court train station which is just across the river from the palace.

The **Royal Apartments** are divided into six thematic walking tours, which are numbered and colour-coded. There's not a lot of information in any of the rooms, but **guided tours**, each lasting half an hour or so, are available at no extra charge for the state apartments; all are led by period-costumed historians, who do a fine job of bringing the place to life. In addition, the King Henry VIII's Apartments, the Tudor Kitchens, the King's Apartments and the Georgian Rooms are served by an **audioguide**, available (again at no extra charge) from the information centre on the east side of Clock Court. If your energy is lacking – and Hampton Court is a huge complex – the most rewarding sections are **Henry VIII's State Apartments** (aka the Tudor Rooms), the **King's Apartments** (remodelled by William III) and the **Tudor Kitchens**. And be sure not to miss out on the **Maze**.

audioguide, which helps to evoke the scene with contemporary accounts.

The Gardens and the Maze

If you're coming from the Royal Apartments, you'll probably emerge onto the magnificent Broad Walk, which runs along Wren's austere east front and is lined with superbly maintained herbaceous borders. Halfway along is the indoor Royal Tennis Court (50p), established here by Henry VIII – if you're lucky, you might catch a game of this arcane precursor of modern tennis.

Fanning out from the Broad Walk is the Fountain Garden, a grand, semicircular parterre featuring conical dwarf yew trees. To the south of the palace is the more formal Privy Garden (£3; free with palace ticket) which feature magnificent wrought-iron riverside railings by Jean Tijou. The Pond Gardens, originally constructed as ornamental fish ponds stocked with freshwater fish for the kitchens, feature some of the gardens' most spectacularly colourful flowerbeds. Further along, protected by glass, is the palace's celebrated Great Vine, grown from a cutting in 1768 by

▲ SWANS IN BUSHY PARK

Capability Brown and averaging about seven hundred bunches of Black Hamburg grapes per year.

Close by stands the Wren-built Lower Orangery, now a dimly lit gallery for Andrea Mantegna's luminous richly coloured masterpiece, *The Triumphs of Caesar*. Painted around 1486 for the Ducal Palace in Mantua, Mantegna's home town, these heroic paintings are among his best works, characterized by an accomplished use of perspective and an obsessive interest in archeological and historical accuracy.

The most famous feature of the palace gardens, however, is the yew hedge Maze (£3; free with palace ticket), laid out in 1714. It's a deceptively tricky labyrinth that's a winner with kids and adults alike.

Bushy Park

Bushy Park is the perfect place to escape the crowds and head off into the semi-wilderness, home to copious herds of fallow and red deer. Wren's mile-long royal road, Chestnut Avenue, cuts through the park and is at its best in May when the horse chestnuts are in blossom. Off to the west of Chestnut Avenue, it's worth heading off to the Waterhouse Woodland Gardens, created in 1949, and at their most colourful each spring when the rhododendrons, azaleas and camellias are in bloom.

Pubs

King's Arms

Lion Gates, Hampton Court Road. Bare bricks, wood panelling and mosaic floor tiles combine to recreate the feel of a Georgian coaching inn. Popular pub food and Badger beers.

Accommodation

Accommodation

Hotels, B&Bs and hostels

Compared with most European cities, **accommodation** in London is expensive. The cheapest option is a dorm bed at one of the numerous independent **hostels**, followed closely behind by the official YHA (ⓦwww.yha.org.uk) places. Even the most basic **B&Bs** struggle to bring their tariffs below £50 for a double with shared facilities, and you're more likely to find yourself paying £60 to £70 or more. For a decent **hotel** room, you shouldn't expect much change out of £100 a night. In upmarket hotels – particularly those in or near the City – prices are significantly higher during the week. Unless otherwise stated, all accommodation is marked on the maps in this chapter.

Westminster

City Inn 30 John Islip St ☎020/7630 1000, ⓦwwwcityinn.com. Vast, modern, hotel close to Parliament; rooms are well insulated from outside noise and the breakfasts are epic. Doubles from £165.
Melbourne House Hotel 79 Belgrave Rd ☎020/7828 3516, ⓦwww .melbournehousehotel.co.uk. Family run, well furnished place, offering clean and bright en-suite rooms, excellent communal areas and friendly service. Doubles from £85.
Oxford House Hotel 92–94 Cambridge St ☎020/7834 6467. The best-value near Victoria station. Pristine shared facilities, full English breakfast is included. Doubles from £50.
Sanctuary House Hotel 33 Tothill St ☎020/7799 4044, ⓦwww.fullershotels .co.uk. Situated above a Fuller's pub, and decked out like one, too, in smart, pseudo-Victoriana. Breakfast is extra. Doubles from £85.

Booking a room

London doesn't really have a **low season**, though things do slacken off a little in the months just after Christmas. It's wise, therefore, to try and **book your accommodation in advance**, particularly if you want to stay in one of the more popular places. If you book by phone, many places will ask for a credit card number, others for written or faxed confirmation, while a few may even ask for a deposit.

If you're stuck, all London tourist offices (see p.210) operate a **room-booking service**, for which around £5 is levied. You can also **book online** for free at ⓦwww.visitlondon.com; payment is made directly to the hotel on checking out, and discounts can be excellent. Other useful websites include ⓦwww.lastminute .com, which almost always offers discounts, and ⓦwww.hotelsengland.com.

In addition, **Thomas Cook** has accommodation desks at Gatwick Airport (☎01293/529372) and will book anything from youth hostels through to five-star hotels for a £5 fee. There are also **British Hotel Reservation Centre** (BHRC; ⓦwww.bhrc.co.uk) desks at Heathrow (☎020/8564 8808), and Gatwick (☎01293/502433) airports, and several in and around Victoria train station (☎020/7828 2425). Most offices are open daily from 6am till midnight, and there's no booking fee.

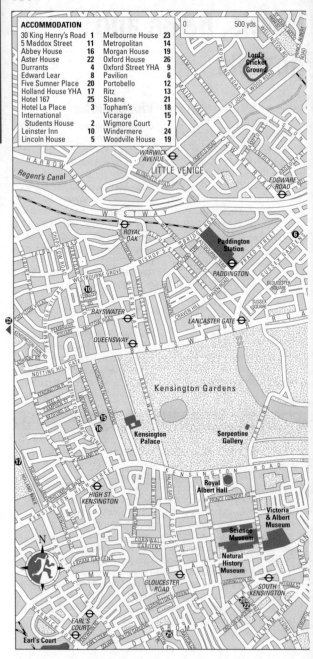

ACCOMMODATION

30 King Henry's Road	1	Melbourne House	23
5 Maddox Street	11	Metropolitan	14
Abbey House	16	Morgan House	19
Aster House	22	Oxford House	26
Durrants	4	Oxford Street YHA	9
Edward Lear	8	Pavilion	6
Five Sumner Place	20	Portobello	12
Holland House YHA	17	Ritz	13
Hotel 167	25	Sloane	21
Hotel La Place	3	Topham's	18
International		Vicarage	15
Students House	2	Wigmore Court	7
Leinster Inn	10	Windermere	24
Lincoln House	5	Woodville House	19

0 — 500 yds

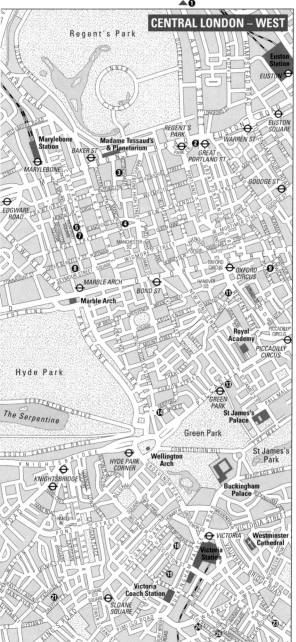

CENTRAL LONDON – WEST

© Crown copyright

Topham's Hotel 26 Ebury St ☎020/7730 8147, ⊛www.tophams.co.uk. Charming family-owned hotel in the English country-house style. Sumptuously furnished en-suite twins or doubles, and full English breakfast included. Doubles from £130.

Windermere Hotel 142–144 Warwick Way ☎020/7834 5163, ⊛www .windermere-hotel.co.uk. Tastefully decorated, quietly stylish place, with mostly en-suite rooms and a tasty restaurant downstairs. Doubles from £90.

Woodville House & Morgan House 107 & 120 Ebury St ☎020/7730 1048 & 7730 2384, ⊛www.woodvillehouse.co.uk & ⊛www.morganhouse.co.uk. Two above-average B&Bs, run by the same vivacious couple. Great breakfasts, patio garden and an iron and a fridge for guests to use. Doubles from £65.

Piccadilly and Mayfair

The Metropolitan Old Park Lane ☎020/7447 1000, ⊛www.metropolitan .co.uk. This terrifyingly trendy hotel adheres to the fad for pared-down minimalism. Its Japanese restaurant is outstanding, and the bar is very fashionable. Doubles from around £250.

No. 5 Maddox Street 5 Maddox St ☎020/7647 0200, ⊛www .5maddoxstreet.com. With a very discreet entrance, this complex of suites is all bamboo flooring and trendy minimalist decor. Each has an open fireplace, workstation, TV, kitchen and decked balcony, and muji foldaway bikes are available. Suites from £230.

The Ritz 150 Piccadilly ☎020/7300 2308, ⊛www.theritzhotel.co.uk. In a class of its own, with extravagant Louis XVI interiors and air of decadent luxury. Rooms maintain the opulent French theme. Doubles from around £350.

Marylebone

Durrants Hotel George St ☎020/7935 8131, ⊛www.durrantshotel.co.uk. This Georgian terrace hotel is a great exercise in period-piece nostalgia, with doormen, lots of wood panelling and old prints. Doubles from £140.

Edward Lear Hotel 28–30 Seymour St ☎020/7402 5401, ⊛www.edlear.com. Great location, lovely flower boxes and a plush foyer. Though the rooms themselves need a bit of a makeover, the low prices reflect both this and the fact that most have shared facilities. Doubles from £70.

Hotel La Place 17 Nottingham Place ☎020/7486 2323, ⊛www.hotellaplace.com. Small, good-value place; the en-suite rooms are equipped with lots of gadgets and comfortably furnished. Doubles from £120.

Lincoln House Hotel 33 Gloucester Place ☎020/7486 7630, ⊛www .lincoln-house-hotel.co.uk. Wood panelling gives this Georgian B&B a ship's cabin feel; rooms are en suite and well equipped. Doubles from £80.

Wigmore Court Hotel 23 Gloucester Place ☎020/7935 0928, ⊛www .wigmore-court-hotel.co.uk. Better than average Georgian B&B, boasting comfortable rooms en suite, as well as a laundry and a basic kitchen for guests' use. Doubles from £75.

Soho

The Fielding Hotel 4 Broad Court, Bow Street ☎020/7836 8305, ⊛www .the-fielding-hotel.co.uk. Quiet, traffic-free location that's a firm favourite with visiting performers, since it's just a few yards from the Royal Opera House. Breakfast is extra. Doubles from £100.

Hazlitt's 6 Frith St ☎020/7434 1771, ⊛www.hazlittshotel.com. Early eighteenth-century hotel of real character and charm, offering en-suite rooms decorated as close to period style as convenience and comfort allow. Continental breakfast (served in the rooms) is extra. Doubles from £230.

Manzi's 1–2 Leicester St ☎020/7734 0224, ⊛www.manzis.co.uk. Above a restaurant of the same name, this is one of very few easily affordable West End hotels, although noise might prove to be a nuisance. Continental breakfast is included.

Doubles from £70.

Oxford Street YHA 14 Noel St
℡020/7734 1618,
✉oxfordst@yha.org.uk. The West End
location and modest size mean booking
ahead is essential here. No café, but a large
kitchen. Dorms from £25.

Bloomsbury

The Academy 21 Gower St ℡020/7631
4115, ✇www.theetoncollection.com.
Very smart place popular with business folk.
Service is excellent, all rooms are air-conditioned, with luxurious bathrooms, and there
are two lovely patio gardens. Doubles from
£180.

Ashlee House 261–265 Gray's Inn Rd
℡020/7833 9400,
✇www.ashleehouse.co.uk. Basic, clean
and friendly hostel in a converted office
block. Breakfast is included. Dorm beds for
around £20; twins from £50.

Hotel Cavendish 75 Gower St
℡020/7636 9079, ✇www
.hotelcavendish.com. A real bargain, with
welcoming owners, a lovely walled garden
and some quite well-preserved original features. All rooms have shared facilities.
Doubles from £50.

**Crescent Hotel 49–50 Cartwright
Gardens** ℡020/7387 1515, ✇www
.crescenthoteloflondon.com.
Comfortable and tastefully decorated B&B,
with a lovely blacked-up range in the
breakfast room. All rooms are en suite.
Doubles from £90.

**Generator Compton Place, off Tavistock
Place** ℡020/7388 7666, ✇www
.the-generator.co.uk. Huge, funky hostel
tucked away down a cobbled street. The
post-industrial decor may not be to everyone's taste, but it's a bargain. Breakfast
included. Dorms from around £15; doubles
from £25.

Jenkins Hotel 45 Cartwright Gardens
℡020/7387 2067, ✇www.jenkinshotel
.demon.co.uk. Smartly kept, family-run
place with just fourteen fairly small but well-
equipped rooms, most of which are en suite.
Doubles from £85.

Museum Inn 27 Montague St
℡020/7580 5360,
✇www.astorhostels.com. Quiet Astor
hostel (for under 30s), set in a lovely
Georgian house. No bar, though still a
sociable, laid-back place with a small
kitchen, TV lounge, Internet access and
breakfast included. Dorms from £15; doubles from £45.

**myhotel 11–13 Bayley St, Bedford
Square** ℡020/7667 6000, ✇www
.myhotels.co.uk. Feng shui hotel, with
small, double-glazed, air-conditioned rooms,
a gym, a very pleasant library and a sushi
restaurant. Doubles from £220.

Ridgemount Hotel 65–67 Gower St
℡020/7636 1141, ✇www
.ridgemounthotel.co.uk. Old-fashioned,
very friendly family-run place, with small
rooms – half with shared facilities – a
garden, free hot-drinks machine and a
laundry service. Cash only. Doubles from
£50.

Hotel Russell Russell Square
℡020/7837 6470,
✇www.lemeridien.com. From its grand
1898 exterior to its opulent interiors of
marble, wood and crystal, this late-
Victorian landmark fully retains its period
atmosphere in all its public areas. Rooms
live up to the grandeur of the lobby, if not
necessarily to its style. Doubles from
£130.

St Pancras YHA 79–81 Euston Rd
℡020/7388 9998 ✉stpancras@yha.org
.uk. Big hostel with very clean, bright,
triple-glazed, air-conditioned dorms and
private rooms, some even en suite. Dorms
from £25; twins from £50.

Thanet Hotel 8 Bedford Place
℡020/7636 2869, ✇www.thanethotel
.co.uk. Small, friendly, family-run B&B
close to the British Museum. Rooms are
clean, bright and freshly decorated, all with
en-suite showers and tea- and coffee-mak-
ing facilities. The same people run the
neighbouring *Pickwick* hostel. Doubles from
£95.

Covent Garden

One Aldwych 1 Aldwych ℡020/7300
1000, ✇www.onealdwych.com. Very
fashionable, minimalist luxury hotel with
underwater music in the hotel pool, oodles

Hotels, B&Bs and hostels

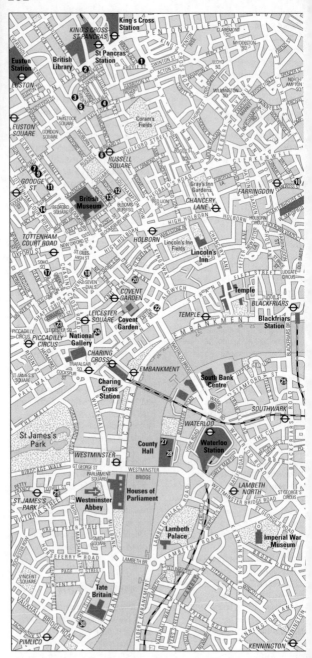

CENTRAL LONDON – EAST

ACCOMMODATION

Academy	11	Great Eastern	15
Ashlee House	1	Hazlitt's	17
Cavendish	7	Jenkins	3
City Hotel	16	Mad Hatter	25
City Inn	30	Malmaison	8
City of London YHA	21	Manzi's	23
County Hall		Marriott London	
Travel Inn	28	County Hall	27
Crescent	5	Museum Inn	13
Fielding	20	myhotel	14
Generator	4	One Aldwych	22

Ridgemount	9
The Rookery	10
Russell	6
St Christopher's	
Village	26
St Martin's Lane	24
St Pancras YHA	2
Sanctuary House	29
Seven Dials	18
Thanet	12
Threadneedles	19

of modern art, and TVs in the bathrooms. Rooms from around £225.

St Martin's Lane 45 St Martin's Lane ☏020/7300 5500 or 0800/634 5500, ⊛www.ianschragerhotels.com. Self-consciously chic "boutique hotel" from the New York-based Ian Schrager chain, with the startling *Light Bar* and the sushi *Sea Bar* on site. Doubles start around £250.

Seven Dials Hotel 7 Monmouth St ☏020/7681 0791, ⊛www.infotel.co.uk. Pleasant, small, family-run hotel in an outstanding location; the en-suite rooms have TV and tea/coffee-making facilities. Doubles from £75.

Smithfield and Clerkenwell

Malmaison Charterhouse Square ☏020/7012 3700, ⊛www.malmaison .com. The Victorian red-brick facade gives way to modern, understated decor in muted tones; well-equipped rooms have enormous beds and the restaurant is very good. Doubles from £165.

The Rookery 12 Peter's Lane, Cowcross Street ☏020/7336 0931, ⊛www .rookeryhotel.com. Rambling Georgian town house that makes a fantastically discreet little hideaway. Decor is a deliciously camp, modern take on the Baroque period. Doubles from £265.

The City

City of London YHA 36 Carter Lane ☏020/7236 4965, ℮city@yha.org.uk. Crowded, 200-bed hostel opposite St Paul's Cathedral. Dorms from £25; twins from £50.

Great Eastern Hotel Liverpool St ☏020/7618 5010, ⊛www.great -eastern-hotel.co.uk. This venerable late-nineteenth-century station hotel has had a minimalist makeover, yet manages to retain much of its clubby flavour. Doubles from around £150 at the weekend.

Threadneedles 5 Threadneedle St ☏020/7657 8080, ⊛www .theetoncollection.com. Magnificent former Midland Bank building, now converted into a boutique hotel, with every mod con from plasma TV screens to cordless digital telephones. Doubles from around £150.

Hoxton and Spitalfields

City Hotel 12 Osborn St ☏020/7247 3313, ⊛www.cityhotellondon.co.uk. Spacious, clean and modern with plainly decorated en-suite rooms, some with kitchens; four-person rooms are a bargain for families or small groups. Doubles from £150.

Docklands

Four Seasons Hotel Canary Wharf 46 Westferry Circus ☏020/7510 1999, ⊛www.fourseasons.com. A spectacular riverfront setting, ultra-modern interiors, pool, fitness centre, spa, tennis courts and the option of taking the boat into town. Doubles from £175. See map on p.136.

South Bank

London County Hall Travel Inn Belvedere Rd ☏020/7902 1619, ⊛www.travelinn.co.uk. No river views at these prices, but the County Hall location is pretty good. Decor and ambience are functional, but the flat-rate rooms are a bargain. Rooms from £80.

Mad Hatter 3–7 Stamford St ☏020/7401 9222, ⊛www.fullershotels.co.uk. Situated above a pub on the corner of Blackfriars Road. Breakfast is extra, weekend deals are good and the location is great. Doubles from £85.

Marriott London County Hall Hotel County Hall ☏020/7928 5200, ⊛www.marriott.com. Expensive and plush County Hall hotel, with the majority of rooms offering river views (many have small balconies too). Full-size indoor pool and well-equipped gym. Doubles from around £200.

Bankside and Southwark

St Christopher's Village 161–165 Borough High St ☎020/7407 1856, ⊛www.st-christophers.co.uk. Efficiently run hostel, with upbeat, cheerful decor and a party-animal ambience. Dorms from £10; twins from £55.

Hyde Park and Kensington Gardens

Leinster Inn 7–12 Leinster Square ☎020/7229 9641, ⊛www.astorhostels.com. Biggest and liveliest of the Astor hostels for under 30s, with a party atmosphere. Dorms from £15; twins from £45.

South Kensington, Knightsbridge and Chelsea

Aster House 3 Sumner Place ☎020/7581 5888, ⊛www.asterhouse.com. Pleasant, non-smoking B&B in a luxurious white-stuccoed street; there's a lovely garden at the back and a large conservatory, where breakfast is served. Doubles from around £140 a night.
Five Sumner Place 5 Sumner Place ☎020/7584 7586, ⊛www .sumnerplace.com. Discreetly luxurious B&B in a pretty white-stuccoed terrace; all rooms are en suite and breakfast is served in the lovely conservatory. Doubles from £130.
Hotel 167 167 Old Brompton Rd ☎020/7373 3221, ⊛www.hotel167.com. Small, stylishly furnished B&B with en-suite facilities, double glazing and fridges in all rooms. Continental buffet-style breakfast is served in the attractive morning room/reception. Doubles from £90.
Sloane Hotel 29 Draycott Place ☎020/7581 5757, ⊛www.sloanehotel.com. Discreet hotel hidden in a terrace of red-brick mansions, sumptuously stuffed full of antiques. There's

also a fab roof terrace for breakfast (which costs extra). Doubles from £230.

High Street Kensington to Notting Hill

Abbey House 11 Vicarage Gate ☎020/7721 7395, ⊛www .abbeyhousekensington.com. Inexpensive Victorian B&B in a quiet street just north of Kensington High Street, maintained to a very high standard by its attentive owners. Rooms are large and bright – prices are kept down by sharing facilities. Full English breakfast. Cash only. Doubles from £75.
Holland House YHA Holland Walk ☎020/7937 0748 ⊛hollandhouse@yha.org.uk. Idyllically situated in the wooded expanse of Holland Park, this extensive hostel offers a decent kitchen and an inexpensive café. Dorms from around £20.
The Pavilion Hotel 34–36 Sussex Gardens ☎020/7262 0905, ⊛www .msi.com.mt/pavilion. The successful rock star's home from home, with outrageously over-the-top decor and every room individually themed. Doubles from £100.
Portobello Hotel 22 Stanley Gardens ☎020/7727 2777, ⊛www .portobello-hotel.co.uk. Elegant Victorian hotel with individually designed double rooms of varying sizes and prices, the most expensive overlooking the private gardens. Breakfast is included and there's a restaurant and 24hr bar. Doubles from £160.
Vicarage Hotel 10 Vicarage Gate ☎020/7229 4030, ⊛www .londonvicaragehotel.com. Ideally located B&B with clean rooms (some with shared facilities), and a full English breakfast included. Cash only. Doubles from £80.

Regent's Park and Camden

30 King Henry's Road 30 King Henry's Road ☎020/7483 2871, ⊛eingram@30kinghenrysroad.co.uk. Handsome Victorian terraced house B&B

with spacious rooms, resident dog and a real homely feel. Doubles from around £100.

International Students House 229 Great Portland St ☎020/7631 8300, ⊛**www.ish.org.uk.** Hundreds of beds in a vast complex at the southern end of Regent's Park. Beds from around £15.

Hampstead and Highgate

The places listed below appear on the map on pp.176–7.

Hampstead Heath YHA 4 Wellgarth Rd ☎020/8458 9054, ⊛**hampstead@yha.org.uk.** Large and well-appointed hostel, with its own garden and the wilds of Hampstead Heath nearby. Dorms from £20; twins from £45.

Hampstead Village Guesthouse 2 Kemplay Rd ☎020/7435 8679, ⊛**www.hampsteadguesthouse.com.** Lovely B&B in an old house set in a quiet backstreet near the Heath. Rooms (not all en suite) have "lived-in" clutter. Doubles from £75.

Langorf Hotel 20 Frognal ☎020/7794 4483, ⊛**www.langorfhotel.com.** Pristinely maintained, tastefully decorated hotel in a trio of red-brick Victorian mansions, with a walled garden. Doubles from £100.

Essentials

Essentials

Arrival

London's international **airports** are all less than an hour from the city centre, and the city's **train** and **bus** terminals are all pretty central, and have tube stations close at hand.

By plane

Heathrow Airport (☎0870/000 0123; ☯www.baa.co.uk), 15 miles west of central London, has four terminals and is served by two train/tube stations: one for terminals 1, 2 and 3, and another for terminal 4. The **Heathrow Express** (☎0845/600 1515, ☯www.heathrowexpress.co.uk) travels non-stop to Paddington Station (every 15min; 15–20min) for £13 each way or £25 return (£2 more if you buy your ticket on board). Cheaper but slower is the Piccadilly **Underground** line into central London (every 5–9min; 50min) for £3.70 one-way. If you plan to make several journeys on your arrival day, buy a Travelcard (see p.210) rather than a single-destination ticket. **National Express** (☎0870/580 8080, ☯www.go-by-coach.com) run buses from Heathrow's central bus station direct to central London's Victoria Coach Station (every 30min; 1hr), while **Airbus** #2 (☎0870/574 7777) runs from outside all four Heathrow terminals to several destinations in the city (every 30min; 1hr); tickets for either cost £10 single, £15 return. After midnight, you'll have to take **night bus** #N9 to Trafalgar Square (every 30min; 1hr) for a bargain fare of £1. A **taxi** will cost £45 to central London, and take an hour (longer in the rush hour).

Gatwick (☎0870/000 2468; ☯www .baa.co.uk), 30 miles to the south, has two terminals, North and South, connected by a monorail. The **Gatwick Express** (☎0870/ 530 1530, ☯www.gatwickexpress.co.uk) train runs non-stop between the South Terminal and Victoria Station (every 15–30min; 30min) for £11 single, £21.50 return. A taxi ride into central London will set you back £90 or more, and take at least an hour.

Stansted (☎0870/000 0303; ☯www.baa.co.uk) lies 35 miles northeast, and is served by the **Stansted Express** to Liverpool Street (every 15–30min; 45min), which costs £13 single, £23 return. **Airbus** #6 also runs 24 hours a day to Victoria Coach Station (every 30min; 1hr 30min), and costs £10 single, £15 return. A taxi into central London will cost around £75, and take at least an hour.

Luton airport (☎01582/405100; ☯www.london-luton.com) is roughly 30 miles north of London, and mostly handles charter flights. A free shuttle-bus takes five minutes to transport passengers to Luton Airport Parkway station, connected by **Thameslink** trains to King's Cross and other stations (every 15min; 30–40min) for £10 single, £20 return. Alternatively, **Green Line** buses (☎0870/608 7261, ☯www.greenline.co.uk) run from Luton to Victoria Station (every 30min; 1hr 15min), costing £8 single, £11.50 return. A **taxi** will cost around £70 and take at least an hour to reach central London.

City airport (☎020/7646 0000, ☯www.londoncityairport.com), the capital's smallest, is situated nine miles east of central London in the Docklands area. It handles European flights only, and is connected by shuttle-bus with Canning Town tube (every 5min; 5min; £2.50), Canary Wharf (every 10min; 10min; £3), and Liverpool Street (every 10min; 30min; £6). A taxi into the city's financial sector will cost around £20 and take half an hour or so.

By train and coach

Eurostar (☎0870/160 6600, ☯www.eurostar.com) trains arrive at Waterloo International station in central London. Trains from the Channel ports arrive at the equally central Charing Cross or Victoria, while boat trains from Harwich arrive at Liverpool Street, just east of the centre and linked to the tube network. Arriving by **train** (☎0845/748 4950, ☯www.nationalrail.co.uk) from elsewhere in Britain, you'll come into one of London's numerous main-line stations, all of which have adjacent Underground stations linking into the city centre's tube network. Coming into London **by coach** (☎0870/580 8080, ✆www.go-by-coach .com), you're most likely to arrive at Victoria Coach Station, a couple of hundred yards south down Buckingham Palace Road from Victoria train station and tube.

Information

The main tourist office is the **Britain and London Visitor Centre**, near Piccadilly Circus at 1 Regent Street (Mon–Fri 9am–6.30pm, Sat & Sun 10am–4pm; ☎020/7808 3864, ✆www.visitbritain .com). The **London Visitor Centre**, run by the capital's own tourist board, Visit London, is in Waterloo International train station (Mon–Sat 8.30am–10.30pm, Sun 9.30am–10.30pm; ✆www.visitlondon .com).

Individual London boroughs also run **tourist offices**, the most useful of which are: on the south side of St Paul's Cathedral (May–Sept daily 9.30am–5pm; Oct–April Mon–Fri 9.30am–5pm; ☎020/7332 1456); in Greenwich's old Royal Naval College (daily 10am–5pm; ☎0870/608 2000); and inside Richmond's Old Town Hall (Mon–Fri 10am–5pm; Easter–Sept also Sat & Sun 10.30am–1.30pm; ☎020/8940 9125).

For "**what's on**" information, buy the weekly listings magazine *Time Out* (£2.20), published every Tuesday after-noon. In it you'll find details of all the latest exhibitions, shows, films, music, sport, guided walks and events in and around the capital.

Websites

✆ **www.24hourmuseum.co.uk** Up-to-date information on virtually every single museum, large or small, in London.

✆ **www.londonnet.co.uk** A virtual guide to London with useful up-to-date listings on eating, drinking and nightlife.

✆ **www.myvillage.com** Huge site that covers every district/borough in London, giving club, music, cinema and theatre listings, restaurant reviews, plus local gossip and messageboards.

✆ **www.streetmap.co.uk** Type in the London address you want and this site will locate it for you in seconds.

✆ **www.thisislondon.com** Website of The *Evening Standard*, London's only daily newspaper, with constantly updated news and listings.

City transport

London's transport network is among the most complex and expensive in the world. You can get a free transport map from any tube station, or from one of the more comprehensive Transport for London (TfL) **travel information offices**, at Piccadilly Circus tube station (daily 8.45am–6pm); there are other desks at the arrivals at Heathrow (terminals 1, 2, & 4), Oxford Circus and St James's Park (Mon–Fri only) tubes, Victoria Coach Station, and Euston, King's Cross, Liverpool Street, Paddington and Victoria train stations. There's also a 24-hour phone line and a website for transport information (☎020/7222 1234; ✆www.tfl.gov.uk). If you can, avoid travelling during the **rush hour** (Mon–Fri 8–9.30am & 5–7pm) when tubes become unbearably crowded, and some buses get so full they won't let you on.

Travelcards

To get the best value out of the public transport system, buy a **Travelcard**. Available from machines and booths at all tube and train stations (and at some newsagents as well), a Travelcard is valid for the bus, tube, Docklands Light Railway, Tramlink and suburban rail networks. **Day Travelcards** come in two varieties: Off-Peak – which are valid after 9.30am on weekdays and all day during the weekend – and Peak, valid at all times. An Off-Peak Day Travelcard costs £4.30 for the central zones 1 and 2, rising to £5.40 for zones 1–6 (including Heathrow); the Peak Day Travelcard starts at £5.30 for zones 1 and 2. **Weekend Travelcards**, for unlimited travel on Saturdays and Sundays, start at £6.40 for zone 1 and 2. **Weekly Travelcards** begin at £20.20 for zones 1 and 2. Travelcards also give you discounts on boat services (see p.210).

The tube

Except for very small journeys, the Underground – or **tube** – is by far the quickest way to get about. Each line has its own colour and name – all you need to know is which direction you're travelling in: northbound, eastbound, southbound or westbound. Services operate from around 5.30am Monday to Saturday, and from 7.30am on Sundays, and end around 12.30am every day; you rarely have to wait more than five minutes for a train between central stations.

Tickets must be bought in advance from the machines or booths in station entrance halls; if you cannot produce a valid ticket, you will be charged an on-the-spot Penalty Fare of £10. A single journey in the central zone costs an unbelievable £2, but if you're intending to travel about a lot, a Travelcard is a better bet.

The driverless **Docklands Light Railway** (see p.134), which connects the City with Docklands, Greenwich and parts of the East End, is an integral part of the tube system. Travelcards are valid on the DLR, which also has its own selection of tickets and passes.

Buses

Tickets for bus journeys within London cost £1; unless you have a Travelcard, you must buy your ticket beforehand from one of the machines by the bus stop. The only exception is on those routes covered by older Routemaster buses, staffed by a conductor and with an open rear platform. Note that at request stops (easily recognizable by their red sign) you must stick your arm out to hail the bus you want (or ring the bell if you want to get off). In addition to the Travelcards mentioned opposite, a **One-Day Bus Pass** (zones 1–4) is also available for £2.50 and can be used before 9.30am.

Regular buses run between about 6am and midnight; **night buses** (prefixed with the letter "N") operate outside this period. Night bus routes radiate out from Trafalgar Square at approximately twenty to thirty-minute intervals, more frequently on some routes and on Friday and Saturday nights. Fares are the same as for daytime buses and Travelcards are valid. Useful bus routes appear on the front-cover flap map.

Taxis

Compared to most capital cities, London's metered **black cabs** are an expensive option – a ride from Euston to Victoria, for example, costs around £10, more at weekends and after 8pm on weekdays. The **meter** will show two amounts: one calculates distance and time, while the other is the fixed charge for passengers, luggage and any off-peak extras – after these are totalled, a small tip is customary. A yellow light over the windscreen tells you if the cab is available – just stick your arm out to hail it. To order a black cab in advance, phone ☎020/7272 0272.

Minicabs are considerably cheaper, but can only be phoned for in advance and are something of a law unto themselves. Avoid taxi touts as they are illegal, and always establish the fare beforehand as minicabs are not metered.

Sightseeing tours and guided walks

Standard **sightseeing bus tours** in open-top double-deckers with live commentary are run by several rival companies. The Original Tour (☎020/8877 1722, ⊛www.theoriginaltour.com) and the Big Bus Company (☎0800/169 1365, ⊛www.bigbus.co.uk) run several buses on various routes (daily 9am–5pm; every

15–20min; around £17) and you can get on and off as often as you like. Pick-up points include Victoria station, Marble Arch, Trafalgar Square and other conspicuous tourist spots.

Walking tours are infinitely more appealing and informative, covering a relatively small area in much greater detail,

mixing solid historical facts with juicy anecdotes in the company of a local specialist. They cost £5 and take around two hours; normally you can simply show up at the starting point and join. Details of walks appear in *Time Out* magazine (see p.210); alternatively, contact Original London Walks (☎020/7624 3978, ✆www.walks.com).

Entertainment

On any night of the week London offers a bewildering range of things to do after dark, ranging from top-flight opera and theatre to clubs.

Theatre

The **West End** is the heart of London's "Theatreland", with Shaftesbury Avenue its most congested drag. All of the shows are listed in the weekly *Time Out* and at ✆www.albemarle-london.com.

Tickets under £10 are restricted to the Fringe; the box-office average is closer to £15–25, with £30–40 the usual top-whack. Agencies such as Ticketmaster (☎020/7344 4444, ✆www.ticketmaster .co.uk) or First Call (☎020/7497 9977, ✆www.firstcalltickets.com), can get seats for most West End shows, but add up to ten percent on the ticket price. The Society of London Theatre (✆www.officiallondontheatre.co.uk) runs the **tkts ticket booth** in Leicester Square (Mon–Sat 10am–7pm, Sun noon–3pm), which sells on-the-day tickets for all the West End shows at discounts of up to fifty percent, though they tend to be in the top end of the price range, are limited to four per person, and carry a service charge of £2.50 per ticket. What follows is a list of those West End theatres that offer a changing roster of good plays, along with the most consistent of the Off West End and Fringe venues.

Theatres

Almeida Almeida St ☎020/7359 4404, ✆www.almeida.co.uk. Excellent new plays and excitingly reworked classics.

Barbican Centre Silk St ☎020/7638 8891, ✆www.barbican.org.uk. The two venues here see everything from puppetry and musicals to new drama works and, of course, Shakespeare, courtesy of the Royal Shakespeare Company. See p.119.

Donmar Warehouse Thomas Neal's, Earlham St ☎020/7369 1732, ✆www.donmar-warehouse.com. Noted for new plays and top-quality reappraisals of the classics.

Drill Hall 16 Chenies St ☎020/7307 5060, ✆www.drillhall.co.uk. This studio-style venue specializing in gay, lesbian, feminist and politically correct new work.

ICA Nash House, The Mall ☎020/7930 3647, ✆www.ica.org.uk. The ICA attracts the most innovative practitioners in all areas of performance; the hits outweigh the misses.

King's Head 115 Upper St ☎020/7226 1916. The oldest and probably most famous of London's thriving pub-theatres, staging adventurous performances in a pint-sized room.

National Theatre South Bank Centre, South Bank ☎020/7452 3000, ✆www.nationaltheatre.org.uk. Three performance spaces, each attracting the country's top actors and directors in programmes ranging from Greek tragedies to Broadway musicals. See p.142.

Open Air Theatre Regent's Park, Inner Circle ☎020/7486 2431, ✆openairtheatre.org. Summer programme of Shakespeare, musicals, plays and concerts.

Royal Court Sloane Square ☎020/7565 5000, ✆www.royalcourttheatre.com. Best place in London to catch radical new writing.

Shakespeare's Globe New Globe Walk ☎020/7902 1400, ✆www.shakespeares-globe.org. Solid, fun Shakespearean shows from mid-May to mid-September, with "groundling" tickets (standing-room only) for around £5. See p.148.

Opera

English National Opera Coliseum, St Martin's Lane ☎020/7632 8300, ✆www.eno.org. The cheaper and more experimental of London's two opera houses, with all operas sung in English. Ticket prices start from as little as £3, rising to just over £60; day seats are also available to personal callers after 10am on the day of the performance, with balcony seats going for just £3. Three hours before the performance, standbys (all tickets that are unsold) go on sale at £12.50 to students and £18.00 to senior citizens and the unemployed.

Royal Opera House Bow St ☎020/7304 4000, ✆www.royaloperahouse.org. The Floral Hall hosts regular free lunchtime recitals, and there are modestly priced, small-scale productions in the studio-sized Linbury Theatre. The ROH main auditorium remains over-priced (over £120 for the best seats). A small number of day seats (for £30 or under) are put on sale from 10am on the day of a performance – these are restricted to one per person, and you need to get there by 8am for popular shows. Four hours before performances, low-price standbys (subject to availability) can be bought for around £15 by students, senior citizens etc. See p.108.

Dance

London Coliseum St Martin's Lane ☎020/7632 8300, ✆www.eno.org. Performances here by the touring company of the English National Ballet (ENB; ✆www.ballet.org.uk) include a regular Christmas slot.

The Place 17 Duke's Rd ☎020/7387 0031, ✆www.theplace.org.uk. New choreographers and student performers, and some fine small-scale contemporary dance from across the globe.

Royal Ballet Royal Opera House, Bow St ☎020/7304 4000, ✆www.royaloperahouse.org. Recent refurbishment of the ROH has added two small performing spaces, where experimental ballets are staged. You should be able to get decent seats for around £25 if you buy early, though sell-outs are frequent (see Royal Opera House, above, for details of day tickets and standbys).

Sadler's Wells Rosebery Ave ☎020/7863 8000, ✆www.sadlers-wells.com. Home of Britain's best contemporary dance companies, and visited by many of the finest international companies. As well as the main auditorium, the Lilian Baylis space, tucked around the back, puts on smaller-scale shows.

Comedy

Comedy Café 66 Rivington St ☎020/7739 5706, ✆www.comedycafe.co.uk. Long-established, purpose-built club in Hoxton, often with impressive lineups. Free admission for the new-acts slot on Wednesday. Wed–Sat.

Comedy Store Haymarket House, 1a Oxendon St ☎020/7344 0234, ✆www.thecomedystore.co.uk. Closed Mon. Improvisation on Wednesdays and Sundays, in addition to a stand-up bill; Friday and Saturday are the busiest nights, with two shows, at 8pm and midnight – book ahead.

Jongleurs Camden Lock Dingwalls Building, 36 Camden Lock Place, Chalk Farm Road; box office ☎020/7564 2500, information ☎0870/7870707, ✆www.jongleurs.com. The chain store of comedy, doling out high quality stand-up and post-revelry disco-dancing on Fridays. Book well in advance.

Live music and clubs

Astoria 157 Charing Cross Rd ☎020/7454 9592, ✆www.meanfiddler.com. One of London's best and most central medium-sized venues, generally hosting slightly alternative bands (from underground US hip-hop to thrashing rock). Club nights on Friday and Saturday.

Bagley's King's Cross Goods Yard, off York Way ☎020/7278 2777. Vast warehouse-style venue in a post-apocalyptic industrial estate. Perfect for enormous raves.

Bar Rumba 36 Shaftesbury Ave ☎020/7287 2715, ⓦwww.barrumba.co.uk. Fun, smallish venue with an adventurous mix of nights ranging from future-jazz on Mondays to glamorous house sessions at weekends.

Cargo 83 Rivington St ☎020/7739 5446, ⓦwww.cargo-london.com. Club and live music venue offering modern-genre mixups that blend jazz with Brazilian, Latin and African music, often complemented by DJs.

The End 18 West Central St ☎020/7419 9199, ⓦwww.the-end.co.uk. Large and spacious, with chrome minimalist decor and a devastating sound system. Best for tech-house at weekends, or anything-goes bacchanalia on Mondays.

Fabric 77a Charterhouse St ☎020/7336 8898, ⓦwww.fabriclondon.com. Cavernous three-room underground space holding 2500 people. Fridays are Fabric Live, a mix of drum'n'bass and hip-hop that features lives acts, while Saturdays see cutting-edge house from big-name DJs.

Jazz Café 5 Parkway ☎020/7916 6060, ⓦwww.jazzcafe.co.uk. Futuristic venue with an adventurous booking policy exploring Latin, rap, funk, hip-hop and musical fusions.

Ministry of Sound 103 Gaunt St ☎020/7378 6528, ⓦwww.ministryofsound.co.uk. Vast, state-of-the-art enterprise with an exceptional sound system and the pick of visiting US and Italian DJs. Corporate clubbing and full of tourists, but it still draws the top talent, especially on Saturdays.

Ronnie Scott's 47 Frith St ☎020/7439 0747, ⓦwww.ronniescotts.co.uk. London's most famous jazz club: small, smoky and still going strong. *The* place for top-line names, – book a table, or you'll have to stand.

Scala 278 Pentonville Rd ☎020/7833 2022, ⓦwww.scala-london.co.uk. Unusual and multi-faceted nights that take in film, live bands and music ranging from quirky hip-hop to drum'n'bass and deep house.

Shepherds Bush Empire Shepherds Bush Green ☎020/8771 2000. Grand old theatre that now plays host to the finest cross-section of mid-league UK and US bands in the capital.

12 Bar Club 22–23 Denmark Place ☎020/7916 6989, ⓦwww.12barclub.com. A combination of live blues and contemporary country seven nights a week.

Turnmills 63 Clerkenwell Rd ☎020/7250 3409, ⓦwww.turnmills.com. Famed for the glorious gay extravaganza, Trade, which begins on Sunday morning at 4am, this is the place to come if you want to sweat from dusk till dawn.

Wigmore Hall 36 Wigmore St ☎020/7935 2141, ⓦwww.wigmore-hall .org.uk. Popular classical music venue, boasting near-perfect accoustics, that's best-known for performances of chamber music, and for recitals from some of the world's greatest singers. Mid-morning Sunday performances are especially busy.

Festivals and events

January 1
London Parade A procession of floats, marching bands, clowns, American cheerleaders and classic cars wends its way at noon from Parliament Square to Berkeley Square. ☎020/8566 8586, ⓦwww.londonparade.co.uk.

Late January/Early February
Chinese New Year Celebrations Chinatown explodes in a riot of dancing dragons, firecrackers and heaving crowds. ⓦwww.chinatown-on-line.org.uk.

Late March/Early April
Oxford and Cambridge Boat Race Since 1845, Oxford and Cambridge university rowers have battled it out on a four-mile, upstream course on the Thames from

Putney to Mortlake.
🌐 www.theboatrace.org.

Third Sunday in April
London Marathon The world's most popular city marathon, with over 40,000 runners sweating the 26.2 miles from Greenwich Park to Westminster Bridge. ☎ 020/7620 4117, 🌐 www.london-marathon.co.uk.

May Bank Holiday Weekend
IWA Canal Cavalcade Lively celebration of the city's inland waterways held at Little Venice (near Warwick Avenue): decorated narrowboats, Morris dancers and children's activities. 🌐 www.waterways.org.uk.

Third or Fourth Week in May
Chelsea Flower Show The world's finest horticultural event, with the public admitted only for the closing stages (the last two days). Tickets must be bought in advance: ☎ 0870/906 3781, 🌐 www.rhs.org.uk.

Late May/Early June
Beating Retreat Annual military display held on Horse Guards' Parade over three evenings, marking the old custom of drumming the troops back to base at dusk, followed by a floodlit performance by the Massed Bands of the Queen's Household Cavalry. ☎ 020/7739 5323, 🌐 www.army .mod.uk/ceremonialandheritage.

June–August
Morris Dancing This ancient, peculiarly English form of folk dancing can be seen outside Westminster Abbey every Wednesday evening.

Second Saturday in June
Trooping the Colour The Queen's official birthday celebrations, featuring massed bands, gun salutes and fly-pasts. Tickets for the ceremony itself must be applied for before the end of February, but there are free rehearsals (minus Her Majesty) on the two preceding Saturdays. ☎ 020/7414 2479.

Last Week of June and First Week of July
Wimbledon Lawn Tennis Championships This Grand Slam tournament is one of the highlights of the sporting and social calendar. ☎ 020/8946 2244, 🌐 www.wimbledon.org.

Early July
Pride in the Park/Mardi Gras Colourful, whistleblowing lesbian and gay march through the city streets followed by a huge, ticketed party in a London park. 🌐 www.londonmardigras.com.

Mid-July to Mid-September
BBC Henry Wood Promenade Concerts The Proms are a series of outstanding nightly classical concerts at the Royal Albert Hall, with standing-room tickets from as little as £3. ☎ 020/7589 8212, 🌐 www.bbc.co.uk/proms. See p.156.

Last bank holiday weekend in August
Notting Hill Carnival The two-day free festival is the longest-running, best-known and biggest street party in Europe, a tumult of imaginatively decorated floats, eye-catching costumes, thumping sound systems, irresistible food and huge crowds. 🌐 www.lnhc.org.uk.

Third Weekend in September
Open House Peek inside hundreds of buildings around London, many of which are normally closed to the public. 🌐 www.londonopenhouse.org.

September–November
Dance Umbrella Six-week season of often ground-breaking new dance work at various venues across town. ☎ 020/8741 5881, 🌐 www.danceumbrella.co.uk.

Late October/Early November
State Opening of Parliament The Queen arrives by horse-drawn coach at the Houses of Parliament at 11am, accompanied by the Household Cavalry and gun salutes. ☎ 020/7219 4272, 🌐 www.parliament.uk.

November
London Film Festival Three-week cinematic season, with scores of new international films screened at the National Film Theatre and other central venues. ☎ 020/7928 3232, 🌐 www.bfi.org.uk or (nearer the time) 🌐 www.rlff.org.uk.

Early November

London Jazz Festival Ten-day international jazz fest held in all London's jazz venues, large and small, in association with BBC Radio 3. ☎020/7405 9900, ⊛www.bbc.co.uk/radio3.

November 5

Bonfire Night In memory of Guy Fawkes – who tried to blow up King James I and the Houses of Parliament in 1605 – effigies are burned on bonfires all over London, and numerous council-run fires and fireworks displays are staged. ☎020/8365 2121.

Second Saturday in November

Lord Mayor's Show The newly appointed Lord Mayor sets off at 11.10am, in the 1756-built State Coach at the head of a vast ceremonial procession from the Guildhall to the Strand and back. Later, there's a big fireworks display on the Thames. ☎0207606 3030, ⊛www.cityoflondon.gov.uk.

Christmas (6–24 December)

Trafalgar Square carols In gratitude for British help in liberating the country from the Nazis, Norway supplies a mighty spruce tree for Trafalgar Square. Decorated with lights, it becomes the focus for carol singing versus traffic noise each evening (from 5pm) until Christmas Eve.

New Year's Eve

The New Year is welcomed en masse in Trafalgar Square as thousands of inebriated revellers stagger about and slur to Auld Lang Syne at midnight. London Transport runs free public transport all night.

Directory

AIRLINES Aer Lingus ☎0845/084 4444, ⊛www.aerlingus.com; Air France ☎0845/084 5111, ⊛www.airfrance.com /uk; Alitalia ☎0870/608 6001, ⊛www .alitalia.co.uk; American Airlines ☎020/7365 0777, ⊛www.aa.com; British Airways ☎0845/773 3377, ⊛www .britishairways.com; Buzz ☎0870/240 7070, ⊛www.buzzaway.com; Canadian Airlines ☎0870/524 7226, ⊛www .aircanada.ca; Delta ☎0800/414767, ⊛www.delta.com; easyJet ☎0870/600 0000, ⊛www.easyjet.com; KLM ☎0870/ 575 0900, ⊛www.klm.com; Lufthansa ☎0845/606 0310, ⊛www.lufthansa .co.uk; Qantas ☎0845/774 7767, ⊛www.qantas.com.au; Ryanair ☎0871/ 246 0000, ⊛www.bookryanair.com; Virgin ☎01293/450150, ⊛www.virgin-atlantic .com.

AMERICAN EXPRESS 30–31 Haymarket ☎020/7484 9600 (and other branches); ⊛www.americanexpress.com. Mon–Sat 9am–6pm, Sun 10am–5pm.

BOAT TRIPS The most central departure point for pleasure cruises along the Thames is Westminster Pier. The most popular trip is to Greenwich (every 30–40min; 1hr); typical fares are around £6.50 single, £8 return. From April to October, you can also take a boat from Westminster via Kew and Richmond to Hampton Court (3hr 30min; £12 single, £18 return); shorter trips to the Tower of London (around £3 single) are also available. For a full list of operators, pick up the Thames River Services booklet from a TfL travel information office, phone ☎020/7222 1234, or visit ⊛www.londontransport.co.uk.

CAR RENTAL Avis ☎0870/606 0100, ⊛www.avis.com; easyCar ☎0906/333 3333, ⊛www.easycar.com; Global Leisure Cars ☎0870/241 1986, ⊛www.globalleisurecars.com; Hertz ☎0870/599 6699, ⊛www.hertz.com.

CINEMAS

Electric 191 Portobello Rd ☎020/7299 8688, ⊛www.the-electric.co.uk; **ICA Cinema** Nash House, The Mall, SW1 ☎020/7930 3647, ⊛www.ica.org.uk; **BFI London IMAX Centre** South Bank, ☎020/7902 1234, ⊛www.bfi.org.uk /imax; **National Film Theatre** South Bank ☎020/7928 3232, ⊛www.bfi .org.uk/nft; **Prince Charles** 2–7 Leicester

Place ☎020/7494 3654, ⊛www
.princecharlescinema.com.

CONSULATES AND EMBASSIES
Australia, Australia House, Strand
☎020/7379 4334, ⊛www.australia.org
.uk; Canada, Canada House, Trafalgar
Square ☎020/7528 6533,
⊛www.canada.org.uk; Ireland, 17
Grosvenor Place ☎020/7235 2171,
⊛ireland.embassyhomepage.com; New
Zealand, New Zealand House, 80
Haymarket ☎020/7930 8422,
⊛www.nzembassy.com; USA, 24
Grosvenor Square ☎020/7499 9000,
⊛www.usembassy.org.uk.

DENTISTS Emergency treatment: Guy's
Hospital, St Thomas St ☎020/7955 4317
(Mon–Fri 9am–3pm).

DOCTORS Walk-in consultations are
available at Great Chapel Street Medical
Centre, Great Chapel St ☎020/7437
9360 (phone for surgery times).

ELECTRICITY Electricity supply in London
conforms to the EU standard of
approximately 230V.

EMERGENCIES For police, fire and
ambulance services, call ☎999.

HAIRDRESSERS Basecuts 252
Portobello Rd ☎020/7727 7068; **Charles
Worthington** 7 Percy St, London and
other branches ☎020/7631 1370,
⊛www.charlesworthington.co.uk; **Fish**
30 D'Arblay St ☎020/7494 2398,
⊛www.fishweb.co.uk; **Terry Jacks** 2
Bathurst St ☎020/7706 7030; **Toni &
Guy** 8 Marylebone High St and many
other branches ☎020/7240 6635,
⊛www.toniandguy.co.uk; **Trevor Sorbie**
27 Floral St ☎020/7379 6901,
⊛www.trevorsorbie.com; **Windle** 41
Shorts Gardens ☎020/7497 2393,
⊛www.windle-hair.com.

HOSPITALS For 24hr accident and
emergency: Charing Cross, Fulham
Palace Rd ☎020/8846 1234; Chelsea &
Westminster, 369 Fulham Rd ☎020/8746
8000; Royal Free, Pond St ☎020/7794
0500; Royal London, Whitechapel Rd
☎020/7377 7000; St Mary's, Praed St
☎020/7886 6666; University College,
Grafton Way ☎020/7387 9300;
Whittington, Highgate Hill ☎020/7272
3070.

ICE SKATING Leisurebox, 17 Queensway
(☎020/7229 0172), is a centrally located
year-round ice rink. From October to
March, there's the Broadgate outdoor ice
rink (☎020/7505 4068,
⊛www.broadgateestates.co.uk/ice/frame
set.htm); in the Christmas and New Year
period there are outdoor rinks at
Somerset House (⊛www.somerset-
house.org.uk) and Marble Arch
(⊛www.marblearchicerink.com).

INTERNET Most hotels, B&Bs hostels and
libraries will have Internet access; there
are also Internet cafés (£2–5 per hour)
dotted around the city;
⊛www.easyEverything.com is the
biggest chain, with eight branches.

LEFT LUGGAGE Charing Cross (daily
7am–11pm); Euston (Mon–Sat
6.45am–11.15pm, Sun 7.15am–11pm);
Victoria (daily 7am–10.15pm); Waterloo
International (daily 7am–10pm).

LOST PROPERTY Airports Gatwick
☎01293/503162 (Mon–Sat 8am–7pm,
Sun 8am–4pm); Heathrow ☎020/8745
7727 (daily 8am–4pm); London City
☎020/7646 0000 (Mon–Fri
5.30am–10pm, Sat 5.30am–1am, Sun
10am–10pm); Stansted ☎01279/680500
(daily 6am–midnight). **Buses** ☎020/7222
1234, ⊛www.londontransport.com
(24hr). **Heathrow Express** ☎020/8745
7727, ⊛www.heathrowexpress.co.uk
(daily 8am–4pm). **Taxis** (black cabs only)
☎0791/82000 (Mon–Fri 9am–4pm). **Train
stations** Euston ☎020/7387 8699
(Mon–Fri 9am–5.30pm); King's Cross
☎020/7278 3310 (Mon–Fri 9am–5.30pm);
Liverpool Street ☎020/7247 4297
(Mon–Fri 9am–5.30pm); Paddington
☎020/7313 1514 (Mon–Fri 9am–5.30pm);
Victoria ☎020/7922 9887 (daily
7am–midnight); Waterloo ☎020/7401
7861 (Mon–Fri 7.30am–8pm). **Tube trains**
London Regional Transport ☎020/7486
2496, ⊛www.londontransport.co.uk.

MARKETS Brick Lane Brick Lane,
Cygnet St, Sclater St; Bacon St, Cheshire
St, Chilton St. Sun 8am–1pm. Fruit and
veg, cheap goods, bric-a-brac.
Brixton Electric Avenue, Pope's Rd, Brixton
Station Rd, Atlantic Rd. Mon, Tues &
Thurs–Sat 8am–6pm; Wed 8am–3pm.

African and Caribbean foods, hair and beauty products, records, clothes. **Camden** Camden High St to Chalk Farm Rd. Daily 10am–6pm. A conglomeration of markets, selling food, clothes, jewellery, gifts, records, arts and crafts. **Columbia Road** Columbia Rd. Sun 8am–1pm. Flowers and plants. **Covent Garden** The Piazza, and Jubilee Market, off Southampton St. Daily 9am–5pm. Crafts, gifts, clothes and (on Mon only) antiques. **Greenwich** Greenwich High Rd, Stockwell St, and College Approach. Thurs–Sun 10am–5pm. Antiques (Thurs, Sat & Sun), crafts, clothes, food (Sat), bric-a-brac, books and furniture. **Petticoat Lane** Middlesex St and around. Mon–Fri 10am–2pm, Sun 9am–2pm. Cheap clothes. **Portobello** Portobello Rd and Golborne Rd. Mon–Wed, Fri & Sat 8.30am–6pm, Thurs 8.30am–1pm. Antiques (Sat), fruit and veg, clothes, furniture and bric-a-brac. **Old Spitalfields** Commercial St, between Brushfield St and Lamb Streets. Organic food, crafts and clothes.

MONEY The basic unit of currency is the pound sterling (£), divided into 100 pence (p). Coins come in denominations of 1p, 2p, 5p, 10p, 20p, 50p, £1 and £2; notes come in denominations of £5, £10, £20 and £50. For exchange, you"ll find a branch of at least one of the big four high-street banks (NatWest, Barclays, Lloyds TSB and HSBC) in every area; opening hours are generally Mon–Fri 9.30am–4.30pm. Outside banking hours go to a bureau de change; these can be found at train stations and airports in most areas of the city centre.

POLICE Central police stations include: Charing Cross, Agar St, WC2 ☎020/7240 1212; Holborn, 70 Theobalds Rd, WC1 ☎020/7404 1212; King's Cross, 76 King's Cross Rd, WC1 ☎020/7704 1212; West End Central, 10 Vine St, W1 ☎020/7437 1212; City of London Police, Bishopsgate, EC2 ☎020/7601 2222.

PUBLIC HOLIDAYS On the following days, all banks and offices are closed, while everyone else pretty much runs to a Sunday schedule: New Year's Day (January 1); Good Friday (late March/early April); Easter Monday (late March/early April); Spring Bank Holiday (first Monday in May); May Bank Holiday (last Monday in May); August Bank Holiday (last Monday in August); Christmas Day (December 25); Boxing Day (December 26). Note that if January 1, December 25 or December 26 falls on a Saturday or Sunday, the holiday falls on the following weekday.

SAUNAS Turkish baths: Ironmonger Row Baths, Ironmonger Row (☎020/7253 4011) and Porchester Spa, 226 Queensway ☎020/7792 3980. **Women-only**: The Sanctuary, 12 Floral St ☎0870/770 3350, ⊛www.thesanctuary.co.uk. **Gay**: Chariots 1, 201–207 Shoreditch High St; ☎020/7247 5333, ⊛www.gaysauna.co.uk.

SWIMMING Outdoor and indoor pools at Covent Garden's Oasis Sports Centre, 32 Endell St ☎020/7831 1804. Outdoor swimming at the Serpentine Lido in Hyde Park (June–Aug daily 10am–6pm; £3), or the open-air pools on Hampstead Heath (daily 7am–9pm or dusk).

TELEPHONES There should be a public payphone within five minutes' walk of wherever you're standing. Most take all coins from 10p upwards, though some take only phonecards (available from post offices and newsagents).

TIME Greenwich Mean Time (GMT) is used from October to March; for the rest of the year the country switches to British Summer Time (BST), one hour ahead of GMT.

TIPPING Porters, bellboys and table waiters rely on being tipped to bump up their often dismal wages. It's not normal, however, to leave tips in pubs, although bar staff are sometimes offered drinks, which they may accept in the form of money. Taxi drivers expect tips on long journeys – add about ten percent to the fare – as will traditional barbers.

TRAIN ENQUIRIES For national rail enquiries, call ☎0845/748 4950 or visit ⊛www.nationrail.co.uk.

TRAVEL AGENTS STA Travel, 33 Bedford St ☎020/7240 9821, ⊛www.statravel.co.uk; Trailfinders, Lower Ground Floor, Waterstone's, 203–205 Piccadilly ☎020/7292 1888, ⊛www.trailfinders.co.uk.

ROUGH GUIDES TRAVEL...

UK & Ireland
Britain
Devon & Cornwall
Dublin
Edinburgh
England
Ireland
Lake District
London
London Mini Guide
Scotland
Scottish Highlands
  & Islands
Wales

Europe
Algarve
Amsterdam
Andalucía
Austria
Baltic States
Barcelona
Belgium &
  Luxembourg
Berlin
Brittany &
  Normandy
Bruges & Ghent
Brussels
Budapest
Bulgaria
Copenhagen
Corfu
Corsica
Costa Brava
Crete
Croatia
Cyprus
Czech & Slovak
  Republics
Dodecanese & East
  Aegean
Dordogne & Lot
Europe
Florence
France
Germany
Greece
Greek Islands
Hungary

Ibiza & Formentera
Iceland
Ionian Islands
Italy
Languedoc &
  Roussillon
Lisbon
The Loire
Madeira
Madrid
Mallorca
Malta & Gozo
Menorca
Moscow
Netherlands
Norway
Paris
Paris Mini Guide
Poland
Portugal
Prague
Provence & the
  Côte d'Azur
Pyrenees
Romania
Rome
Sardinia
Scandinavia
Sicily
Slovenia
Spain
St Petersburg
Sweden
Switzerland
Tenerife & La
  Gomera
Turkey
Tuscany & Umbria
Venice
Vienna

Asia
Bali & Lombok
Bangkok
Beijing
Cambodia
China
Goa
Hong Kong &
  Macau

India
Indonesia
Japan
Laos
Malaysia,
  Singapore &
  Brunei
Nepal
Philippines
Singapore
South India
Southeast Asia
Thailand
Thailand's Beaches
  & Islands
Tokyo
Vietnam

Australasia
Australia
Melbourne
New Zealand
Sydney

North America
Alaska
Baltic States
Big Island of Hawaii
Boston
California
Canada
Chicago
Florida
Grand Canyon
Hawaii
Honolulu
Las Vegas
Los Angeles
Maui
Miami & the Keys
Montréal
New England
New Orleans
New York City
New York City Mini
  Guide
Pacific Northwest
Rocky Mountains
San Francisco

Seattle
Southwest USA
Toronto
USA
Vancouver
Washington DC
Yosemite

**Caribbean
& Latin America**
Antigua & Barbuda
Argentina
Bahamas
Barbados
Belize
Bolivia
Brazil
Caribbean
Central America
Chile
Costa Rica
Cuba
Dominican Republic
Ecuador
Guatemala
Jamaica
Maya World
Mexico
Peru
St Lucia
South America
Trinidad & Tobago

**Africa & Middle
East**
Cape Town
Egypt
The Gambia
Jerusalem
Jordan
Kenya
Morocco
South Africa,
  Lesotho &
  Swaziland
Syria
Tanzania
Tunisia
West Africa

Rough Guides are available from good bookstores worldwide. New titles are
published every month. Check www.roughguides.com for the latest news.

...MUSIC & REFERENCE

Zanzibar
Zimbabwe

Travel Theme guides
First-Time Around the World
First-Time Asia
First-Time Europe
First-Time Latin America
Gay & Lesbian Australia
Skiing & Snowboarding in North America
Travel Online
Travel Health
Walks in London & SE England
Women Travel

Restaurant guides
French Hotels & Restaurants
London
New York
San Francisco

Maps
Algarve
Amsterdam
Andalucia & Costa del Sol
Argentina
Athens
Australia
Baja California
Barcelona
Boston
Brittany
Brussels
Chicago
Crete
Croatia
Cuba
Cyprus
Czech Republic

Dominican Republic
Dublin
Egypt
Florence & Siena
Frankfurt
Greece
Guatemala & Belize
Iceland
Ireland
Lisbon
London
Los Angeles
Mexico
Miami & Key West
Morocco
New York City
New Zealand
Northern Spain
Paris
Portugal
Prague
Rome
San Francisco
Sicily
South Africa
Sri Lanka
Tenerife
Thailand
Toronto
Trinidad & Tobago
Tuscany
Venice
Washington DC
Yucatán Peninsula

Dictionary Phrasebooks
Czech
Dutch
Egyptian Arabic
European
French
German
Greek
Hindi & Urdu
Hungarian
Indonesian

Italian
Japanese
Mandarin Chinese
Mexican Spanish
Polish
Portuguese
Russian
Spanish
Swahili
Thai
Turkish
Vietnamese

Music Guides
The Beatles
Bob Dylan
Cult Pop
Classical Music
Country Music
Cuban Music
Drum'n'bass
Elvis
Hip Hop
House
Irish Music
Jazz
Music USA
Opera
Reggae
Rock
Techno
World Music (2 vols)

100 Essential CDs series
Country
Latin
Opera
Rock
Soul
World Music

History Guides
China
Egypt
England
France

Greece
India
Ireland
Islam
Italy
Spain
USA

Reference Guides
Books for Teenagers
Children's Books 0–5
Children's Books 5–11
Cult Fiction
Cult Football
Cult Movies
Cult TV
Digital Stuff
Ethical Shopping
Formula 1
iPods & iTunes
The Internet
Internet Radio
James Bond
Kids' Movies
Lord of the Rings
Man Utd
Muhammad Ali
PCs & Windows
Pregnancy & Birth
Shakespeare
Superheroes
Travel Health
Travel Online
Unexplained Phenomena
The Universe
Videogaming
Weather
Website Directory

also! More than 120 Rough Guide music CDs are available from all good book and record stores. Listen in at www.worldmusic.net

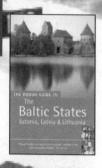

The ROUGH GUIDE to
Walks in London and Southeast England

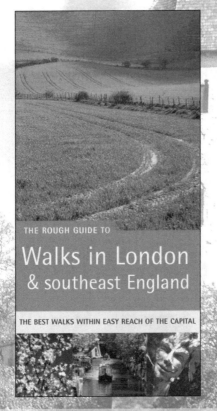

THE ROUGH GUIDE TO
Walks in London
& southeast England

THE BEST WALKS WITHIN EASY REACH OF THE CAPITAL

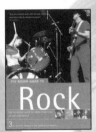

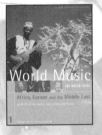

Index and small print

A Rough Guide to Rough Guides

London DIRECTIONS is published by Rough Guides. The first *Rough Guide to Greece*, published in 1982, was a student scheme that became a publishing phenomenon. The immediate success of the book – with numerous reprints and a Thomas Cook prize shortlisting – spawned a series that rapidly covered dozens of destinations. Rough Guides had a ready market among low-budget backpackers, but soon also acquired a much broader and older readership that relished Rough Guides' wit and inquisitiveness as much as their enthusiastic, critical approach. Everyone wants value for money, but not at any price. Rough Guides soon began supplementing the "rougher" information about hostels and low-budget listings with the kind of detail on restaurants and quality hotels that independent-minded visitors on any budget might expect, whether on business in New York or trekking in Thailand. These days the guides offer recommendations from shoestring to luxury and a large number of destinations around the globe, including almost every country in the Americas and Europe, more than half of Africa and most of Asia and Australasia. Rough Guides now publish:

• Travel guides to more than 200 worldwide destinations
• Dictionary phrasebooks to 22 major languages
• Maps printed on rip-proof and waterproof Polyart™ paper
• Music guides running the gamut from Opera to Elvis
• Reference books on topics as diverse as the Weather and Shakespeare
• World Music CDs in association with World Music Network

Visit **www.roughguides.com** to see our latest publications.

Publishing Information

This 1st edition published May 2004 by **Rough Guides Ltd**, 80 Strand, London WC2R 0RL. 345 Hudson St, 4th Floor, New York, NY 10014, USA.

Distributed by the Penguin Group
Penguin Books Ltd, 80 Strand, London WC2R 0RL
Penguin Group (USA), 375 Hudson Street, NY 10014, USA
Penguin Group (Australia), 487 Maroondah Highway, PO Box 257, Ringwood, Victoria 3134, Australia
Penguin Group (Canada), 10 Alcorn Avenue, Toronto, Ontario, Canada M4V 1E4
Penguin Group (NZ), 182–190 Wairau Road, Auckland 10, New Zealand
Typeset in Bembo and Helvetica to an original design by Henry Iles.
Printed and bound in Italy by Graphicom.

240pp includes index
A catalogue record for this book is available from the British Library

ISBN 1-84353-316-2

The publishers and authors have done their best to ensure the accuracy and currency of all the information in **London DIRECTIONS**, however, they can accept no responsibility for any loss, injury, or inconvenience sustained by any traveller as a result of information or advice contained in the guide.

1   3   5   7   9   8   6   4   2

Help us update

We've gone to a lot of effort to ensure that the first edition of **London DIRECTIONS** is accurate and up-to-date. However, things change – places get "discovered", opening hours are notoriously fickle, restaurants and rooms raise prices or lower standards. If you feel we've got it wrong or left something out, we'd like to know, and if you can remember the address, the price, the time, the phone number, so much the better.

We'll credit all contributions, and send a copy of the next edition (or any other DIRECTIONS guide or Rough Guide if you prefer) for the best letters. Everyone who writes to us and isn't already a subscriber will receive a copy of our full-colour thrice-yearly newsletter. Please mark letters: **"London DIRECTIONS Update"** and send to: Rough Guides, 80 Strand, London WC2R 0RL, or Rough Guides, 4th Floor, 345 Hudson St, New York, NY 10014. Or send an email to **mail@roughguides.com**

Have your questions answered and tell others about your trip at **www.roughguides.atinfopop.com**

Rough Guide Credits

Text editor: Polly Thomas
Layout: Katie Pringle, Dan May, Andy Hilliard
Photography: Victor Borg
Cartography: Ed Wright

Picture research: Sharon Martins, Joe Mee
Proofreader: Amanda Jones, Karoline Densley
Production: Julia Bovis
Design: Henry Iles

The author

Rob Humphreys has lived in London since the late 1980s and has written several Rough Guides. When not working, he can usually be found capsizing in the city's reservoirs, spotting bitterns or steering a Norfolk reed cutter up and down the Thames.

Acknowledgements

Rob Humphreys would like to thank editor Polly Thomas; Sharon Martins and Joe Mee for photo research beyond the call of duty; and Ed Wright for all his hard toil on the maps.

Polly Thomas would like to thank Rob for good humour, spiritual counsel and captions that went against the grain; Sharon for focus; Ed for painstaking attention to detail; Katie for her patience and luscious layouts; Helena for all her pertinent suggestions; Kate for overall guidance; Karoline for proofing under pressure; and the couriers of London for their initiative and panache.

Photo credits

All images © Rough Guides except the following:

p.1 Old Bond Street sign © Dave Bartruff/CORBIS
p.2 Face sculpture, British Museum © Robert Harding
p.4 Taxi light © Mark Thomas
p.5 Neon Piccadilly © Mark Thomas
p.5 Brick Lane with Bollywood posters © Timothy Allen/AXIOM
p.6 Berkeley Square © Tim Allen/AXIOM
p.6 Thames at sunset © Mark Thomas
p.7 Soho at night © Inge Yspeert/CORBIS
p.7 Cutty Sark © Adam Woolfitt/CORBIS
p.7 Covent Garden Piazza © Alamy
p.8 Diplodocus skeleton, Natural History Museum © Bill Varie/CORBIS
p.10 Tate Modern exterior © Biniam Ghezai/Travel Ink
p.11 Chapel of Henry VII, Westminster Abbey © www.britainonview.com
p.11 Van Eyck's Arnolfini Portrait © National Gallery/CORBIS
p.12 New Tayyab dining room © New Tayyab
p.14 Somerset House ice rink © Mark Thomas
p.16 Old Compton Street © Alex Segre/REX
p.17 Mardi Gras © Paul Brown/REX
p.19 Cheshire Cheese sign © Rupert Horrox/CORBIS
p.20 Manet's Bar at the Folies-Bergère © Courtauld Institute
p.20 Courbet's Young Ladies on the Bank of the Seine © National Gallery/CORBIS
p.21 Tate Modern exterior © Alamy
p.21 Iveagh Bequest, Kenwood House © Bill Batten/English Heritage
p.21 Wallace Collection gallery © Michael St Maur Sheil/Collections

p.21 Tate Britain © Alamy
p.22 Trooping the Colour © Sean Dempsey/PA Photos
p.23 Imperial Crown of India, Tower of London © Tim Graham/CORBIS
p.23 Royal Mews © Matthew Fearn/PA Photos
p.24 Harrods Food Hall © Harrods
p.25 Paul exterior © Paul
p.26 Lewis chessmen, British Museum © British Museum
p.26 Imperial War Museum guns © Barclay Graham/CORBIS
p.27 Cast Courts, V&A Museum © Sandro Vannini/CORBIS
p.27 Sir John Soane's Museum © Massimo Listri/CORBIS
p.27 Science Museum © PNS/REX
p.27 National Maritime Museum © National Maritime Museum
p.29 Temple Church © Alamy
p.31 London Central Mosque © Chris Capstick/REX
p.32 London Aquarium © Tony Kyriacou/REX
p.33 Syon Park © Syon Park
p.33 No. 11 bus © Mark Thomas
p.33 Child with monkey © Natural History Museum
p.33 Diana Memorial Playground © Graham Tim/CORBIS
p.34 Koi Carp Lounge © The Sanctuary
p.35 Charles Worthington salon © Charles Worthington
p.35 Cocktails at the Savoy © Savoy
p.40 Karl Marx tomb, Highgate Cemetery © Nils Jorgensen/REX

p.41 Gilt-bronze tomb, Westminster Abbey © Angelo Horak/CORBIS

p.41 Wellington monument, St Paul's Cathedral © Angelo Horak/CORBIS

p.45 Evensong at St Paul's Cathedral © www.britainonview.com

p.48 Proms © Robbie Jack/CORBIS

p.48 Carnival © Arena-Pal

p.49 IWA Cavalcade, Little Venice © Michael Freeman/CORBIS

p.49 Durbar Court, Foreign Office © Peter Aprahamian/CORBIS

p.49 Dance Umbrella © Dance Umbrella

p.49 Wimbledon © Nils Jorgensen/REX

p.50 Chamber of Horrors © Madame Tussauds

p.51 London Dungeon © Cordaiy Photo Library/CORBIS

p.51 Old Operating Theatre © Michael Jenner/Collections

p.52 Shakespeare's Globe production © Julian Nieman/Collections

p.52 National Theatre © Hideo Kurihara/Collections

p.53 Donmar Warehouse production © Robbie Jack/CORBIS

p.53 Comedy Café © Inge Yspeert/CORBIS

p.54 Royal Opera House © David Paterson/Collections

p.54 Jazz Café © Jazz Café

p.55 Wigmore Hall © Wigmore Hall

p.55 Shepherds Bush Empire © Mark Thomas

p.55 Guitar man © Mark Thomas

p.56 Lloyds Building © Mark Thomas

p.56 Swiss Re © Barry Beattie/Collections

p.57 Serpentine Gallery summer pavilion © Alamy

p.57 Millennium Bridge © Rachel Royse/CORBIS

p.58 Globe Theatre © Yann Arthus-Bertrand/CORBIS

p.59 Middle Temple Hall © Michael Jenner/Collections

p.59 Ham House © www.britainonview.com

p.59 Hampton Court Palace © Mecky Fogeling

p.60 Freud Museum © Freud Museum

p.61 Leighton House © Leighton House

p.61 Handel House Museum © Handel House

p.61 James Joyce's Finnegan's Wake manuscript, British Library © HIP/Scala

p.61 2 Willow Road © National Trust

p.62 Ritz © Ritz

p.62 Savoy © Savoy

p.63 Dorchester © Dorchester

p.63 Claridge's © Claridge's

p.63 Lanesborough © Lanesborough

p.64 Big Ben reflection © Alamy

p.69 Uccello's Battle of San Romano © Archivo Iconografico/CORBIS

p.70 Isambard Brunel, National Portrait Gallery © Hulton-Deutsch Collection/CORBIS

p.78 Blake's Newton, Tate Britain; Newton © Bettman/CORBIS

p.98 Soho at night © Inge Yspeert/CORBIS

p.100 Martini © CORBIS

p.109 Somerset House fountains © Peter Durant/Somerset House Trust

p.128 White Cube, Hoxton Square © Mark Thomas

p.142 Royal Festival Hall © Jeremy Horner/CORBIS

p.144 Dali sculpture with Big Ben in background © Doug McKinlay/AXIOM

p.148 Tate Modern interior © Timothy Allen/AXIOM

p.158 Diplodocus skeleton, Natural History Museum © Bill Varie/CORBIS

p.160 Stephenson's Rocket, Science Museum © Science & Society Picture Library

p.161 Miniature zebra painting, V&A © Stapleton Collection/CORBIS

p.167 Trellick Tower © Alberto Arzoz/AXIOM

p.186 Lion sculpture, Hampton Court Palace © Sandro Vannini/CORBIS

Index

INDEX

240